Wakefield Press

Matthew Flinders:
The Man behind the Map

Gillian Dooley is Honorary Senior Research Fellow at Flinders University. She is the co-editor of Matthew Flinders' *Private Journal* (2005), of the 2019 Wakefield Press anthology *The First Wave: Exploring Early Coastal Contact History in Australia* (with Danielle Clode), and (with Philippa Sandall) of *Trim: The Cartographer's Cat* (2019), a new authoritative edition of Flinders' *Biographical Tribute*. She also writes on authors including Jane Austen and Iris Murdoch.

Matthew Flinders:
The Man behind the Map

GILLIAN DOOLEY

Wakefield Press

Wakefield Press
16 Rose Street
Mile End
South Australia 5031
www.wakefieldpress.com.au

First published 2022
Reprinted 2023

Copyright © Gillian Dooley, 2022

All rights reserved. This book is copyright. Apart from
any fair dealing for the purposes of private study, research,
criticism or review, as permitted under the Copyright Act,
no part may be reproduced without written permission.
Enquiries should be addressed to the publisher.

Text designed and typeset by Michael Deves, Wakefield Press
Printed in Australia by Pegasus Media & Logistics

ISBN 978 1 74305 920 3

NATIONAL LIBRARY OF AUSTRALIA   A catalogue record for this book is available from the National Library of Australia

CORIOLE
McLAREN VALE

Wakefield Press thanks
Coriole Vineyards for
continued support

Contents

Abbreviations		vii
Introduction		1

Part 1. The Private Man and the *Private Journal*

1	Matthew Flinders: The Man behind the Map of Australia	9
2	Matthew Flinders' *Private Journal*	22
3	From Timor to Mauritius: Matthew Flinders' Island Identity	44

Part 2. The Journeys

4	'To perfect the discovery of that extensive country': Matthew Flinders' Achievements in the Exploration of Australia	57
5	Matthew Flinders in South Australia, January to April 1802	68
6	Matthew Flinders and the Limits of Empathy: First Encounters with Aboriginal Peoples	74

Part 3. Family, Friends, Patrons, Companions

7	Matthew Flinders of Donington	97
8	Ann Chappelle of Partney	108
9	Matthew Flinders and his Friends	117
10	'The sporting, affectionate, and useful companion of my voyages': Matthew Flinders and Trim	135

Part 4. Writing, Reading, Music

11	Matthew Flinders, Life-writer	147
12	'Well it is for me that I have books': Books in Matthew Flinders' Life	160
13	'When tired of writing, I apply to music': Music in Matthew Flinders' Life	166
14	The Library at Soho Square: Matthew Flinders, Sir Joseph Banks and the Publication of *A Voyage to Terra Australis* (1814)	173

Part 5. Occasional Pieces

Address for the Bicentenary of Matthew Flinders' Death, 19 July 2014	195
Book Reviews	199
Inspired by Flinders: Fridays at the Library, March 2002	213
Music of the Ships: Adelaide Baroque, August 2020	216
Epilogue: Flinders as Romantic Hero through the Generations	221
Bibliography	232
Notes	237
Index	247

Abbreviations

The sources listed here will be cited in the text with the following abbreviations plus volume and page numbers (if applicable). For all other references, see the Bibliography.

AC Flinders, Matthew. *Australia Circumnavigated: The Voyage of Matthew Flinders in HMS Investigator, 1801–1803* edited by Kenneth Morgan. 2 Vols. London: Hakluyt Society, 2016.

FPNMM *Flinders Papers: Letters and Documents about the Explorer Matthew Flinders (1774–1814)*. National Maritime Museum, Greenwich. Online.

GP Flinders, Matthew (Snr). *Gratefull to Providence: The Diary and Accounts of Matthew Flinders, Surgeon, Apothecary and Man-Midwife 1775–1802* edited by Martyn Beardsley and Nicholas Bennett. 2 Vols. Woodbridge: Boydell Press, 2009.

JFMFA *James Fairfax Matthew Flinders Electronic Archive*. State Library of New South Wales. Online.

MFNC Ingleton, Geoffrey C. *Matthew Flinders: Navigator and Chartmaker*. Guildford: Genesis Publications, 1986.

PJ Flinders, Matthew. *Private Journal 1803–1814* edited by Anthony J. Brown and Gillian Dooley. Adelaide: Friends of the State Library of SA, 2005.

PL Flinders, Matthew. *Matthew Flinders: Personal Letters from an Extraordinary Life* edited by Paul Brunton. Sydney: Hordern House, 2002.

TCC Flinders, Matthew, Philippa Sandall and Gillian Dooley. *Trim: The Cartographer's Cat*. Oxford: Adlard Coles, 2019.

VTA Flinders, Matthew. *A Voyage to Terra Australis*. 2 Vols. London: Nicol, 1814.

Introduction

Matthew Flinders has long been an iconic figure in the Australian imagination, and not just because of his heroic exploits. His achievements, when you consider his career lasted only a few short years, were extraordinary. However, many biographers, novelists and poets have been more fascinated by his marriage to Ann Chappelle, followed so soon by their unhappy parting and long separation; his imprisonment by the French on Mauritius; and the two or three fatal mistakes he made. He has inspired not just admiration, but affection, across the generations.

W.H. Langham wrote in 1925 of his 'personality of singular strength and charm.' Miles Franklin called him her 'beloved Flinders'. Ernestine Hill wrote a nation-building historical novel about him during the Second World War. Much poetry has been based on his life and legend. More than a dozen biographies have been published, as well as volumes of his letters, his journals, and his own biography of his cat, Trim, in several modern editions. Extensive archival material relating to his life and work can be found at the State Libraries of NSW and Victoria, and the National Maritime Museum in Greenwich. So why do we need yet another book about Matthew Flinders?

Like many other authors who have written on Flinders, I have found myself drawn to this complex and contradictory man and his extraordinary life story. Over the years I have written many essays and presented many lectures on various aspects of his life, some of which are not so well known, and I thought there might be some interest in having my scattered research and reflections on these subjects brought together in one place.

As my home discipline is literature, my initial reaction on first encountering Flinders was to the quality and extent of his writing. At the time I was the Special Collections Librarian at Flinders University, South Australia. Throughout 2002 there was a major historical celebration of what is known in SA as 'The Encounter' – the meeting between Flinders and Captain Nicolas Baudin, the commander of the French expedition sent to chart the Australian coast. The meeting took place on 8 April 1802 in a bay – now called Encounter Bay – off the lands of the Ngarrindjeri people, south of where Adelaide is now situated.

In preparation for the various Encounter events, researchers were visiting Special Collections frequently to access the Flinders Collection, and I got to know many of them. In particular, I met the late Tony Brown, who was preparing a scholarly edition of Flinders' *Private Journal*. He accepted my offer of help with this mammoth task, and the *Private Journal* was published in 2005 by the Friends of the State Library of South Australia.

Many people, when they think of Flinders' 'journal', mean the official published account of his expedition, titled *A Voyage to Terra Australis* and published in London in 1814, just days before his death. This was his major work: he spent the last three years of his life researching and writing it, perfecting the maps and charts, and correcting proofs. After a lengthy introduction detailing previous explorations in Australian waters – at over 200 pages, possibly the longest introduction that had ever been written to a published voyage at the time – the account is in the form of a journal: a day-by-day account of the preparations for and progress of the *Investigator* voyage.

It is enlightening to compare this published account with the captain's log from the *Investigator*, written day by day as the voyage proceeded, and recently published under the title *Australia Circumnavigated*, edited by Kenneth Morgan. This is more or less the same material, without the benefit of hindsight and without the prospect of public exposure, although it was still an official document which would be lodged with the Admiralty at the end of the voyage.

However, the *Private Journal* is something completely different. Upon their return to their home port, naval officers were required to surrender to the Admiralty all logs and journals written on board ship in the course of an expedition. Any journals they kept when on shore, on the other hand, were their own private property – hence 'private journal'. And the fascination of Flinders' *Private Journal* is the deeply personal nature of much of what he wrote.

He began writing this journal on the first day of what turned out to be a lengthy and frustrating stay on the island of Mauritius, then called Île de France and under French rule.[1] The island's governor, Charles Mathieu Isidore Decaen, refused to accept his passport, declared he was a spy, and imprisoned him and his crew, impounding his ship and all its cargo, books and paperwork. It is debatable to what extent Flinders exacerbated Decaen's mistrust by his angry and proud reaction, but the combination of unfortunate circumstances and clashing personalities led to his detention on the island for more than six and a half years.

His journal was certainly intended to keep a careful record of what happened during his time ashore, and he based some later official reports on this information. But he was also, especially as time went on, recording much intimate personal information about his activities, his opinions, his health both physical and mental, his emotions, and his relationships with the people amongst whom he found himself.

This kind of reflection is not entirely absent from his captain's logbook, or from the published *Voyage* – where he sometimes apologised for 'sentimental conjectures and exclamations' that he felt some readers might find ill-suited to an official account (VTA I: 356). There is an extraordinary passage describing his visit to Timor which seems to have been included in the logbook almost by accident. However, more than anywhere else, it is in the *Private Journal*, along with his voluminous personal correspondence, that the nature of Flinders as an individual is revealed most clearly. We can find out how he liked to spend his time, the qualities he treasured in his friends, what made him angry, and what made him happy.

In 2014 I was very honoured to be invited to deliver the 'Royal Society Matthew Flinders Memorial Lecture' at the Royal Society of Victoria. I took as my theme a broad topic: 'the man behind the map', using as a starting point the list of qualities I had rattled off in response to a radio interviewer's simple question, 'what was Flinders like?' In my talk I managed to cover about one quarter of these qualities.

Determined	Proud
Stubborn	Patriotic
Ambitious	Studious
Romantic	Hardworking
Loyal	Shy/reserved
Adventurous	Good leader and teacher
Courageous	Meticulous
Curious	Thrifty
Scientific	Temperate
Enlightened	Affectionate
Sceptical	Generous
Literate	Practical
Good at languages	Resourceful
Musical	'Candid'
Conservative	Sensitive
Courteous	Self-disciplined
	Authoritative

My early talks and essays on Flinders dealt with my own encounter with the *Private Journal* and his other writings. In later talks, even though I am not a naval historian and couldn't explain the difference between a brig and a schooner, let alone a jib and a topgallant, I ventured into more mainstream maritime history territory and spoke about his voyage and how it compared with what he had hoped to achieve, and his activities in various parts of the country.

An important turning point for me came when I was reading the newly published ship's log in *Australia Circumnavigated*. I realised that I had previously neglected to foreground the dealings that Flinders and his ship's company had, on their travels, with the Indigenous inhabitants on the shores of Australia. This led to the edited book, *The First Wave: Exploring Early Coastal Contact History in Australia*, which was published by Wakefield Press in 2019 and launched in London in June that year.

*****

In this book I have revisited and revised many of the pieces I have written on Flinders since 2001. Although some themes recur in different contexts,

I have removed a lot of duplication – thus two early essays on the *Private Journal* have been merged, and other talks and essays have been trimmed. The different purposes for which these pieces were written will account for some variation in tone and register between them. I have not attempted to impose a uniform style: some are more 'academic', some are downright chatty; some are longer and more densely argued than others.

This is not a biography, although it contains much biographical information: there are already many excellent biographies, written from different perspectives. And it is not intended to be comprehensive in any way. There is much more that can and will be said about the life and times of Matthew Flinders.

The book is divided into five sections. First comes a group of essays about 'The Private Man and the *Private Journal*'. I begin here, since this was my introduction to Flinders and remains the first point of reference for all my research on his life. Next is a section titled 'The Journeys', which includes essays on his achievements measured against his ambitions, his explorations of the South Australian coast, and a discussion of his encounters with the Aboriginal inhabitants whom he often referred to as Australians.

Thirdly, there is a section titled 'Family, Friends, Patrons, Companions'. Flinders had numerous friends and used the word to denote a large variety of relationships, including, most importantly, his family, his wife Ann, his patron Sir Joseph Banks, and his cat Trim. In Chapter Nine, 'Matthew Flinders and his Friends', I survey a small selection of his many friends, some well-known, others less so. The next section is on Writing, Reading and Music – activities which took up much of his time during his lengthy detention on Mauritius, as recorded in his *Private Journal*. Reading and music were both resources for solitude and sociable activities shared with his new French friends and neighbours. This section also contains an evaluation of the research Flinders undertook for his *Voyage* especially in Sir Joseph Banks' personal library.

Lastly, I have collected together a miscellany of smaller pieces – short talks for specific occasions, book reviews, and program details for Flinders-themed events I have been involved with. And as an epilogue, I include a recent essay on Flinders the romantic hero as reflected both in what he wrote himself, and what was written by those who came later – his successors in exploration, poets, novelists, and biographers.

One of the most exciting things to have happened over the past few years in the world of Flinders enthusiasts is the statue created by Mark Richards for the bicentenary of Flinders' death in 2014. In 1911, the Australian writer George Gordon McCrae described his ideal for a statue of Matthew:

> The figure, of course, of heroic size, and in a working undress of the period, the pose easy and natural, the feet planted on a coralline rock, with a few sea shells and weed, and perhaps a star-fish 'en evidence' – his quadrant laid against the inner surface of his flexed left arm, while he reads off the bearing from the vernier of the instrument, the fingers of the right hand grasping the pencil, with which he is about to record it.[2]

Mark Richards was not familiar with this quotation when he designed his statue, but although there are differences in detail, this is the spirit in which he conceived his Flinders. In most statues of Flinders, he is standing in a heroic pose, gazing into the distance. Richards' Flinders is intent on the task at hand, concentrating his attention on the map of Australia which is taking shape beneath his feet, a pair of compasses spanning a blank section of the coastline. When I first saw the statue in person at Euston Station in September 2014, I recognised the Flinders I feel I know, the man I encounter when I read his journals and letters: not a hero but a human being making his way in the world with an intelligent and curious mind, taking risks, working meticulously at his chosen profession, dealing with disappointments and setbacks with a mixture of ingenuity, indignation and resignation. A loyal friend, a conscientious brother, a loving husband. And an unexpectedly able writer.

Part 1

The Private Man and the *Private Journal*

Part 1

1

Matthew Flinders: The Man behind the Map of Australia

THE ROYAL SOCIETY
MATTHEW FLINDERS MEMORIAL LECTURE, 2014.[1]

Today – the one hundred and fifty first anniversary of the birth of Matthew Flinders, the Discoverer of South Australia – is a fitting occasion for a short appreciation of his character and work, and, since character exceeded achievement, I propose to present the man rather than his famous voyages, which have hitherto a little overlaid and obscured a personality of singular strength and charm.

This is quoted from an article by W.H. Langham in the Adelaide *Register*, Monday 16 March 1925, titled 'Matthew Flinders: The Indefatigable'.[2] Flinders' 240th birthday fell in 2014, as well as the bicentenary of his death, and I echo Langham's sentiment.

Matthew Flinders' most obvious claim to fame is that he captained the *Investigator*, the first ship to circumnavigate continental Australia, charting the sections of the coast which were unknown to Europe at the time. He is an established member of the Australian canon of the great, and the unveiling of his statue at Euston Station, London in July 2014 has perhaps raised his profile in his native country, where he has not been so celebrated.

His was a life of action and achievement thwarted by a run of bad luck in 1803 and cut short by his early death in 1814. When I co-edited his *Private Journal*, written between these years, I was interviewed for a West Australian regional radio station. It was a live interview and I forget many of the details, but I do remember that I was asked what Flinders was like. I immediately reeled off a long list of qualities (which I have included in the Introduction). During the three years or so that I had spent working on the edition I had built up what felt like a rounded picture of the man, almost as if I knew him personally.

So when I was invited to give this lecture, I decided to use some of these qualities as the structure of my talk. I have already written about Flinders' achievements. I have written about him as a reader, as a writer, even as a musician. He is someone I admire deeply, but he was not perfect. He has been worshipped as a hero across the years, often by Australians wishing to recruit him for the national pantheon. For example, Ernest Scott, in the Preface to his 1914 biography, wrote, 'He was … a downright Englishman of exceptionally high character, proud of his service and unsparing of himself in the pursuit of his duty.'[3] An article in the Melbourne *Argus* in 1925 announcing the unveiling of the Melbourne statue of Flinders concludes, 'He was a great and good man, an able and accomplished scientist, an inspired navigator. No one since Cook has left such an indelible mark upon the annals of this country.'[4]

To counterbalance this, there has more recently been a trend towards iconoclasm – calling Flinders arrogant and inexperienced. For example, Sidney Baker's 1962 book *My Own Destroyer* takes a psychoanalytical approach: 'The flaw in Flinders's character was a tendency to underestimate authority together with a rigidity of outlook that neither understood impulsive generosity nor deemed it worthy of personal pursuit.'[5] This is a startling misreading of Flinders' character, as I think will become clear. Geoffrey Ingleton sums up his character thus:

> Flinders' failing was vanity and arrogance – usual with British naval officers of that period – and these two unfortunate traits were responsible for most of his tribulations. He was, in some ways, his own worst enemy. His brother Samuel judged him a fatally-clever man, who, confiding in his own discernment, too easily believed that no branch of knowledge was beyond his reach. (MFNC 425)[6]

In what follows, I try to give my impression of this young man, dead at 40 and stymied before his 30th birthday by what he called, in his *Voyage*, 'a train of ills' (VTA 2:428), mostly caused by sheer bad luck magnified by risky decisions which, if they had been attended with success, would have made him even more of a hero. As he himself wrote to Sir Joseph Banks in March 1806, 'After a misfortune has taken place we all see very well the proper steps that ought to have been taken to avoid it' (PL 144). He was not impetuous, and always calculated risks and benefits, but the caution that might have prevented both disasters and great achievements came to him only with time and experience. My portrait of him is built up from his own letters and journals and some precious accounts of him from contemporaries.

Against the wishes of my friends
The first quality I will mention is determination, or stubbornness. There is much mythmaking about Flinders' boyhood – including, perhaps, his own statement in later life that he had been 'induced to go to sea against the wishes of friends from reading *Robinson Crusoe*'[7] – 'friends', in this case, meaning what we used to call our 'elders and betters', and almost certainly, in this case, his father. What is undisputed is that his father wanted him to follow in his own profession of surgeon and 'man-midwife', and, according to his journal, on 26 April 1790, the month after Matthew's 16th birthday, he went to Lincoln and 'agreed with Mr Dell, who is to give him 10 guineas per Annum' (GP 2:79). Joseph Dell was a surgeon and apothecary, and Matthew was presumably to be his assistant. However, less than three weeks later, on 14 May 1790, a momentous heading appears in Matthew Flinders Senior's journal: 'Matthew going to Sea.' He recounts going with his son 'to Spalding to take the Coach for London, thence to Rochester to Commodore Pasley's, to embark in the *Scipio*.[8] It has long been his Choice, not mine. ... [P]ray God it may be to his advantage. ... I shall heavily miss him' (GP 2:79).

Presumably young Matthew made the agreement with Mr Dell because he despaired of ever having a chance to go to sea, but having done so, he almost immediately received the offer of a midshipman's berth on the *Scipio* with his cousin Henrietta's employer, Commodore Pasley. Henrietta was a governess in Pasley's household. One can only imagine the tense and excited atmosphere in the Flinders' Donington household for the intervening two and a half weeks. Matthew junior knew what he wanted, but he was not (*pace* Baker) by nature one to rebel against authority. Later, when, returning to Port Jackson from his circumnavigation of New Holland in 1803, he received news of his father's death, his reaction is tinged with regret and even guilt:

> The duty I owed him and which I had now a prospect of paying with the warmest affection and gratitude, had made me look forward to the time of our return with increased ardour. I had laid such a plan of comfort for him as would have tended to make his latter days the most delightful of his life. ... Oh, my dearest, kindest father, how much I loved and reverenced you, you cannot now know.

This is from a copy of a letter to his stepmother in his letter-book: he crossed out the following continuation, in which he is still addressing his dead father:

> Everything that I have ever said or done that was displeasing to you now strikes upon my mind like moral guilt. I had indeed a strong propensity to independence of mind [,] of thought and action, and did not attend as I ought to gratify you by my words and actions. I thought indeed that I was certainly not acting wrong, in anything I did, but I was, in not making your ease and happiness the first rule of my ... conduct I have not acted right. (PL 95)

Here we have evidence of stubbornness: from his father, when he says, 'it has long been his choice, not mine', and from himself. But here we can also see his propensity, evident throughout his letters and *Private Journal*, to see things from the other side. I will come back to that.

I have too much ambition ...

He was determined, stubborn, and ambitious. I hardly feel the need to prove his ambition. A young man in Flinders' position could hardly have stumbled blindly into the career he pursued: for this son of an obscure Lincolnshire family to get ahead, it took activity, planning, determination and assiduous attention to everything that would promote it. If we needed documentary evidence, we have it from his own letter to Sir Joseph Banks, written from Mauritius in 1804:

> I have too much ambition to rest in the unnoticed middle order of mankind, and since neither birth nor fortune have favoured me, my actions shall speak to the world. In the regular service of the navy there are too many competitors for fame: I have therefore chosen a branch which, though less rewarded by rank and fortune, is yet little less in celebrity.

Note the date: he had already circumnavigated Australia and he had charted all the coastlines he would ever chart by this time. The fact that we are honouring him with lectures and monuments two centuries later is witness to his success, but he was not yet satisfied that he had achieved his aims. His letter continues:

> If adverse fortune does not oppose me, I will succeed; and although I cannot rival the immortalized name of Cook, yet if persevering industry joined to what ability I may possess, can accomplish it, then I will secure the second place.

Fine words, but what follows might fall on modern ears less happily:

> The hitherto obscure name of Flinders may thus become a light by which even the illustrious character of Sir Joseph Banks may one day receive an additional ray of glory: as a satellite of Jove I may reflect back splendour to the gracious primary who, by shining upon me, shall give lustre to my yet unradiated name. (PL 116)

Flinders was child of the Romantic movement as much as of the Enlightenment. Purple prose is not uncommon in the letters he wrote to his wife and family, but this, addressed to his patron, sounds sycophantic. In contrast, his friend George Bass's communications with those in authority are business-like and almost brusque.[9] Banks, however, seems not to have minded. He was assiduous in his efforts to obtain Flinders' liberty from a captivity that he noted in 1807 had been 'supported with manly fortitude'.[10]

Ambition is certainly at the root of much of Flinders' behaviour. Ambition made him disobey his father and flatter his patron. Ambition made him leave his new bride behind in England, with the deadly words, 'I shall give up the wife for the voyage of discovery' (PL 69). He had planned to take her on the voyage, which was strictly speaking contrary to naval regulations although not unheard of at the time. But the Admiralty found out and he was told he would lose his command if he kept her on board. That choice caused both him and his wife agonies which they were still suffering years later, magnified because ambition made him reckless in September 1803. Desperate to get back to England to replace his rotten ship *Investigator* and continue his explorations, and already thwarted by the shipwreck of the *Porpoise*, he set off in a tiny schooner, the *Cumberland*, built in the colony and never designed for such a long voyage. He later admitted himself that 'some ambition of being the first to undertake so long a voyage in such a small vessel' was one of the factors that induced him to Governor Philip Gidley King's offer of the ship (VTA 2:323).

Ambition, of course, is nothing without resourcefulness and intelligence. Flinders had an inquisitive mind and read widely – we know this from his letters to his wife, Ann, from the *Investigator*, as well as his *Private Journal* on Mauritius. His father kept a good library, continually recording the purchase of new books and the sale of old ones in his journal, and one assumes that reading was a habit Flinders began in childhood, and not only with *Robinson Crusoe*. Miriam Estensen writes, 'Tradition holds that on his own Matthew mastered John Robertson's *The Elements of Navigation* and John Hamilton Moore's *The New Practical Navigator*, but it is doubtful that even a clever fifteen-year-old could have done so without help.'[11] This is one of those legends which is difficult to track to its source. Lisette Flinders Petrie, Matthew's great-great-granddaughter, claims that his cousin John Flinders, or Jackey, a naval lieutenant who 'was frustrated in gaining promotion since he had no connections' tried to discourage him from joining the Navy by 'telling him to read Euclid, Robertson's *Navigation*, and Moore's *Practical Navigator*', but that it had the opposite effect.[12] In any case, Flinders certainly came to his first ship well-prepared to profit from the education a good captain would provide to his junior officers, so that when he 'expressed a desire' in 1791 for a long voyage his patron Commodore Pasley was happy to get him 'the situation with Capt. Bligh' on the *Providence*, as his father records in his journal. He goes on, 'He has made much improvement in his knowledge of Navigation. ... If he is Successful this Voyage may be a great means to promotion' (GP 2:94). William Bligh, for all his faults, taught Flinders the navigation and charting skills he had learned from James Cook. Ingleton established that 'Flinders drew at least, seven plans and one chart, while onboard (*sic*) the *Providence*' (MFNC 15).

Overlooking obstacles

Flinders had the essential quality of the successful person: he had what biographer James Mack calls 'nerve'.[13] He actively pursued his goals with resourcefulness and tenacity. As we have seen, Flinders did this in his teenage years. Later in life it became a habit which for some time served him well. He wrote to Henry Waterhouse in 1794 putting himself forward as master's mate for the voyage to New South Wales on the *Reliance*. Then, once he was in New South Wales, he offered himself to Governor Hunter as an explorer of the rivers around Sydney, with his friend George Bass, in an eight-foot boat which they called the *Tom Thumb*. He and Bass continued their exploring when they could, culminating in the circumnavigation of Tasmania in 1798–99. As he wrote, 'the furor of discovery, upon whatever scale it is, is perhaps as strong, and can overlook obstacles, as well as most other kinds of mania.'[14] Then, having gained that experience as an explorer and chart-maker during the four or five years he was based in Sydney in the last years of the eighteenth century, he had the confidence, brashness, or effrontery to write to the most influential man in the world of scientific investigation, the President of the Royal Society, Sir Joseph Banks, on the subject of a proposed expedition to New Holland.

T.M. Perry has shown that this letter was not written out of the blue. Banks and Flinders had already met, and Banks already had Flinders in mind to command the expedition, though there was to be another man included 'to undertake the exploration of the interior'.[15] However, Flinders certainly felt that he was pushing the boundaries of propriety: he excused himself, somewhat jocularly (and surely disingenuously), for 'any informality there may be in thus addressing him, that almost constant employment abroad, and an education among the unpolished inhabitants of the Lincolnshire fens, have prevented me from learning better' (PL 52). Banks did not seem to have been offended by this slight upon their shared county of origin, and promptly used his influence to have Flinders appointed to command the expedition.

The honest indignation of oppressed innocence

It could be argued that this quality of taking bold action to make things happen, which had got him so far in his career, caused things to go disastrously wrong when he landed on Mauritius in December 1803 and encountered Governor Decaen. Unlike Pasley, Governors Hunter and King, and Banks, Decaen was a figure of authority who had no use for Flinders' talents and was not impressed by him; he was suspicious of his motives and doubted his identity. Baudin, who would have spoken well of him, was dead. Pierre Bernard Milius, who would have been a useful friend to have, had sailed from Mauritius the day before Flinders arrived, in command of the *Géographe* in Baudin's place. The previous year, Milius had written in his journal:

> During his time in Sydney, Captain Flinders had often had us to dinner on board his ship. He seemed to be a most distinguished officer and to be very well educated. He has already made several voyages along this coast and we were grateful to him for some very useful information for the next stage of our trip.[16]

But in this new situation his friends in high places were powerless. He had, by a combination of bad luck and miscalculation, been forced to take the *Cumberland* into port to make urgent repairs. He had no way of knowing that Britain was again at war with France (although he knew it was possible), and even if he had, he was confident that the passport issued by the French government would be honoured, even though technically it applied to the *Investigator* rather than the *Cumberland.* He was in a hurry: he wanted to get back to England, find a replacement for the unseaworthy *Investigator* and go on with his unfinished task of mapping the Australian coastline.

So when Decaen stood in his way he was not diplomatic. Apparently he failed to remove his hat, a gross insult that the Captain General recalled years later (MFNC 267). There is a sad irony in the fact that upon his earlier significant encounter with a Frenchman, off the South Australian coast, he had shown his respect to Captain Baudin by taking off his hat, which, as Jean Fornasiero et al. remarked, 'set the scene for the meeting that was about to take place between these explorers from two rival nations.'[17] The language of headwear was potent indeed at that time – it was the absence of a bonnet on the head of Ann Flinders which is said to have alerted the Admiralty to the fact that she was living on the *Investigator* rather than just visiting in May 1801, causing them to suspect that Flinders was planning to take her with him on the voyage.

Flinders described the encounter with Decaen in an 1804 letter to his brother Samuel:

> They formed erroneous opinions of me on my arrival, – they imprisoned me, – I remonstrated, – they were enraged that a prisoner should accuse them of injustice, and determined to punish me. I was too obstinate to sacrifice one tittle to them either of the honour of my country or myself, and therefore prepared myself to suffer. (PL 104)

And suffer he did, but not in silence. The stream of indignant letters and messages he sent to Decaen only made things worse. Neither man softened his stance towards the other. They never met again, although in November 1807 Flinders happened to encounter Decaen on the road with another general and a large retinue: 'I stood a little on one side whilst they passed, and saluted the generals which was returned by the whole party' (PJ 191).

Flinders was a British Naval officer. He was proud of that and objected to anything that threatened it. When he was threatened with having to give up his sword, he attached a label to it with a message, beginning, 'Farewell, thou faithful companion! Thou guardian of my honour, Farewell!' (PJ 35). There was in him, especially in moments of emotional stress, a melodramatic streak not uncommon at the time.

Flinders was independent as well as proud. He disliked receiving favours and feeling himself placed under obligation: this is part of what Baker means when he says that 'he neither understood impulsive generosity nor deemed it worthy of personal pursuit.'[18] From on board the *Cumberland* he wrote a letter to the Governor of New South Wales, Philip Gidley King,

> It is part of my disposition to avoid receiving obligations as much as possible, but when from peculiar circumstances I am brought under the yoke, few retain a stronger sense of them or more desirous of making returns. To balance this, I am but little given to conferring kindnesses. Upon the whole I am more guided by justice than generosity for an act of the latter never escapes me from natural impulse: it is upon mature deliberation if I am ever generous. This is saying but little for myself, but I wish to be known by the few whom I would have for my friends. (PL 109)

When he did regard himself under obligation, he was very generous with his time and attention. An outstanding example of this is his efforts on behalf of French prisoners once he was back in England, advocating for them and lending them money. Less than three weeks after his return, he spent two days and 'near £5' to travel by stagecoach to Odiham in Hampshire, a journey of more than 50 miles, to meet four French prisoners and deliver letters and money from their relatives on Mauritius. They were overwhelmed, finding it difficult to believe that his visit was 'solely on their account' (PJ 330–331).

My earliest friend
Perhaps he hardly knew it himself, and this may seem to contradict what he wrote to King, but one of Flinders' most endearing attributes is his gift for friendship. Although their names are closely linked in Australian colonial history, his friendship with George Bass was tinged with hero-worship and was not the kind of warm mutual bond which he formed with many other people, both men and women. He kept up an affectionate correspondence with two friends from his days on the *Providence* with Bligh, and within weeks of his detention he found that members of the French community in Port Louis were inclined to befriend him. He responded by making of some of them friends for life, even though his country was at war with theirs.

When he was eventually allowed to move to a country residence in the south-western part of Mauritius for the good of his health, he formed a close friendship with his hostess, Madame d'Arifat, and her children. His relationship with Delphine and with her sisters and brothers was partly a pedagogical one. He taught the younger d'Arifat boys mathematics and navigation: as a naval captain, he would have done the same for his junior officers, one of whom, the famous polar explorer John Franklin, called him 'my earliest friend'.[19] He taught the young women English while they taught him French. About two months after their lessons started, he wrote, modestly, 'I am satisfied that one if not both of them make a better progress in English than I do in French' (PJ 110). He made excellent progress in French, however, and was soon quite fluent and able to participate in Francophone society as well as reading French books lent to him by his new friends. It had been brought home to him how important it would be to learn the language, when attending a dinner party in Port Louis in August 1805, just before travelling to his new quarters on Madame d'Arifat's estate:

The post of honour, that of conducting the lady of the house to table was assigned to me; and which as I understood so little French and spoke less, and have moreover been little accustomed to female society, embarrassed me not a little. (PJ 79)

It was equally important to accustom himself to female society, as he was to spend a good deal of time with Madame d'Arifat and her daughters and their female neighbours, but this seems to have come even more easily than learning French. In October, he was able to describe a typical day, consisting of much time spent with the 'ladies', walking round the plantation, learning French, reading, conversing, or playing cards. He often found these 'employments' so 'agreeable … as to prevent me from sleeping' (PJ 102). And although he made friends among the menfolk among the French settler society of Mauritius, he was sometimes uneasy in their company when they teased him, or talked about subjects 'which an Englishman generally thinks it better to keep secret' (PJ 108).

A good boiling in the large kettle

So far you might think that Flinders had no sense of humour. His letters and journals often prove otherwise. From the *Cumberland*, he wrote to his friend Philip Gidley King complaining about its infestation with bugs: 'I have at least a hundred lumps upon my body and arms; and before this vile bug-like smell will leave me, must, I believe, as well as my clothes, undergo a good boiling in the large kettle' (PL 110). You can almost hear him chuckling when he reports the effect on Governor Decaen of an act of disobedience by one of his subjects in his journal in November 1808, 'It is said His Excellency was obliged to make use of a warm bath to prevent his anger from having an effect upon his health' (PJ 237). More evidence of his capacity for humour is his *Biographical Tribute to the Memory of Trim*, which is now well known among Flinders fans. However, originally, in what was perhaps an early draft, it seems he wrote it merely as a French exercise. In January 1807, as he recorded in his journal, 'I have lately employed myself, either in correcting my narrative … – in reading Grants history of the Isle of France and making notes upon it, – or in translating into French the history of my cat Trim, which I wrote out for the purpose' (PJ 150). The whole tone of this delightful essay is playful and affectionate. Here is one short passage:

There are some men so inconsiderate as to be talking when they should be eating, who keep their meat suspended in mid-air till a semi-colon in the discourse gives an opportunity of taking their mouthful without interrupting their story. Guests of this description were a dead mark for Trim: when a short pause left them time to take the prepared mouthful, they were often surprised to find their meat gone, they could not tell how. (TCC 28–29)

Ourselves for instance

His essay on Trim, as well as being a superb piece of writing, contains an illustration of another of Flinders' most attractive traits, his fair-mindedness. It seemed to be an ingrained habit to see things from the other point of view. When Trim disappeared from the Port Louis household where he was staying while Flinders was still imprisoned in the town, Flinders wrote, 'My sorrow may be better conceived than described,' but he went on, 'it is but too probable that this excellent unsuspecting animal was stewed and eaten by some hungry black slave' (TCC 49). Not a wicked slave or a cruel slave: a hungry slave. He even attempts to understand Decaen's conduct which, he thought, 'must have originated in unjust suspicion, been prosecuted in revenge, his dignity being injured at my refusing to dine with him, and continued from obstinacy and pride' (PJ 75). When he wrote the words to a song and sent them to Ann from Mauritius, they were all about her feelings at his abandonment of her, and written from her point of view. And in his *Voyage*, he commented on the behaviour of the Barngarla people at Port Lincoln, South Australia, imagining that he and his compatriots – 'ourselves for instance' – would act in the same way if they were in their situation (VTA 1:146).

The received usages

Another trait which we nowadays might regard as less than admirable is his conventional streak. There were slaves on Mauritius: he never records an objection to slavery. He recounted his interactions with slaves, and observed their activities, as an unremarkable feature of everyday life. In October 1806 he and his servant, John Elder, heard a dog howling on a neighbouring plantation. As I recount in the next chapter, Elder wanted to 'cut the dog loose, being shocked at such cruelty; but I forbid him, preferring to mention it to some one who knew better than we did the consistence of such proceeding with the received usages' (PJ 141). Perhaps this was part of the caution he had had to learn from three years of detention; but I believe that a certain conservatism was part of his nature. He might be bold and adventurous but he was never a rebel: he was patriotic and generally respectful of those in authority, and his ambition was to be useful to the society he belonged to, rather than change it.

An unvaried line of peace and comfort
What can one say to sum up a life which ended so prematurely two hundred years ago? No-one remains unchanged by their experiences, and the impetuous, imperious naval captain of 1803 did indeed, as he foretold in a letter to Ann, 'learn patience in this island, which will perhaps counteract the insolence acquired by having had unlimited command over my fellow men' (PL 122). He apparently carried that patience over into his married life during the short years he and Ann finally spent together. Ernest Scott quotes a letter she wrote to a close friend, during those years, about the happiness of their life together: 'Day after day, month after month passes, and I neither experience an angry look nor a dissatisfied word. Our domestic life is an unvaried line of peace and comfort.'[20] This is impressive, given the irritations Flinders was subject to during these last years in London: battling an indifferent Admiralty for recognition, working day and night to get his *Voyage* finished, moving house no fewer than six times during those three and a half years – and Ann herself was often in poor health.

Oddly enough, I think that despite his adventurousness and ambition, he relished domestic life. He was introspective and somewhat of an introvert, ill at ease in large social gatherings. There is more to be said about this complex and fascinating man, but I will let his cousin, John Franklin, have the last word, to remind us of the reasons for Flinders' enduring fame. In 1842 Franklin, by then the Governor of Tasmania, wrote to Ann:

> I have long been desirous of giving you the full particulars of the monument which I am about to erect on Stamford Hill above Port Lincoln to the memory of your deeply lamented husband – and my earliest friend – not that his undying fame needed such a memento for he must live in the grateful remembrance of every friend of Hydrographical Science and especially of those who navigate the shores of Australia.[21]

2

Matthew Flinders' *Private Journal*[1]

The *Private Journal*

> Saturday December 17th. 1803: At 5 P.M. the health boat came on board and I accompanied the officers on shore, with the commander of the American ship. The captain-general was at dinner and I was kept waiting until eight o'clock and then saw him. He asked in an impetuous manner why I came here in a small schooner with a passport for the Investigator, and after many other questions put with much acumen, he expressed himself unsatisfied with my answers or the business I was upon, saying that I was imposing upon him, for it was not probable that I should be here in so small a vessel. (PJ 9)

So ended Matthew Flinders' active career. He was not yet thirty on the fateful day when he called in to Mauritius to repair his ship, but he would never again command a ship or chart a coastline.

Flinders' *Private Journal*, from which this quote is taken, covers the whole period from his captivity in 1803 until a few days before his death in July 1814, with only a couple of short intervals. In it, he records the many disappointments and frustrations, and the fewer achievements and joys, of the remainder of his life.

Arrival on Mauritius

The sixteenth of December was a bitter day for Matthew Flinders. In 1803 on this day he first encountered French revolutionary authority in the person of Etienne Bolger, the commandant of the District of Savanne on the south coast of the island of Mauritius. Flinders had set out from Port

Jackson in the tiny 29-ton schooner *Cumberland* to sail back to England, still expecting, despite the run of bad luck that began with the condemnation of the *Investigator* as unseaworthy and culminated in the shipwreck of *Porpoise*, that he would meet with no obstacles he could not overcome and that everything would yet turn out well.

Flinders had approached the island to make urgent repairs to the *Cumberland* which was taking water as fast as its defective pumps could expel it. Commandant Bolger insisted that he report to Captain-General Decaen at Port North-West (now Port Louis). He sailed under escort to the port, where Decaen, unimpressed by Flinders' story and his passport, detained him for what turned out to be six and a half years. His luck had run out: this was to be the last time Flinders commanded a vessel in His Britannic Majesty's Navy, or indeed at all.

A lot can be learned from the *Private Journal*, always bearing in mind that it does not tell the whole story. It is tempting to believe that, knowing the Journal, one knows the man. Indeed, it reveals a great deal. Reading through, day by day, one can chart his state of mind without the benefit of hindsight: his bitterness at his captivity and incredulity at the injustice of it. He copied a letter of 21 December 1803 to the Captain General into his journal, explaining in proud and high-flown prose his appointment to and prosecution of his voyage of discovery, the history of its progress and setbacks. He continued:

> Now, Sir, I would beg to ask you whether it becomes the French nation, even independent of all passport, to stop the progress of such a voyage and of which the whole maritime world are to receive the benefit? How contrary to this was her conduct some years since towards captain Cook! I sought protection and assistance in your port, and I have found a prison. Judge for me as a man, Sir, – judge for me as a British officer employed in a neutral occupation, – judge for me as a zealous philanthropist what I must feel at being thus treated. –...
>
> With all the respect due from my situation to the captain general, I am
> Your Excellencys obedient servant
> Matt^w Flinders
> From my confinement – Dec 21st 1803 (PJ 14)

The clash with Governor Decaen

The word 'arrogance' appears often in biographies of Flinders. Geoffrey Ingleton, for example, writes that during his initial interview with General Decaen, 'Flinders had arrogantly and deliberately kept his hat on' (MFNC 267). Paul Brunton calls him 'a man with more than a hint of arrogance and self-will' (PL 10). Miriam Estensen in her excellent biography claims that 'there was in Flinders a vein of self-importance amounting at times to arrogance.'[2]

I would prefer not to use the word 'arrogance'. Matthew Flinders was a man of his time, a naval officer, and the code of honour for such men was of paramount importance. Whatever justification there may have been for his treatment by Decaen, it would have been irreconcilable with Flinders' honour to behave any differently.

He reported an interesting conversation with the governor's aide-de-camp in his journal of Tuesday 27 December 1803:

> Mr Monistrol appeared to be sorry that I had written to the general in the stile that I had done, and he said that even my last letter was not agreeable to him, especially the passage where it is said that my charts and books would furnish me <u>with a better amusement than that of writing letters to His Excellency</u>. As I have found this gentleman was in the generals confidence I opened my mind concerning the treatment I had met with from the first, adding that as I demanded only justice, so I did not think an adulatory stile proper to be used: my rights had been invaded and I used the language of a man so circumstanced. Had I favours to ask or if there were any circumstances that I wished to hide, I should have probably used language more pleasing to the general; but I defied, nay wished them to make the strictest scrutiny into my papers or any way that might tend to detect my falsehood, if such there was. It was not the custom in England when justice only was the object in view to apply for it in the supplicating stile of a criminal, and although I was now to the east of the Cape of Good Hope, yet I retained too much of my native manners to address the captain-general as if he were an eastern monarch from whom I had favours to ask. The officers did not disagree with my sentiments, but still seemed to think that another stile would have much better answered my purpose. (PJ 16)

His attitude might be called arrogance, but Flinders would never see it as anything more than his proper pride as an English officer.

In 2003 Michael Duffy published a book on pioneer Australian pastoralist John Macarthur, who was born in 1766, eight years before Flinders. In it he discusses questions of honour and what it meant for men of the time to be considered gentlemen:

> Macarthur was born at a time of enormous opportunity. Britain had made more progress towards democracy than almost any other nation. Its creative spirit and economy were booming thanks to the scientific and industrial revolutions and the expansion of the empire. The material and social prospects for an ambitious man of Macarthur's background were better than they had ever been. ...
>
> The army of Georgian Britain ... was one of the few means of social and sometimes financial advancement for men of middling birth. Becoming an officer automatically made such a man a gentleman and therefore, at least in theory, an equal in some ways to every man above him on the social scale.[3]

Like Macarthur, Flinders was born in this period to a 'middling' family, and although he chose to become an officer in the navy rather than the army, the same considerations applied: he automatically became a 'gentleman'. Macarthur's code of honour took him to the lengths of fighting three duels during his lifetime. Flinders never went this far, although he commented in his Journal upon a duel which was fought on Mauritius:

> Wednesday October 31st, 1804: Two gentlemen have been just killed here in duelling, a circumstance that rarely occurs amongst the French. They usually fight with small swords and a scratch or prick usually settles the business; but those confounded English weapons, pistols, are getting into vogue, and were used on the above occasions. (PJ 49)

He clearly did not disapprove of duels. On the contrary, he is slightly scathing about the preference of the French to avoid killing each other.

On the first anniversary of his captivity, he wrote a letter to General Decaen, and his remarks upon it in his Journal are extremely revealing:

> To urge every argument to induce the general to comply with my request, and yet not to sacrifice any thing of my own honour or that of my country; not to give up one tittle of the justice of my cause and yet not hurt his pride

by telling him of his injustice. In short to demand justice without offending the oppressor; to beg without lowering the dignity of my cause. I found this a difficult task, and wrote the letter four times over without being able to please myself in the composition; perhaps I never wrote a worse letter where any consideration had been bestowed upon it. So difficult is it to express what the heart does not feel. The honest indignation of oppressed innocence, which might have given energy to my expression, it was necessary to suppress, and the letter is consequently without spirit, and almost hypocritical. It is likely I may be accused of wanting the spirit that I had before shewn – of an Englishman, by having suffered something for it. It may be said that I ought to have set my oppressor at defiance all together, and not have spared him. Perhaps this is very true, but of what advantage would it have been? My letter indeed does not carry accusations, but then I have not flattered my oppressor, or ask for my right as for an indulgence. I have only omitted telling him what would be offensive, but have not at all gone to the opposite extreme. – I have suffered a years imprisonment – am debilitated in health – kept back from my promotion, and the credit arising from my exertions and risks in prosecuting discovery – remain in ignorance of the state of my fortune and family both of which have suffered some late material alterations – and, oh above all, am kept from the arms of a beloved wife. Let any one reflect whether to reverse all these things, he would make the sacrifice of omitting offensive expressions in a letter to his foe and oppressor? – I have done no more. (PJ 54–55)

It can be seen here that he feels he has to justify himself for failing to show proper spirit 'as an Englishman' – what some biographers have called 'arrogance'. Flinders never reproached himself for his behaviour any further than this:

My consolations are, that I am usefully employed, and that in time I shall be set at liberty with honour and perhaps recompense. (PJ 55)

Liberty *without* honour would be an unbearable state. Perhaps he did not prize honour over life, but he certainly prized it over liberty. He was constantly assessing how far his parole – his word of honour – would allow him to go. Although he contemplated escape many times, he would not consider it while his parole was in force.

Anniversaries

In the years that followed, Flinders often marked 16 December with a journal entry. In 1804, as we have seen, he spent the first anniversary writing to Decaen, 'praying to be released,' and went to some lengths in his journal to record how difficult it was to write this letter. It was of paramount importance to him to preserve his self-respect. This is a private journal after all. His only audience was himself.

In 1805 and 1806 he had other distractions on 16 December, but again in 1807, he noted 'the miserable anniversary of my imprisonment in this island, completing the fourth year. I learn that the cartel [the ship on which he had had hopes of leaving] is arming for India with all expedition' (PJ 195). In 1808, he was more offhand: 'it is five years this evening since general De Caen made me prisoner' (PJ 239). But in 1809, he wrote emphatically that 'it is **six years** today since my unfortunate arrival in this island. God grant that it may be the last anniversary I shall see in this place' (PJ 289). And indeed on 16 December 1810 he was in the north of England, making a homecoming tour of his relatives in Lincolnshire.

Much to write and charts to construct

For the first three and a half months, Flinders and his companions were confined to the Café Marengo, which was virtually a prison. He struggled against his frustration and tried to use his time as usefully as he could:

> 11 February: The agitation of my mind, arising from the treatment I have received in this port and being totally ignorant of the causes or consequences, has sometimes prevented me, even for days, from applying seriously to work. I must endeavour to do better, for I have yet much to write and some charts to construct. (PJ 23)

A few days later, on 17 February 1804, he wrote,

> Neither these three days or the preceding one did I see the interpreter or any one else. I have received no answer or the least notice from the captain-general. I am yet a stranger to the cause of my confinement, and to the length of time it is to continue. It is indeed a most cruel suspence in which I am kept. I know not whether death is not almost preferable to it, when accompanied with such contemptuous treatment as is bestowed

upon me. Even in the dusk of the evening when I could see nothing, I am not allowed to stretch my legs with a walk, or to speak to any one except the interpreter, who has lately favoured me with very little of his company. These things with the reflection that I am kept from my country, from my family, from the employment where I expect to reap honour prey sorely on my mind: well it is for me that I have books and charts and employment. It is useless to prove my innocence, for no crime is alleged against me. It is useless to write, for no answer or other notice is returned. It is useless to ask for an audience, for it is denied. What it will end in, God knows, the arm of oppression being once stretched out there is no knowing to what length it will go. (PJ 24)

On 18 May 1804 he was a little calmer. Six weeks earlier he had been moved to the Garden Prison, the Maison Despaux:

My time is now employed as follows. Before breakfast my time is devoted to the latin language, to bring up what I formerly learned. After breakfast I am employed making out a fair copy of the Investigators log in lieu of my own which was spoiled at the shipwreck. When tired of writing, I apply to music, and when my fingers are tired with the flute, I write again until dinner. After dinner we amuse ourselves with billiards until tea, and afterwards walk in the garden till dusk. From thence till supper I make one at Pleyels quartettes; afterwards walk half an hour and then sleep soundly till daylight when I get up and bathe. Thus although the captain general keeps the log book I want and will not allow me my charts and papers to finish up my accounts of the Investigators voyage, which of all things I am most anxious to do, yet my time does not pass wearily or uselessly run. (PJ 33)

He would be at the Maison Despaux until August 1805, when he was allowed to leave the town and live in the country. Here he was allowed at least to walk in the garden and spend time with other English prisoners, and was even able to socialise with some of the French inhabitants of Mauritius.

Friends on Mauritius

One of the most intriguing aspects of Flinders' time on Mauritius was the number of friends he made. Thomi Pitot became a very close friend:

Friday 10 August 1804: Messrs. Pitots, merchants in the town dined today with Mr. Robertson and our mess. They were very agreeable and seemed interested to do him and me service. They have lent us books and music and behaved more liberally than is customary to any strangers, but especially to prisoners and Englishmen. (PJ 40) …

Monday 20 August. Mr. Pitot dined with me today, and I shewed him the letters which I had written to general De Caën, but which he did not much approve. This gentleman is become one of my best friends. He speaks some English and is very conversant with English books, and celebrated men. From him I learn the general opinion which the principal inhabitants of this place entertain of my situation, and which is rather gratifying. (PJ 41)

Another close male friend was Charles Baudin, a French naval officer who had been on Nicolas Baudin's expedition, though no relation to the Captain. Baudin lost an arm in a naval battle against the English during Flinders' detention. Others include Charles Desbassayns, who later married Lise, the youngest daughter of his hostess Madame Louise d'Arifat; Labauve d'Arifat, adult son of his hostess; Toussaint Chazal, a close neighbour. But it was not always easy being the only foreigner amongst these young French men. He remarked, a few months after being released on parole, upon the conversation of three men he accompanied on a hunting party:

> In the evening, Mr. LaB. La Chaise and F. renewed the former conversation upon hunting parties, intermixed with that of their amours; but as I understood nothing of the one subject, and I never make the other a topick of conversation, and besides spoke French very badly I remained silent, lying down upon my mat. On comparing the conversation with that of three young English men of the same age and class, it appeared that they were more brotherly with each other, more kind in their language, each speaking to the other in the second person singular; but they were more free in their language and ideas also, the words bouger, foutu, mâtin, diable &c. compounded with the word sacra, entered constantly into their phrases; and they made no scruple to avow circumstances which an Englishman generally thinks it better to keep secret; yet these young men were not libertines, or did they think themselves so. With us however their language would be thought to exceed the usual bounds of licence that Englishmen permit themselves when there are no women in company. (PJ 108)

So far this is merely an observation on national differences, but after a few years and more familiarity, he begins to find that even his good friends can be tiresome:

> Monday 7th November 1808. My two friends [Thomi Pitot and Charles Baudin] being persuaded to pass the day, I remained also. Persecuted a little upon the subject of politics and national character. These gentlemen and most other Frenchmen that I have seen, take a great pleasure in depreciating the English character; which is ungenerous in the presence of an Englishman and a prisoner. This is done by pleasantries generally, which it is best to answer by reprisals in the same way. Each nation has its manners. The populace in England throw mud at a Frenchman passing in the street, the gentlemen in France augment the misfortune of an Englishman by searching to turn his nation into ridicule; though I have always found at the bottom, that they respected it; and I attribute this to their desire of shewing their wit, joined to a little envy and perhaps hatred, rather than to any want of consideration. After dinner, my two friends returned to town, and I to Vacouas with mixed sensations of anxiety for my poor wounded friend [Baudin], regret at parting with him, and that I cannot go at the same time, and gratitude for the interest he takes to deliver me from my bondage mixed with some displeasure at his national animosity. (PJ 235)

On 28 May 1808 he spent the evening with the Chazals, close neighbours of the d'Arifats, joking that he had been 'handsomely treated and handsomely beaten at chess' (PJ 215–216). Mrs Chazal was a gifted harpsichord player and, Flinders said, 'One of the most agreeable women I have ever met with,' and she often accompanied him on his flute. But a year later, the friendship of Toussaint Chazal is wearing extremely thin:

> Friday 28th April 1809: Had a violent dispute with Chazal, who reproached the English government with injustice and inhumanity in a most prejudiced manner, and even with crimes that I shewed him it was the French and not the English government that had committed them. This is not the first instance I have seen of this gentleman's animosity and egoism; and I think, that if there is a second person in the island who would have treated me as general De Caën has done, notwithstanding the kindness and hospitality I

have personally received from Chazal, it is he who would be capable of it.' (PJ 254)

They continued to socialise, but although he stayed in touch with many of his Mauritius friends after his return to England, Chazal was not one of them.

Plaines Wilhems

The short period in late 1805 was probably one of the happiest times in Flinders' life, certainly the happiest of his time on Mauritius. Having been kept confined within the grounds of the 'Garden Prison' for more than a year, he had been allowed on parole to stay on a plantation at Plaines Wilhems, out in the countryside. Thomi Pitot had found him a congenial hostess in Louise d'Arifat, with three daughters and two young sons at home, in a hospitable neighbourhood. His parole allowed him to roam to the extent of two leagues (about ten kilometres) from the d'Arifat plantation, Le Refuge. This would be his home for more than four years: he lived there for longer than anywhere else during his adult life. He set up his bedroom in one of two 'pavilions' near the house, with his servant, John Elder, occupying the other.

At first, it was like a new love affair. On 27 October 1805 he describes his usual day at home with the d'Arifats, busy and happy, concluding: 'At nine we sup, and at ten retire to bed; where the agreeable employments of the day often occupy so much of my thoughts as to prevent me from sleeping' (PJ 102).

Depression and dreams of escape

The 'honeymoon' did not last. The journal entry for 1 to 3 February 1806 laments: 'These days passed over sadly. I did little' (PJ 114). 1806 was Flinders' worst year. He descended into a deep depression, which he documented carefully in the Journal, faithfully reporting as if to some higher authority. On 22 June 1806, he writes: 'It is some time since I have expressed the state of my sentiments and feelings, except by the letters which I have occasionally written.' He goes on to describe the plans he had made to attempt an escape: 'I had formed a plan of getting back my parole and of making my escape. I had even every thing arranged, but not being able to get back the parole, the design could not be accomplished.' He had thought of escaping while his parole was still in force, but 'the dread of dishonouring my parole made me ... contemplate this plan with a fearful eye.' After the failure of this scheme, he wrote, he 'remained some time in a state of sullen tranquillity' (PJ 129–130).

By September 1806 he had lost even this dubious peace of mind. He wrote that he was 'declining into a state of melancholy and weakness of mind' (PJ 138) that lasted, on and off, until August 1807. At first he made arrangements to retreat from society altogether:

> Friday 26 September 1806: At noon wrote a letter to Mad. D. informing her of the steps I had taken and entreating the continuance of her indulgence and friendship. The afternoon and evening passed in a depression of spirits inconceivable, and before supper I received an answer from Madam D. in which she requested to know what reasons she was to give to the world for my abrupt departure. The uneasiness she seemed to have, tainted with displeasure, added to my chagrin and I retired to my couch in a fever, whose increase, even to the causing my death I ardently desired: happily my servant waked me, from the town, with a packet of letters from England, which afforded me much consolation by the intelligence they contained.
>
> Saturday 27. I mustered spirits enough to go to breakfast with our good family and communicated the happy intelligence I had received, and which with the soothing consolations and reasonings of Madam D. induced me to abandon my ill-omened project, demanding permission to retire to myself at such times as my spirits were too low for society, and which she promised to me without offence. ... I endeavoured by forcing myself into society to re-establish my spirits and the little portion of assurance I possess from nature, and in this and the following day Sunday 28. partly succeeded ...
>
> Monday 29. Weather rainy these two days. Find myself better this morning, and hope to escape the gulph which I cannot contemplate without horror ... (PJ 138–139)

He persisted with his plan to spend more time with his friends, but found that the 'small portion of gaiety' he obtained 'does not penetrate very deep; indeed I fear the state of my mind is too much deranged for any thing but a liberation from this imprisonment to produce a radical cure: my reason is become more and more weak and the imagination more and more strong, what may be the end I fear to think' (PJ 141).

How poignant this is. The man who had thought nothing of sailing halfway round the world in a 29-ton schooner; who had travelled more than 700 miles from Wreck Reef in an open boat to get help for his shipwrecked companions, has become afraid to face dinner with his well-disposed hostess. General Decaen had certainly exacted a heavy penalty on his prisoner. Flinders' active career had been characterised by self-confidence, impetuousness and above all optimism. Many times he had staked his life on the fact that everything would turn out well, and even if things went wrong, he could make them right again. On Mauritius he learned patience, as he promised Ann he would (PL 122). He also learned to be despondent, cynical, cautious and pessimistic.

In December, he was a little better. But still,

> there is a weight of sadness at the bottom of my heart, that presses down and enfeebles my mind. ... The little knowledge I have is not reckoned or is unappreciated; that which I have not is exaggerated. ... In society I have no confidence nor scarcely presence of mind; any little pleasantry either upon myself, or the peculiarities of others, if they have any relation to, or seem to be thought to have any relation to me, puts me out of countenance. I am satisfied nowhere. ... Sleep, that sweet calmer of human woes, is my great resource, and I accordingly sleep much. ... The energy of my mind is I fear lost for ever. ... I now perceive what is meant by the state of a hypochondriac. (PJ 146–147)

Keeping busy

Social enjoyments could only go so far in restoring Flinders' *amore propre*. He threw himself into work. He had already completed what he could of his charts and sent them back to England in late 1804. Now he wrote a Memoir on his imprisonment, and made several copies to send to eminent people in England and France – wherever he judged it to be useful. It was in early 1807 that he wrote what became *A Biographical Tribute to the Memory of Trim* – he mentions 'writing out' the history of his cat, but the final manuscript we have is dated 1809. Although its playfulness is tinged with melancholy, this hardly seems the work of a depressive.

He had been studying French with Delphine d'Arifat and her sister

Sophie since the end of 1805, in return coaching them in English. In early 1807 he began to teach the elements of navigation to the young d'Arifat boys, Marc and Aristide. As a naval captain, it was his duty to instruct his junior officers on board any ship he commanded, and it was no doubt very natural for him to see potential midshipmen in these lads. With an eye always to the advancement of science and commerce, he made notes about the way maize and indigo were prepared on Mauritius. He could not see a mountain, river or lake without speculating on its origin, height or depth. The weather was of constant interest: he had the sailor's habit of recording meteorological observations every day, but his scientific mind was interested in the causes of climatic conditions as well: 'It has lately been forbidden to cut down any of the wood in the upper parts of the mountains, the rains having been found to decrease of late years, owing, as it is thought, to the hills having been nearly stripped of their covering,' he reported on 22 August 1805 (PJ 79).

He read works of science, philosophy and even the occasional novel, borrowed from his increasingly wide circle of friends. He had already sent a paper on the Marine Barometer to Sir Joseph Banks, and it was read before the Royal Society in 1806. In 1808 he began work on his observations on the effect of magnetism on a ship's compass, which eventually led to the invention of the Flinders Bar, an innovation which would make him better known in international naval circles than his exploration of Australia.

Decaen could not break his spirit entirely, but in December 1807 Flinders commented, on hearing yet another hopeful rumour of his impending release, 'I have been so often flattered with similar hopes and so often deceived, that I am almost become callous to prospects of being set at liberty' (PJ 196). And indeed, when the news finally came in 1810, he was understandably slow to believe it.

Delphine d'Arifat
Flinders' friendship with Madame d'Arifat's eldest daughter Delphine has been the subject of much speculation. At first, he was clearly attracted to Delphine. The family arrived at their *habitation* in October 1805, six weeks or so after Flinders had moved there from the Maison Despaux. On 6 November, Flinders wrote:

This family, particularly Mademoiselle D, become daily more interesting. She is indeed an extraordinary young lady, possessing a strength of mind, a resolution, and a degree of penetration which few men can boast of; and to these are joined activity, industry and a desire for information. 'Tis pity she had not been born a man, and in a more extensive field than the Isle of France. (PJ 103)

Flinders wrote an emotionally charged letter to Delphine on New Year's Day 1806 when she was away visiting friends, though he decided not to send it. He offers 'respectful compliments, and best wishes for your happiness', and goes on to write:

> the excellent qualities of the head and heart, both of which you possess, receive a double value in my estimation from the circumstance of their being combined in the person of one who distinguishes me by the title of friend. Remember the expression à jamais, and if the word doucement! escapes your lips, remember the pain it once caused me. Your beauty – but this is the affair of your lover, and therefore no concern of mine (PL 139–141).

The expressions *à jamais* [for ever] and *doucement* [slowly, or perhaps 'slow down!'] seem to hint at something a little more than innocent friendship. Later there was a falling out.

> 19 July 1807: A little quarrel with my friend D. which has now kept us at some distance for five or six weeks still continues and gives me uneasiness. I was the party that had a right to be offended at what was said to me, but wished to pass it over; for which I am punished by opposition and neglect as if the case was the reverse. (PJ 171)

There is little more than this tantalisingly general reference. There is no evidence that their friendship, however romantic, ever deepened into a love affair. And it is highly unlikely that this was the case. Flinders was, as I have said, a man whose notions of honour were extremely important to him. Having an affair with the daughter of his hostess would certainly not be consistent with his moral code, and that he could then have continued to live as a respected member of the d'Arifat household, as he did, is unlikely in the extreme. In the absence of proof to the contrary it is perhaps too much to insist that Flinders remained faithful to his wife Ann during their whole nine years separation, but not too much to insist that there was no affair with Delphine.

Delphine married M. Pailleux, a friend of Charles Desbassayns, her brother-in-law, in April 1813.

Living on Mauritius, dreaming of home

There is a very slight dissonance between his letters and his Journal at one stage. During his first weeks with the d'Arifat family, he reported:

> At present I rise every morning with the sun, and go out to bathe in the river, which is tolerably cool work; afterwards I dress, and either accompany the ladies in a walk round the plantation to visit their poulaillers [hen-houses]; or read till half past seven, which is the usual breakfast time.–After breakfast, I retire to my pavilion to read and write for two or three hours; after which I take my dictionary and grammar, some paper and a book, and translate French into English, and English into French, and read French under the correction of Mesdemoiselles Delphine and Sophie; and they do the same in English to me: these last until or very near dinner time; which is at two o'clock. After dinner I read and write, or sometimes walk, and sometimes sleep until about 5 o'clock, when I join the ladies again, either in a walk, or in conversation before the house. After tea, which is usually served at half past six, we retire to the parlour for the evening, which is passed in reading French and English, in conversation, or sometimes in singing and flute playing, or sometimes at cards. At nine we sup, and at ten retire to bed; where the agreeable employments of the day often occupy so much of my thoughts as to prevent me from sleeping. (PJ 102)

Just a few days earlier, he had written to Ann, 'I am now very happy; and yet I often retire to the little pavilion which is my study and bed room, and with my flute in my hand and sometimes tears in my eyes I warble over the little evening song of which I sent thee a copy. Ah my beloved, then my heart overleaps the distance of half a world and wholly embraces thee' (PL 135). The sincerity of his longing for Ann and home is not really ever in question: she was never far from his thoughts even during his happiest hours. At first he refrained from even telling the d'Arifats 'that amongst my other grievances I had a beloved wife in England who was expecting my return in sickness and in tears; because I saw that the scene would become too interesting, and oblige me to retire' (PJ 97), and when he received letters from home, he took them back to his room to read, 'for when I have anything that touches me very closely, solitude is preferable to any company' (PJ 101).

Politics and geophysics

Near the beginning of his time in Plaines Wilhems, he allowed himself a rather self-conscious meditation upon political philosophy, brought to mind by his observations of the geomorphology of Mauritius:

> 21 October 1805. Whilst waiting for my friend, I made some reflexions upon the formation of these cascades. It appeared to me that originally there had been only one great cascade or declivity at the mouth of the valley, but that the water draining through the crevices of the rock above caused pieces to fall down, forming another cascade. The same thing happening further and further back in the course of time, has brought them to what we now find them; and it is still going on. A large mass will soon fall from the top of the grand cascade into the basin below and its height will be there by decreased. The regular progress then is, that the cascades should diminish in height and increase in number. The masses that fall, are carried to the low land or to the sea; the cut of the river, which is the valley, becomes deeper, the sides fall in and are also carried out to the sea, and thus nature proceeds in reducing all things to a level as well in the moral as the physical world. The greater the inequalities are, (the higher the mountains are above the valleys, or that kings are above other men) the more is a sudden fall or revolution to be apprehended. The steep mountains cannot retain vegetable earth on the sides, it is washed into the vallies to raise them; but those that have a more gentle slope will retain a part, and do not diminish near so fast; nor is any violent change to be apprehended from the breaking off of masses, as from the steep mountains. (PJ 99–100)

However, he was not much given to such abstractions in his journal. He was not especially religious, and his politics, such as they were, tended to be careful and conservative. He made no comment on the morality of the slave trade, seeming to accept the status quo quite readily. A fellow prisoner, Walter Robertson, was allowed to leave in November 1804, but reluctantly left his 'negro boy' behind:

> The ship in which he goes to America being bound to Salem he is obliged to leave his black slave behind, the good quakers of that place not allowing a black man to be brought to their town: the poor boy is left to go to England with me, when it shall please God and general De Caën to permit it. (PJ 51)

Later correspondence revealed that the 'boy', Etienne, left Mauritius with Flinders' colleague John Aken in May 1805, and appears to have been reunited with Robertson in India.

A revealing little incident is related in the *Private Journal* in October 1806:

> For several days I have heard from my pavilion the continual howling of a dog upon a neighbouring plantation, and my servant tells me that it arises from the proprietor of a small habitation having tyed a dog in his field of Indian corn for the purpose of frightening the monkies: in order to make him cry continually, he gives him nothing to eat; so that he cries for two or three days and then dies of hunger and fatigue: he added that two or three dogs had already received this treatment. Elder said he would go and cut the dog loose, being shocked at such cruelty; but I forbid him, preferring to mention it some one who knew better than we did the consistence of such proceeding with the received usages. On mentioning the circumstance to Mr. Labauve, he said, it was a common custom amongst the smaller proprietors, who could not afford slaves to watch their corn, to tye dogs up in that manner, and did not seem to think much of it, though far from approving it. (PJ 141)

Flinders does not particularly approve of the practice, but Elder shows more impulsive humanitarian sentiments, itching to release the dog and prevent this cruelty. Flinders, more conservative and disinclined to interfere in this society where he still felt himself to be somewhat of an outsider, prefers to find out first whether it is 'the done thing' to use dogs this way before acting rashly and offending his hostess's neighbours: he refuses to interfere with something that is consistent 'with the received usages'.

Religion and social morality

He seldom invokes the deity, except in a formulaic way – 'God knows' or 'thank God'. Of the personal qualities Flinders developed during his stay on Mauritius, piety is not uppermost. He viewed religion, like many other subjects, with a scientific, detached and sometimes satirical eye. His friend Captain William Fitzwilliam Owen, who was a prisoner of war on Mauritius during Flinders' last years there, addressed him as a 'Man of your Science and precision'[4] and referred to 'our difference of Opinion on the Government of this Ball of Earth & Water and things thereon — You say General Principles. I say particular providence.'[5] At the marriage of his friend Charles Desbassayns with the daughter of his hostess, Lise d'Arifat, he remarked:

> Previous to the mariage ceremony, seven black children were christened. It struck me risibly to see the abbé pronouncing benedictions to these poor devils in Latin, of which neither they nor the god-fathers or mothers understood one word. The greater part of the mariage ceremony was also performed in latin, the two contracting parties kneeling the whole time. I did not remark so much difference from our church in this as in the baptisms, where it seems the first protestants have curtailed with a more lavish hand. (PJ 199)

Back in London, he attended church as often as not, while his wife went with greater regularity. He liked a good sermon: he mentions one or two preachers he found impressive, but religion was not prominent among his concerns, and the one surviving letter written to him by his wife begs him 'to read the holy scriptures, & ... to pray' in a way that suggests it was not his habit to do so.[6]

Nevertheless Flinders had a strong moral sense, and French ways were sometimes a puzzle to him. Commenting on a dance at a neighbour's house, he noted wryly,

> Having been accustomed to our close modest English step, the high vaulting manner of dansing used by the French, did not appear so graceful or so decent as I should perhaps have otherwise thought it. In the dress of the ladies I remarked nearly the same singularity as I have before noticed ...

Very delightful to behold, but not such as I should chuse for females of my own family. (PJ 103)

He made an accurate, but possibly uncharitable, observation when a young wife gave birth to her first child 'thirteen days less than 9 months after her marriage' (PJ 246), and in January 1807 he reported:

In a conversation on religion, I found sentiments of tolerance pushed further even than mine. I believe, that Voltaire is pretty generally read amongst the married ladies here as well as in France; and that their fidelity to their husbands does not arise from religion, nor I think from fear of shame: little slips are spoken of, and laughed at, but do not prevent either one party or the other from being admitted into all societies. (PJ 150)

The implication is that, to Flinders, the role of religion was at least in part to regulate social behaviour.

Last years in England

The introspective journal entries dry up once he returns to England. Naturally enough upon resumption of his married life, we learn nothing of his inner feelings about his wife, beyond a shy reference to 'my Mrs F.' on his first day back in London (PJ 326). The birth of his daughter on 1 April 1812 is recorded only briefly, among his own occupations: 'Occupied in correcting the bearing book, by a just proportionate variation. This afternoon Mrs. Flinders was happily delivered of a daughter; to her great joy and to mine' (PJ 400). It must indeed have been a joy and relief, since Ann miscarried more than once: she was 42 when little Anne was born. Worries about the child's health find their way into the journal, but we must go to the letters to find out what he thought of fatherhood: 'This child has the most varied and expressive physiognomy, I have ever seen in one so young. ... I begin to love the child myself, now that it shows signs of intelligence,' he wrote to Madame d'Arifat on 25 November 1812, when Anne was nearly eight months old (PL 228).

Flinders confided to his journal more freely his frustration with Sir Joseph Banks, who had not helped him in his dealings with the Admiralty as much as he had hoped: on 8 August 1811, he spent the day working at his *Voyage* and 'meditating upon the general conduct of Sir J.B. towards me; in which I find many things not easy to be explained' (PJ 373).

Towards the end of 1813 the journal entries become a catalogue of work done on the *Voyage* and irritable references to interruptions. A regular visitor, Captain Farquharson Stuart, who had connections with Mauritius, was so assiduous in his weekly evening calls that Flinders finally wrote to him asking him 'to do away his regular Monday visits' (PJ 453) until the work was finished. Perhaps only long habit kept him writing his daily journal, which must have become something of a chore.

Final illness

Abruptly, in February 1814, with the work just about finished, Flinders reports having consulted a doctor about his illness, 'which appears to be either stone or gravel in the bladder. It is troubled me more within some months and become painful' (PJ 466). From then on, the journal entries are concerned more and more with the painful course of his condition, and the series of unpleasant and ineffective remedies he tried at the suggestion of his medical advisers. Ever the empirical observer, he describes his symptoms meticulously. On 20 March he went for a walk as suggested by his doctor, but he reports being 'obliged to move very snail-like' (PJ 468). He reports without comment that Ann's half-sister Isabella arrives to help her with the nursing, but remarks on 16 June that the naturalist from *Investigator*, Robert Brown, 'called upon me today, and he has been very kind in doing so several times lately' (PJ 482). Like-minded in their scientific attitude, they would have discussed the illness, and Brown, as Sir Joseph Banks' librarian, helped Flinders find some scientific papers which they thought might assist in his treatment.

In the light of modern medical knowledge, it can be seen that this treatment was worse than useless. Flinders probably died from a urinary infection originally introduced by treatment for venereal disease administered on board the *Providence* when he was still a teenager. In our edition of his *Private Journal*, we included a medical opinion by Dr Stephen Milazzo examining the evidence Flinders provided. He notes that 'Even the last few succinct entries still breathe meticulous objectivity, and display no rancour or self-pity.'[7]

The last entry in the Journal is from Sunday 10 July 1814: 'Did not rise before two being I think, weaker than before' (PJ 485). Nine days later he died.

The *Private Journal*: Light and shade
The *Private Journal* begun on 17 December 1803 is to a large extent a record of adversity faced with fortitude and intelligence, if occasionally tinged with impatience or complaint. There are passages of intense melancholy and soul-searching. But it has its lighter moments. After a visit to the Chazals, he reports that he had been 'handsomely treated and handsomely beaten at chess' (PJ 216). In a cheerfully forgetful moment in 1809, he describes a series of losses at cards as 'the strangest persecution of bad luck I ever experienced,' discounting shipwrecks, rotting leaky ships and imprisonment (PJ 244). Back in London, he writes lightheartedly on Good Friday 1811 that he and Ann 'breakfasted, as in duty bound, off hot-cross buns, one a penny' (PJ 355).

England and France
A loyal subject of King George the third, Flinders usually marked the 4th of June with a tribute to 'the birthday of my gracious sovereign,' although by 1811 he had become 'the poor king'. But his patriotism did not extend to chauvinistic prejudice against the French. His cordial dealings with Nicolas Baudin during the time of war are famous, and while on Mauritius he made friends with many of the French inhabitants. He rarely approved of the proceedings of the French government, still less the Governor of Île de France, but at a personal level went out of his way to help anyone who claimed his loyalty, whatever their nationality, and despite the strains he occasionally felt at being the sole defender of England's honour among even his closest friends. Learning not to take offence, placing the value of friendship above the honour of himself and his country, was perhaps one of the more difficult lessons he had to learn during his detention, along with patience and the necessity of accepting that there were some things in life he could not change by feats of daring and endurance.

The Romantic conservative and cat-lover
Of all the biographers, Miriam Estensen agrees best with the Matthew Flinders I have got to know during my work on his *Private Journal*. In spite of her use of that word 'arrogance', she immediately tempers her judgement by saying, 'he was a naval officer of his time, a time when this was an attitude virtually intrinsic to naval or military rank. … Imperious when

his rightful authority was challenged, he knew his place in his particular world.'[8] As she says, he had 'strong affections and loyalties,' for both men and women. In spite of his conservatism, he had a strong romantic streak, typical of his time. He read and enjoyed novels as well as historical and scientific works. And he loved his cat, Trim.

> Sunday 11 January 1807. When not otherwise occupied, I have lately employed myself, either in correcting my narrative, of which Elder is employed making a fresh copy, – in reading Grants history of the Isle of France and making notes upon it, – or in translating into French the history of my cat Trim, which I wrote out for the purpose. (PJ 150)

Trim is not mentioned in any other context in the Journal, even during the initial weeks spent confined in the Café Marengo, when, according to the *Biographical Tribute*, Trim 'by his gay humour contributed to soften our strait captivity' (TCC 46).

So the Journal does not give the full picture of Flinders. It can be read in conjunction with his letters and other writings, like *Trim*, and with the more official documents intended for publication like his *A Voyage to Terra Australis*. However, it is both fascinating and revealing, and an essential source for the study of the last quarter of his life. It shows the qualities of determination and pride which enabled him to overcome the severe temptations of self-pity and melancholy, to employ his time usefully and survive his detention, while gaining a maturity intensified by misfortune and tempered by the kindness of many who were formally his enemies.

3

From Timor to Mauritius: Matthew Flinders' Island Identity[1]

In the official journal that Matthew Flinders kept on the *Investigator* there is a passage describing his visit to an estate on the island of Timor in April 1803. This does not appear in any form in his later account of the Voyage and unlike the rest of the journal is decidedly personal. He writes, 'I could not prevent my ideas from dwelling upon the happiness that a man whose desires were moderate might enjoy in this delightful retreat with the beloved of his heart'. But, following this train of thought, he decides that there 'could be no collision of mind upon mind', without which even reading would pall. 'I energetically exclaimed No – I was not meant for this' (AC 2:337–338). The island life was not for him.

In December of the same year, Flinders put into the island of Mauritius in the *Cumberland*, seeking a safe harbour to repair his tiny schooner, and was detained there by the French colonial governor until 1810. In October 1805, when he had been on Mauritius for two years, he ruminated in his *Private Journal* about his situation, 'a prisoner on a mountainous island in the Indian Ocean, lying under a cascade in a situation very romantic and interior' (PJ 101). On Mauritius he was without 'the beloved of his heart' – his wife Ann, who was waiting for him in England – but there were unexpected compensations for his enforced sojourn: new friendships, and time to read, think and mature. His view of the drawbacks of island life was confirmed in one respect: the pace of his life on the island necessarily slackened, or relaxed; but this allowed, or forced, the ambitious over-achiever to 'learn patience'. As chronicled in his journal, he developed in ways he could not foresee.

In this chapter I will explore the island identity that Flinders developed during his long stay on Mauritius, in the context of his vision of islands as sites of romance, contemplation and intellectual stagnation.

* * * * *

Islands and isolation

Matthew Flinders knew a thing or two about islands. One of his early claims to fame, in 1798–9, was proving that Tasmania is an island, and his major voyage was, as he explains in the first paragraph of *A Voyage to Terra Australis*, designed to discover whether the bits of Australia that had so far been mapped, 'instead of forming one great land, be no other than parts of different large islands'.[2] Establishing whether previously charted islands and peninsulas had been correctly identified was part of the routine as he circumnavigated the island continent. I see from the Project Gutenberg text of the *Voyage* that the word 'island' is mentioned more than 1000 times in the first volume alone.

To a naval captain, an island provides an opportunity to rest the men, repair the ship and replenish the stores during a long ocean voyage. But if not laid down accurately in existing charts, they represent peril as well as the possibility of rescue. On the voyage out in 1801, he explains that he spent some time looking (in vain) for the island of St Paul, whose position had not yet been satisfactorily mapped:

> I was desirous of ascertaining the true position of this, and of some other small islands, laid down in the neighbourhood of the equator. They are placed so much in the tracks, both of outward and homeward bound ships, that it was not improbable some one of the vessels missed at different times, might have suffered shipwreck upon them; and the hope that we might be the happy means of restoring to their country and friends some unfortunate fellow creatures, perhaps countrymen, was an additional incitement to look after them. (VTA 1:29)

The trope of the island castaway was, of course, ubiquitous in the literature Flinders knew, most notably Daniel Defoe's *Robinson Crusoe*. Here, in his official *Voyage*, he inserts himself imaginatively into the romance of shipwreck as the benevolent rescuer. Towards the end of his short life, he named reading *Robinson Crusoe* as the most important influence on his choice of a career.[3] The allure of travelling to distant and isolated places translated into a life of practical challenges and difficulties, many of which involved islands. Having returned from the triumphant circumnavigation of Tasmania with George Bass, he wrote to his friend, Ann Chappelle, whom he would marry in 1801, that he was having misgivings about his 'profession': '*Sea*: I am thy servant;' he wrote, 'but thy wages must afford me more than a bare subsistence; I do not mean to be always insulated' (PL 39).[4] From the context, by 'insulation' he means cut off from his friends – 'cooped up in a wooden box; year after year' (PL 39) – in effect, isolated (from the same Latin root) – made into an island.

Pelican Island

But islands never quite lost their aura of romance for him. In his *Voyage* he allowed himself a digression on islands and, implicitly, their potential for allegory:

> There are four small islands in the eastern branch [of Nepean Bay]; one of them is moderately high and woody, the others are grassy and lower; and upon two of these we found many young pelicans, unable to fly. Flocks of the old birds were sitting upon the beaches of the lagoon, and it appeared that the islands were their breeding places; not only so, but from the number of skeletons and bones there scattered, it should seem that they had for ages been selected for the closing scene of their existence. Certainly none more likely to be free from disturbance of every kind could have been chosen, than these islets in a hidden lagoon of an uninhabited island, situate upon an unknown coast near the antipodes of Europe; nor can any thing be more consonant to the feelings, if pelicans have any, than quietly to resign their breath, whilst surrounded by their progeny, and in the same spot where they first drew it.

He apologised for inserting this digression into the official voyage, but it was not the only time he allowed himself personal reflections in his public writings. In the *Investigator* logbook, there is a passage describing his visit to the estate of a planter in Timor which is startling in its emotional candour.

The Island of Timor

This visit to Timor occurred in April 1803, at a time when the voyage had taken a turn for the worse. There had been a violent clash with the Yolŋgu in Blue Mud Bay, on Morgan's Island, which led to injuries on the British side and fatalities among the Yolŋgu. Although he says little in the official accounts about the effect this had on him, an anonymous memoir written shortly after his death relates 'the agony of mind he is stated to have suffered' when this happened.[5] Meanwhile, the ship had been taking more and more water, and on the carpenter's examination it was found to be rotten, and scarcely able to weather a storm. With the monsoon coming, Flinders had made the unhappy but inevitable decision to interrupt the voyage of exploration and return to Port Jackson. Before setting out on the safer but more circuitous route around the west coast of Australia, they put into Timor to replenish their supplies of food and water – an unfortunate necessity, as the water brought with it dysentery which killed several members of the ship's company.

So Flinders was not in the happiest frame of mind when they arrived on the island of Timor. He had recently written an anguished letter to Ann wondering about the effect their long separation might be having on her continued fidelity and affection for him, imaginings brought on by reading about Eve in John Milton's *Paradise Lost*. He wrote to other friends and relatives wondering plaintively why they hadn't written to him. He was in the mood to seek some consolation.

After dinner one evening he took a walk 'up a stony parched-up road to the house of a Mrs Van Este', 'black, but very rich'. His dwells in appreciative detail on various adjustments to the environment – tree plantings, buildings and engineering works – which provide relief from the island's dry and fatiguing heat:

> The way to the house lies amongst cocoanut trees, amongst which little streams of water wind every way. The house is situated in a wood of these and two other kinds of palm ... which give together so much shade that, except when vertical, the sun can scarcely see the ground here. In one place is a square cistern into which the water is occasionally let from one of the streams, and when required a hole can be opened in another part by which the water will run out: this is meant to bathe in. In another part is a larger

[hole] through which the water slowly drains constantly, and keeps it full: this is a fish pond ... In some distance round the house, under the shade of the cocoanut trees, are many huts which I suppose to be the habitations of the slaves. Facing the north from the house are stone pillars forming a portal, and without this others, forming a square all about which are shady trees planted but not yet grown up. Without the outer portal is the sea, from whence in the summer months the wind comes, and by means of the skreens that surround the verandas of the house can be admitted more or less.

I thought this to be a little paradise, and infinitely superior to anything I expected in Timor; and I could not prevent my ideas from dwelling upon the happiness that a man whose desires were moderate might enjoy in this delightful retreat with the beloved of his heart; for here the summer sun could not scorch, nor was there any dread of winters cold. Simple aliments were abundant, slaves were numerous and obedient, and a look was all the exertion that was necessary to have ones wants gratified; such wants at least as would be excited[6] in a mind regular moderate and agreeable to simple nature. I thought such a life as well fitted for philosophical and religious contemplation, as it was for love and all its train of domestic enjoyments: In a delightful reverie, all these ideas passed through my mind as we walked along the sea beach back to Coupang. ...

Pursuing my reverie further, and considering myself in possession of this retreat, I considered well, how shall I employ and amuse myself when books weary and my plantation does not require my care? I saw no employment, of amusement, or society; it was too warm for anything laborious, the roads were scarcely fit to walk upon, as little fit for a horse, and impassable to any kind of carriage; and moreover there was nothing but rocks, and parched-up roads, and here and there a plantation not half so beautiful as my own; there were owners indeed to these, people of property, but then they were men and women without an idea beyond Timor and chewing beetel. With such I could not communicate any knowledge I might possess or acquire, and except from books could make no further acquisition. Conversation upon books is a stimulus to read, but here could be no collision of mind upon mind; I feared that reading would under such circumstances pall with me, and that in the end I should fall a sacrifice to surrounding circumstances and become that mere inactive animal, or rather vegetable – a native of

Timor. I energetically exclaimed No – I was not meant for this: my reverie upon Madam Van Este and her plantation house ended here, for I saw that it owed its beauty to the shade it afforded from the sun of an oppressively warm climate; and said I we have no need of this in England. (AC 2:337–8)

This is Flinders at his most candid and revealing. He has no objection to slavery, except inasmuch it might make him indolent. He is snobbish about the inhabitants of Timor – he considers them not worth his friendship. He doesn't even seem to regard 'the beloved of his heart', his wife Ann, who in this reverie would be joining him in Timor, as a potential intellectual equal, despite indications to the contrary in his letters to her.

Circumnavigation, shipwreck and rescue
Shortly after this visit, the *Investigator* sailed from Timor, heading westward and making its anti-clockwise way around Australia. They arrived in Sydney three months later after a harrowing voyage, with twelve men seriously ill. Several others had not survived.

And Flinders' troubles were far from over. He had to abandon the *Investigator* as it was unseaworthy, so Governor King arranged for him to travel back to England on the *Porpoise* to find another ship suitable to continue his explorations. 730 miles out from Sydney, the *Porpoise* was wrecked on an uncharted reef off the coast of Queensland. Although he had been travelling as a passenger on the ship, as the senior officer he took charge of the salvage and rescue effort. At last he was in the position of rescuer: 'I got back to the port [Sydney] in a six-oared cutter, and being furnished with a ship and two schooners by ... Governor King, returned to the relief of the companions of my misfortune, who had remained six weeks upon a small sand bank' (AC 2: 403). One of the schooners sailed back to Sydney with some of the castaways, the ship, the *Rollo*, sailed for China, while he took himself off for England in the tiny schooner *Cumberland*, with a handpicked volunteer crew of twelve men.

The *Cumberland*
You might almost say he was begging for trouble, taking such a huge risk. The imaginative tendencies we have already seen – in his meditation on the pelicans, in his worries about his marriage, and in his 'reverie' on life

in Timor – sprang into action again. The *Cumberland* was leaky and infested with vermin. He knew it was too small for the trip: as he later admitted, he had 'some ambition of being the first to undertake so long a voyage in such a small vessel' (VTA 2:323).

The trouble he encountered this time was less exciting and more trying than surviving shipwrecks and rescuing castaways, though. On 15 December 1803, when it became obvious that they wouldn't make it to England, or even to the Cape of Good Hope, he put in to the island of Mauritius, then a French possession, assuming that the Peace of Amiens still held. It didn't: war had resumed in May that year, but the news hadn't reached Sydney by the time he left. He was stuck there for six and a half years as a prisoner of the French. As he fumed to the island's hostile governor, 'I sought protection and assistance in your port, and I have found a prison' (PJ 14).

The Island of Mauritius

Here he was, on an island considerably smaller than Timor (2,040 km^2 to 30,777 km^2), among his country's enemies. How did he cope? We have an excellent source of information, because on 17 December, the day he came ashore at Port Louis, he began making daily entries into a journal which he maintained for most of the rest of his life.

For one thing, he refused to vegetate, as he expected he would have if he had decided to live on Timor. He often recorded the activities of a typical day – reading, studying, writing, playing his flute – and once he was given a little more freedom, conversing with friends, discussing books and ideas with them, learning French from them. When he had been there a year, he wrote to Ann, 'I shall learn patience in this island, which will perhaps counteract the insolence acquired by having had unlimited command over my fellow men' (PL 122). He did learn patience, along with the French language. And, incidentally, the possible effect of deforestation on rainfall on the island:

> **Monday 15 April** A gale of wind has blown for these two days, but cleared up this day at noon. It is extraordinarily late for such rainy weather as we have had now for two or three weeks, January and February being the usual rainy months in these two islands, and the time that hurricanes take place

when they do happen, which appears however to have not been seen for some years. The cutting down of the wood upon the hills is supposed to be cause of their cessation, and also of less rain having fallen in the latter years. No rain of any consequence fell this year until the month of March. (PJ 62).

He never stopped learning and thinking and testing ideas. At his most Romantic and scientific, we find him sitting under a waterfall, contemplating the analogy between geophysics and politics, as related in Chapter Two. By this time, he had moved to the estate of Madame d'Arifat, a place romantically named Le Refuge. His parole allowed him to travel up to two leagues from her property without permission. This island 'prison', or refuge, was to be his home for longer than any other place in his adult life.

He cut a path through the woods to a lookout from where he could see the coast, and was able to keep himself informed of some of the shipping movements in that way. He had friends, and he often describes passing time 'agreeably'. But there were bouts of depression. In December 1806, he wrote;

> It is some time that I have not spoken of the state of my mind. I have so far overcome my propensity to melancholy reflexion, as no longer to experience that poignant anguish that oppressed me in September and October last; but there is a weight of sadness at the bottom of my heart, that presses down and enfeebles my mind. Every thing with respect to myself is viewed on the darkest side. The little knowledge I have is not reckoned or is unappreciated; that which I have not is exaggerated. ... I may truly say, that I have no pleasure in life: the nearest approximation to it is to forget my pain. (PJ 146–147)

I find it fascinating that he wrote this in his *Private Journal* – for himself alone. It is so beautifully phrased that it surely must have done him good to put this into words. The journal seems to act as a confessor: he starts by almost apologising for not having 'spoken of the state of [his] mind'. Much of it is in the passive voice, allowing him to distance himself from his feelings of dejection. On the subsequent days his journal entries show him to be more cheerful and sociable.

The reality of life on Mauritius was both better and worse than the Timorese fate he had so vividly imagined for himself – 'in the end I should fall a sacrifice to surrounding circumstances and become [a] mere inactive animal, or rather vegetable' (AC 2:338). There was intellectual stimulation – 'the collision of mind on mind' – although sometimes his French friends made him uncomfortably aware of his foreignness. Even when alone with his thoughts and his books, though, he never became other than his thinking, feeling, imaginative self. He matured, he 'learned patience', and caution, and cynicism. One might imagine that the young man who would dare to sail from Australia to England in a 29-ton schooner because nobody had done it before would have few scruples about trying to escape from his detention when there was a sliver of a chance, but when he was contemplating this in October 1807 he let his friends dissuade him.

The Island of Britain

Finally allowed to leave in June 1810, after many false hopes, he wrote to one of his French friends, 'Now that I am certain of going, the pleasure I had in contemplating this event in perspective, is vanished. My heart is oppressed at the idea of quitting my friends here, perhaps forever' (PL 199). He arrived back on the island of Britain in October 1810. The yearning romantic in him seems to have gone underground. When away from home for a week or two in 1812, his matter of fact letters to Ann were signed 'thy affectionate husband', without the heartfelt professions of undying love which had concluded the letters during his years of absence. He wrote to his friend James Wiles about his plans for the future:

> I shall retire, and render my happiness independent of the will of others; for although I have neither acquired nor inherited a fortune, I have learned to be content upon a little, an advantage perhaps equal to the other. (PL 211)

Flinders looked forward to a time when he could return to Mauritius, now a British possession. He wrote affectionate letters to his French friends there for the rest of his short life, imagining plans for bringing his wife with him to meet his island companions. But it was not to be. The chore of writing his *Voyage* 'grew upon him', as he phrased it, to such an extent that it used up all his remaining time. He died in London the day after his book was published, his account of charting and circumnavigating the island continent, and a mere fortnight after placing an order for a copy of a new edition of *Robinson Crusoe*, the island narrative which sparked his obsession with the travelling across the sea and visiting all the islands that he could find, a fascination of which his enforced sojourn on the *Isle of France* didn't cure him.

Part 2

The Journeys

4

'To perfect the discovery of that extensive country': Matthew Flinders' Achievements in the Exploration of Australia[1]

In a letter to Sir Joseph Banks in May 1801, Matthew Flinders wrote that he hoped his forthcoming voyage would 'preclude the necessity of any one following after me to explore' (PL 69). Unfortunately, however, other circumstances intervened and he was not able to complete the work he set out to do. In this chapter, I compare what Flinders intended to do when he left England in July 1801 with what he actually achieved during those nine years: what he was prevented from doing by his six and a half years' detention, and the compensations (trivial though they might be) he managed to extract from his enforced idleness during that time.

The traveller returns
On 24 October 1810, Matthew Flinders stepped onto English soil, 'having been absent from England', as he wrote in *A Voyage to Terra Australis*, 'nine years and three months, and nearly four years and a half without intelligence from any part of my connexions' (VTA 2:493). While held captive on Mauritius since December 1803, he had been unable to maintain regular correspondence with his family because of the English blockade of the island. He had sent letters whenever an opportunity arose, but the last letter he received from his wife Ann before he arrived back in England was written in July 1806.

He arrived in London by the mail coach at 7 o'clock the next morning, as he relates in his *Private Journal*:

> Went to Mr Bonner from whom I learned that Mrs Flinders was in town. Took a lodging at the Norfolk Hotel, and went thence to the admiralty, where

I saw Messrs Croker and Barrow, the two secretaries, and was treated with flattering attention. ... At noon, my Mrs F. came to me with Mrs Procter. I was obliged to leave them in order to send up my card to Mr Yorke the first lord of the Admiralty. (PJ 326)

The voyage of discovery, and Flinders' devotion to duty, was still interfering with his married life, nine and a half years after he had written to Sir Joseph Banks, 'whatever may be my disappointment, I shall give up the wife for the voyage of discovery. ... I would beg of you ... to be assured that even this circumstance will not damp the ardor I feel to accomplish the important purpose of the present voyage' (PL 69). Ann's feelings on being sidelined again like this already, on the day of their reunion after a long and uncertain separation, are not recorded. But she was surely used to this man by then, and resigned to his ambitions. He had protested to her, in a letter of 7 July 1801, that

> discovery no doubt has its portion in me, but it is only the stepping stone by which I hope to enjoy thy love undisturbed; and believe me my best beloved, had I a moderate competence for thee, I should not grieve if the discovery of New Holland should be reserved to another. (PJ 75)

However, James Stanier Clarke, in his memoir, wrote 'that to his friends he has frequently been heard to say, that, "if a plan of a Discovery-Voyage were read over his grave, he should rise up, awakened from death"' (MFNC 423). The following three and a half years, all the time Matthew and Ann had together before his death in July 1814, were, as can be seen from the *Private Journal*, busy with the absorbing and often frustrating work of getting his *Voyage* written and the charts completed, and ended in an agonising illness, thought by Ann to have been 'brought on by unremitting attention to his work, an attention so close, that he neither allowed himself recreation, nor time for proper exercise.'[2]

Instructions for the voyage

In his *Voyage*, he records the instructions he received from the Lords of the Admiralty on 17 July 1801. Here are some excerpts:

> Whereas the sloop you command has been fitted and stored for a voyage to remote parts; And whereas it is our intention that you should proceed

in her to the coast of New Holland for the purpose of making a complete examination and survey of the said coast, on the eastern side of which His Majesty's colony of New South Wales is situated; You are hereby required and directed to put to sea the first favourable opportunity of wind and weather, and proceed with as little delay as possible in execution of the service above-mentioned ... you are to make the best of your way to the coast of New Holland;... and on your arrival on the coast, use your best endeavours to discover such harbours as may be in those parts; and in case you should discover any creek or opening likely to lead to an inland sea or strait, you are at liberty either to examine it, or not, as you shall judge it most expedient, until a more favourable opportunity shall enable you so to do.

... When you shall have completely examined the whole of the coast from Bass's Strait to King George the third's Harbour, you are ... to proceed to and explore the north-west coast of New Holland, where, from the extreme height of the tides observed by Dampier, it is probable that valuable harbours may be discovered. Having performed this service, you are carefully to examine the Gulf of Carpentaria, and the parts to the westward thereof, between the 130th and 139th degrees of east longitude; taking care to seize the earliest opportunity to do so, when the seasons and prevalent winds may be favourable for visiting those seas. When you shall have explored the Gulf of Carpentaria and the parts to the westward thereof, you are to proceed to a careful investigation and accurate survey of Torres' Strait, and when that shall have been completed, you are to examine and survey the whole of the remainder of the north, the west, and the north-west coasts of New Holland, and especially those parts of the coast most likely to be fallen in with by East-India ships in their outward-bound passages. And you are to examine as particularly as circumstances will allow, the bank which extends itself from the Trial Rocks towards Timor, in the hope that by ascertaining the depth and nature of the soundings thereon, great advantage may arise to the East-India Company's ships, in case that passage should hereafter be frequented by them. So soon as you shall have completed the whole of these surveys and examinations as above directed, you are to proceed to, and examine very carefully the east coast of New Holland, seen by captain Cook, from Cape Flattery to the Bay of Inlets;

During the course of the survey, you are to use the tender under your command [the Lady Nelson] as much as possible; moving the Investigator onward from one harbour to another as they shall be discovered, in order that the naturalists may have time to range about and collect the produce of the earth, and the painters allowed time to finish as many of their works as they possibly can on the spot where they may have been begun: ... And whereas you have been furnished with a plant cabin for the purpose of depositing therein such plants, trees, shrubs, etc., as may be collected during the survey above-mentioned; ... you are ... to cause to be planted therein during the survey, such plants, trees, shrubs, etc., as they may think suitable for the Royal Gardens at Kew;... In this last mentioned cabin the naturalist and gardener are to place the plants, trees, shrubs, etc., which may have been collected during the survey, in order to their being brought home for His Majesty ... (VTA 1:8–12)

Landfall, encounter and circumnavigation

For the first year and a half all went well, apart from minor variations, with this ambitious program. The first landfall was on 6 December 1801 at the south-westernmost tip of Western Australia, and they worked eastwards along the south coast until they met Nicolas Baudin, who had been exploring and charting in the other direction, in April 1802 at Encounter Bay, as Flinders later named it.

As their encounter made continuing to explore the south coast in detail redundant, the *Investigator* then made for Port Jackson, with only a couple of stops to explore Port Phillip and King Island in Bass Strait, arriving in May 1802. In Port Jackson, they undertook the necessary maintenance on the ship and restocked their supplies, and they then headed north in July, up the east coast and through Torres Strait and on to the Gulf of Carpentaria until, on 23 November 1802, at anchor near Sweer's Island at the southern end of the Gulf, the Master, John Aken, and the carpenter, Russel Mart, dropped a bombshell:

> 'in a strong gale, with much sea running, the [Investigator] would hardly escape foundering; so that we think she is totally unfit to encounter much bad weather. ... From the state to which the ship seems now to be advanced, it is our joint opinion, that in twelve months there will scarcely be a sound

timber in her; but that if she remain in fine weather and happen no accident, she may run six months longer without much risk.'

Flinders continued, after quoting this passage:

> I cannot express the surprise and sorrow which this statement gave me. According to it, a return to Port Jackson was almost immediately necessary; as well to secure the journals and charts of the examinations already made, as to preserve the lives of the ship's company; and my hopes of ascertaining completely the exterior form of this immense, and in many points interesting country, if not destroyed, would at least be deferred to an uncertain period. My leading object had hitherto been, to make so accurate an investigation of the shores of Terra Australis that no future voyage to this country should be necessary; ... and with the blessing of GOD, nothing of importance should have been left for future discoverers, upon any part of these extensive coasts; but with a ship incapable of encountering bad weather—which could not be repaired if sustaining injury from any of the numerous shoals or rocks upon the coast—which, if constant fine weather could be ensured and all accidents avoided, could not run more than six months—with such a ship, I knew not how to accomplish the task. (VTA 2: 142–143)

He continued surveying for a few months, but eventually, on 6 March 1803, at Wessel's Islands, he decided to postpone the examination and return, regretfully, to Port Jackson, making best use of the prevailing winds by sailing around the longer anti-clockwise route which incidentally gave him one of his chief claims to fame, that of being the first circumnavigator of Australia. But this was not on his mind at the time:

> We had continued the survey of the coast for more than one-half of the six months which the master and carpenter had judged the ship might run without much risk, provided she remained in fine weather and no accident happened; and the remainder of the time being not much more than necessary for us to reach Port Jackson, I judged it imprudent to continue the investigation longer. ... It was not, however, without much regret that I quitted the coast; both from its numerous harbours and better soil, and its greater proximity to our Indian possessions having made it become daily more interesting; and also, after struggling three months against foul winds,

from their now being fair as could be wished for prosecuting the further examination. (VTA 2: 247–248)

The health of the people

Ten days out from Port Jackson, on 30 May, he passed through Bass Strait which he had first explored with George Bass in 1798 in the colonial sloop *Norfolk*:

> It was a great mortification to be thus obliged to pass Hunter's Isles and the north coast of Van Diemen's Land, without correcting their positions in longitude from the errors which the want of a time keeper in the Norfolk had made unavoidable; but when I contemplated eighteen of my men below, several of whom were stretched in their hammocks almost without hope, and reflected that the lives of the rest depended upon our speedy arrival in port, every other consideration vanished; and I carried all possible sail, day and night, making such observations only as could be done without causing delay. (VTA 2: 271–272)

The ship's doctor, Hugh Bell, had just three days earlier complained that he wasn't 'making all possible speed to port' in consideration of the state of the sick on board, and Flinders had replied on the 29 May with an indignant letter, setting out the contrast between what he had done, given the constraints of his crew's health, and what he would like to have done:

> Had the health of the people been the great object of my duty as it is of yours, and I had been permitted to follow my own plan for their preservation, I should certainly have kept them on shore in their native country, and not have exposed them to the danger of the seas and enemies, and to pernicious changes of climate; to all of which the execution of my orders makes it necessary to expose them. (PL 92)

Shipwreck and detention

Flinders, despite all his efforts, was not able to complete the survey he abandoned on 6 March 1803. In consultation with Governor Philip Gidley King, it was decided that the best option for a speedy completion of the work would be for Flinders to take a passage back to England in the *Porpoise* to allow him to present his charts to the Admiralty and to request another ship.

The *Porpoise* sailed on 10 August 1803, under the command of Robert Fowler, former First Lieutenant in *Investigator*. The *Porpoise* was accompanied by two merchantmen, the *Bridgewater* and the *Cato*. During the night of 17 August, a week out from Port Jackson, the two leading vessels, *Porpoise* and *Cato*, struck hard upon an uncharted reef, some 240 kilometres off the east coast and nearly 1200 kilometres from Sydney. The *Bridgewater* narrowly escaped, but next morning her captain made only a perfunctory search for survivors before continuing his voyage to India, later claiming that he saw no sign of life. In a striking case of poetic justice, however, the *Bridgewater* was lost with all hands on the way back to England (MFNC 242).

Thanks largely to the leadership of Flinders and Fowler, all but three of the wrecked ships' crews survived. Leaving Fowler in command at the sandbank, Flinders, with the *Cato*'s captain and twelve men, set off in one of the two six-oared cutters saved from the wreck to seek help at Port Jackson. They completed the journey in thirteen days. On their arrival, Governor King immediately contracted the Indiaman *Rolla*, in port and bound for China, to go to the castaways' rescue. He also provided two colonial-built schooners, the *Francis* and the *Cumberland*, to accompany her. Sympathising with Flinders' wish to return to England without further delay, King offered him the *Cumberland*, 'a small vessel of 29 tons, a mere boat' (PJ 14), for the purpose: in her he could make a speedy passage through Torres Strait, rather than take the longer route via China.

The *Cumberland* proved to be an unfortunate choice. Always leaking, and close to sinking in the Indian Ocean, the ship limped into port on 16 December 1803 at Mauritus. Flinders was unaware that the peace negotiated between Great Britain and France in March 1802 had ended in May 1803 and that he was therefore entering enemy territory. His passport for the *Investigator* was deemed invalid for the *Cumberland* by the short-tempered Governor Charles Decaen, whom Flinders did nothing to appease, and he was detained as a spy. He was only allowed to leave the island in June 1810 when it became clear that the British were about to invade.

He fulminated against his detention in futile and counterproductive letters to Decaen:

I was chosen by that great patron of the sciences Sir Joseph Banks President of the Royal Society of London, and one well known by all the literati throughout the world, to retrace part of the track of the immortal captain Cook, to complete what in New Holland and its neighbourhood he had left unfinished, and to perfect the discovery of that extensive country. ... Now, Sir, I would beg to ask you whether it becomes the French nation, even independent of all passport, to stop the progress of such a voyage and of which the whole maritime world are to receive the benefit? (PJ 14)

However, despite his frustration, Flinders eventually had to resign himself to an indefinitely extended detention.

Activities on Mauritius

After about eighteen months of real confinement, he was allowed to move to the countryside and live on the estate of Madame d'Arifat at Plaines Wilhems on the south-west of the island, and life was in many ways pleasant and social, as recorded in the *Private Journal*. He did not waste the time he spent detained on Mauritius. He accomplished as much as he could, without consulting sources only available in England, which included the astronomical records at Greenwich, towards the task he knew awaited him on his return: completing his charts and the account of his voyage of discovery. He sent two papers to the Royal Society, one on the differences in the magnetic needle arising from an alteration in the direction of the ship's head, and the other on the uses of the marine barometer. Both were read at the Society and published in their *Transactions*. He read voraciously, in English and French, recording what he had been reading in his journal. He studied the geology and geophysics of the island, and wrote detailed observations in his journal on the local methods of processing products like indigo and maize. He instructed the younger sons of Madame d'Arifat in mathematics and navigation. He had become fluent in French, and formed friendships which lasted for the rest of his life with the local French settlers. He practised his flute and played chamber music with his friends and neighbours, and even wrote the lyrics to a song, which he sent to Ann in 1805. The only full-sized portrait of Flinders was painted by Toussaint Chazal, his neighbour at Madame d'Arifat's, in 1806–7. At his best, while on Mauritius he could say,

Time has softened (*sic*) my disappointments, I have my books, am making acquisitions in knowledge, enjoy good health, and innocent amusements for which I have still a relish, and look forward to the hope of overcoming all objections and difficulties with honour to myself; and to this I add, with heart-felt pleasure, that the consciousness of being perfectly innocent of any thing, that ought to have caused the suspicions that have been or are entertained against me. (PJ 96)

Writing the *Voyage*

Back in England, his task was to finish writing the *Voyage* and complete his charts. In his Preface, he notes that 'the publication in 1814 of a voyage commenced in 1801, and of which all the essential parts were concluded within three years, requires some explanation.' Shipwreck and detention were, of course, major reasons for the delay, but there were other challenges:

the Greenwich observations [were] found to differ so much from the calculated places of the sun and moon, given in the Nautical Almanacks of 1801, 2 and 3, as to make considerable alterations in the longitudes of places settled during the voyage; and a reconstruction of all the charts [became] thence indispensable to accuracy. (VTA 1: iii).

This meticulous work he carried out with the help, not always gracefully rendered, of his brother Samuel, second lieutenant on the *Investigator*. He succumbed to his illness almost as soon as the work was finished, and the *Voyage* was published just days before his death on 19 July 1814. Along the way, in 1812, he performed experiments on the effect on the compass of the magnetism of ships, which led to the invention of the Flinders Bar, a device for correcting the navigation errors caused by the iron in the hull of a ship.

In addition to the charting of the Australian coastline, Flinders' sailing directions referred to the collection of natural history specimens. The naturalist on the voyage was Robert Brown (1773–1858). For three and a half years Brown did intensive botanic research in Australia, collecting about 3400 species, of which about two thousand were previously unknown. Brown remained in Australia until May 1805. He then returned to Britain where he spent the next five years working on the material he had gathered. He published numerous species descriptions; in Western

Australia alone he is the author of nearly 1200 species. In 1810, he published the results of his collecting in *Prodromus Florae Novae Hollandiae et Insulae Van Diemen*, the first systematic account of the Australian flora. In addition to Brown's descriptions, landscapes and coastal views were painted by William Westall, and Ferdinand Bauer produced exquisite paintings of flora and fauna. Bauer, like Brown, stayed in Australia until 1805, when he returned to England with eleven cases of drawings containing 1,542 Australian plants, 180 Norfolk Island plants, and over 300 animals. So as far as that aspect of the voyage was concerned, a major contribution to the knowledge of Australian natural history was made, which would not have been possible without Flinders' active collaboration, in allowing the 'scientific gentlemen' time ashore to collect and explore.

Completing the survey

However, although Flinders' 1814 published map of Terra Australis (or Australia as he would have preferred to name it) provided an almost complete outline of the Australian continent, it was left to Governor King's son Phillip Parker King to complete the survey. In 1817 the British government decided that 'circumstances consequent upon the restoration of Peace ... rendered it most important to explore, with as little delay as possible, that part of the coast of New Holland ... not surveyed or examined by the late Captain Flinders', and appointed Lieutenant King to do this.[3] King made four voyages between 1817 and 1822 to complete the work which Flinders could well have completed had he lived beyond the age of forty. As well as filling in the gap Flinders left westward of Wessel's Islands, he surveyed a recently discovered harbour in Van Diemen's Land (now Tasmania). He was the first to give a report of Port Darwin, now the site of the capital of the Northern Territory.

Flinders achieved a spectacular amount of meticulous and important work during his active career, which had begun with smaller expeditions from Port Jackson in the 1790s in company with George Bass. However, a combination of imprudent decisions (which of course would have been vindicated had all gone well) and just plain bad luck prevented him from 'perfecting the discovery' of Terra Australis. The fact that his enforced stay on Mauritius had, as Miriam Estensen puts it, 'a certain ameliorating effect on this ambitious, driven man',[4] would probably not have been felt by him to be worth the pain and frustration he endured by being kept from his active career. But it seems unlikely that he would be quite the same figure of romance and adulation, had he not been cut off in his prime and prevented from achieving all he wished.

5

Matthew Flinders in South Australia, January to April 1802[1]

Entering SA waters

Matthew Flinders didn't know it, but on Tuesday 26 January 1802 he entered South Australian waters at Longitude 129 degrees East. As far as he was concerned he was mapping Nuyts Land, New Holland. He was passing along the coast of the land of the Mirning people.

In the captain's log of the *Investigator* on this day, along with descriptions of the terrain as it could be seen from the ship – low and sandy, with wooded land further back – he describes 'a fire made close down upon the beach, which seemed to be intended for our observation' (AC 1: 283). This interesting intimation that he was aware of being watched from the shore is not repeated in his *Voyage* narrative published in 1814.

The Aboriginal people of South Australia

On 28 January the *Investigator* anchored in what he named Fowler's Bay, after Robert Fowler, his first lieutenant. In both accounts, he describes finding some dogs' footprints, and 'some decayed spears, but no huts or anything that showed them to have been here lately' (AC 1: 286). In fact, though in the captain's log Flinders recounts several direct encounters elsewhere during his circumnavigation of Australia 1801–1803, there were to be no direct encounters with Aboriginal peoples on the shores of South Australia. They saw some Aboriginal people in the distance on Nawu land – at Coffin Bay – and they heard some in the distance, in what is now called Port Lincoln.

Anticipation and catastrophe

The kind of day-to-day official writing Flinders did is not really conducive to the expression of personal opinion and morality, although he sometimes did it anyway. When they entered Spencer's Gulf for the first time, as he wrote ten years later in the Voyage, 'Large rivers, deep inlets, inland seas, and passages into the Gulph of Carpentaria, were terms frequently used in our conversation of this evening, and the prospect of making an interesting discovery, seemed to have infused new life and vigour into every man in the ship' (VTA 1: 132–133). That life and vigour were to be knocked out of them, however, on the very next day.

In a bay at the southern tip of what we know as Eyre Peninsula, the Master, John Thistle, Midshipman William Taylor and six seamen set off for the shore in a cutter to search for water, and they never returned. Flinders assumed that they were caught in the 'dangerous ripplings of tide' (AC 1: 315) that had overturned the boat. The boat was found, and some of their belongings, but no trace of the bodies of their shipmates.

> As every search has now been made for our unfortunate shipmates that we could think had any prospect of being attended with success, I thought it would avail nothing to remain longer on this account; for there was only a small chance of obtaining these bodies when they might rise to the surface, from the number of sharks that we have constantly seen about. Even this small chance of obtaining their bodies would have induced me to wait a few days longer had not the want of water been so pressing to hurry us forward. I caused a stout post to be erected in the cove, and to it was nailed a sheet of copper upon which was engraven the following inscription:
>
> Memory Cove
> His Majestys ship *Investigator* Matt^w Flinders Commander
> Anchored here February 22 1802
> Mr John Thistle the master
> Mr William Taylor midshipman
> And six of the crew were most unfortunately drowned near this place from being upset in a boat. The wreck of the boat was found, but their bodies were not recovered.
> Nautici cavete! (AC 1: 318)

This was the voyage's first fatality, and Flinders felt it keenly. All the boat's crew were 'active and useful young men; and in a small and incomplete ship's company, which had so many duties to perform, this diminution of our force was heavily felt' (VTA 1: 139). But Thistle was a particularly sad loss. He had known Thistle since 1794, when they sailed together on the *Reliance* from England to Sydney, and, as he wrote in the log,

> we have mostly been together since that time. ... His zeal in the cause of discovery had induced him to join the Investigator when at Spithead and ready to sail, although he had returned to England only three weeks before from a distant voyage of six years continuance. (AC 1: 319)

In other words, a man after Flinders' own heart. Flinders wrote to Ann that 'it will grieve thee, as it has me, to understand that poor Thistle was lost upon the south coast. Thou knowest how I valued him: He is however gone.'[2] Thistle Island is named for him, and each of the other seven who were lost had an island named for them. Cape Catastrophe and Memory Cove are also named in commemoration of these lost men.

It is also possible that Flinders' heightened feelings of grief and loss are expressed in the other names he gave to this area: Cape Donington, after the village where he was born and grew up, Port Lincoln after his county of birth, Boston Island for the nearest large town to Donington, and so on.

This is Barngarla land, and their name for Port Lincoln is Galinyala.

Disappointment

They continued up the west coast of Spencer's Gulf, and on 10 March, at the head of the Gulf the 'scientific gentlemen' went ashore to climb Mount Brown, and Flinders also landed on Nukunu land to explore the head of the gulf. It was something of a disappointment to them that the gulf turned out not to be a strait dividing Australia in two – 'passages to the Gulph of Carpentaria' as had been discussed excitedly three weeks earlier (AC 1: 314).

Three weeks after he visited the head of Spencer Gulf, Flinders went ashore at the head of Gulf St Vincent on 30 March. They would have climbed 'the Hummocky Mountain' – now known as South Hummocks – 'had not its distance been found beyond the bounds of returning to the ship in the evening' (AC 1: 352). They surveyed the east coast of the gulf,

Kaurna land, from the ship. They made observations of Mount Lofty but didn't land. He noted that the land 'has a pleasant appearance, being grassy hills of gentle ascent with clumps of trees interspersed; but ... I judge it to be rather barren than fertile. ... The contrast between this low land and the opposite shore is great, that being mountainous and stony' (AC 1: 352). He didn't pick this as a site for what would become one of the world's most liveable cities.[3]

Alas, for the pelicans!

It was only a few days later that he visited Pelican Lagoon on Kangaroo Island and wrote those lines, which in *A Voyage to Terra Australis* were revised to include the immortal phrase 'Alas, for the pelicans!', as discussed in Chapter Three. Kangaroo Island was known to the mainland inhabitants as Karta, the isle of the dead. It had been uninhabited for several thousand years when Flinders arrived.

> The eastern head of the lagoon contains three islands, of which two seem to be breeding places for pelicans: on the third we did not land. These birds were in great numbers, and many of them too young to fly. From the quantity of scattered bones and skeletons upon the islands, I infer that the pelicans not only commence their being here, but that they have selected this retreat for the closing scene of their existence. Here, at a distance from man the great disturber of all, surrounded by his feathered progeny, and in the very same spot where he first emerged from his own shelly prison: in this retreat, the aged pelican can quietly resign his small portion of ethereal flame back to the great eternal source of vitality whence it emanated, without having his last moments interrupted, and perhaps without a pang. Requiescant ossa in pace, barbare! (AC 1: 356)[4]

He apologised, in a note, to his readers for these 'sentimental conjectures and exclamations' and requested them 'to pardon this touch of the melancholy, though not unpleasing, reflections which took hold of my mind on viewing this uncommon cemetery where the young wingless pelican was seen scrambling over the bones of his parent' (AC 1: 356n.4). This entry was written in the log on 5 April 1802.

Flinders called it Kangaroo Island because of the abundance of kangaroos which afforded them their first fresh food for a long time. He notes in his *Voyage* that he killed ten, and the other members of his party another twenty. Even then, he called it 'butchery, for the poor animals suffered themselves to be shot in the eyes with small shot, and in some cases to be knocked over the head with sticks' (VTA 1: 169). He had reason to feel melancholy, and to be contemplating death and mortality, after the loss of his shipmates.

Encounter

Three days later he met Captain Nicolas Baudin on the *Géographe* for the first time, on 8 April 1802 at a place he named Encounter Bay. It was off the lands of the Ngarrindjeri people. This encounter is of course the subject of many accounts by many authors, some quite romantic, some heroic. It is interesting to read the very first accounts of it from Flinders' log.

> On going on board I requested to see their passport [from the British government] which was shewn to me, and I offered mine for inspection, but captain Baudin put it back without looking at it. ... Captain Baudin was sufficiently communicative of his discoveries about Van Diemens Land, and of his remarks upon my chart of Bass's strait, many parts of which he condemned, but I was gratified to hear him say that the north side of VDL was well laid down and the islands near it. ... As Captain Baudin had an imperfect copy of my miscellaneous chart of Bass' Strait, I presented him [the next] morning with a copy of the three charts lately published, and of the small memoir attached to them. ... On my requesting to know the name of the commander of the *Naturaliste*, ... He 'apropos' begged to know mine and finding that it was the same as that of the author of the chart of Bass's strait which he had been criticising, he expressed some surprise and congratulation; but I did not apprehend that my being here at this time, so far along the unknown part of the coast, gave him any great pleasure (AC 1: 356).

Flinders couldn't have known about the tensions on board the *Géographe*, but it is worth noting that Baudin's antagonist François Péron recorded a favourable first impression of Flinders from this time:

> Mr Flinders is a man of 40 to 45 years of age [he was 28], short, thin and spare; he has a sharp and piercing gaze, his face is full of expression and his

features animated ... all of his movements point to an ardent and impetuous character. His manners are those of a prudent and sensitive man, his conduct towards us was tactful and generous.[5]

Later Péron would not be so complimentary, but this is a precious first-person account of what Flinders was like. He often wrote about himself explicitly, usually self-critically, and also revealed his personality and character in what he wrote, but there are not many eye-witness accounts like this.

After the encounter there was no point in duplicating the effort of the French. Flinders naturally ceded naming rights to them for that portion of the coast they had visited before him. So it was only ten days later, on 19 April, that they left South Australian waters and crossed the present border into Victoria, at 140° 58E. They had been 83 days in SA waters.

6

Matthew Flinders and the Limits of Empathy: First Encounters with Aboriginal Peoples[1]

The Romantic era

On his *Investigator* voyage, the 26-year-old Matthew Flinders brought with him to the coasts of New Holland a sensibility influenced both by Enlightenment ideas and the dawn of the Romantic era. Although he did not have the benefit of a university education, his father's diaries show that he came from a household where books were valued, and the habit of reading seems to have taken hold early. His outlook was formed by his studies in navigation, mathematics, and Latin, but equally by reading imaginative literature, such as Daniel Defoe's *Robinson Crusoe* and John Milton's *Paradise Lost*. He had somehow, during his crowded early life, imbibed the heady spirit of Romantic Science described by Richard Holmes in *The Age of Wonder:*

> Romanticism as a cultural force is generally regarded as intensely hostile to science, its ideal of subjectivity eternally opposed to that of scientific objectivity. But I do not believe this was always the case, or that the terms are so mutually exclusive. The notion of *wonder* seems to be something that once united them, and can still do so. In effect there is Romantic science in the same sense that there is Romantic poetry, and often for the same enduring reasons.[2]

Holmes talks of 'the new imaginative intensity and excitement' that romanticism brought to science: 'It was driven by a common ideal of intense, even reckless, personal commitment to discovery.'[3] This is something I have often noted in Flinders' personal writings – 'Sea! I am thy servant,' he wrote to Ann in 1799[4] – and it makes sense that 'the idea of the exploratory voyage, often lonely and perilous, is in one form or another a central and defining metaphor of Romantic science', as Holmes writes.[5]

Sympathy/Empathy

Much of what Flinders wrote is in the nature of scientific reports and factual accounts of his travels, but in his personal letters and his *Private Journal* we can begin to discover the nature of this young man – he was never anything but that, and died at forty – and from these we can perhaps see in what way, if any, his view of the world affected his decisions and behaviour. One aspect of his world view that has always struck me in his writings is a habit of looking at things from the other point of view – what was known as 'sympathy' at the time, and what we now call 'empathy'.[6] I have always thought of this as a typical trait of the eighteenth century, with its Enlightenment emphasis on objectivity, tolerance, and scientific enquiry.[7] It even seems encoded in the balance of the eighteenth-century prose style: the cadences of the style that is so familiar in Jane Austen are to be heard in Flinders' prose, and both, I suspect, can be traced further back into the eighteenth century. Even taking a sample of the prose of Samuel Johnson totally at random, for example, I find:

> Thus they rose in the morning and lay down at night, pleased with each other and with themselves; all but Rasselas, who, in the twenty-sixth year of his age, began to withdraw himself from their pastimes and assemblies, and to delight in solitary walks and silent meditation. He often sat before tables covered with luxury, and forgot to taste the dainties that were placed before him; he rose abruptly in the midst of the song, and hastily retired beyond the sound of music.[8]

The stately rhythms of this prose all come in pairs: they *rose* and *lay*; he *began to withdraw* and *to delight*; he *sat* and *forgot*; he *rose* and *retired*. The writer of sentences like these is looking for the 'tock' to complement his 'tick' (to use Frank Kermode's apt formulation[9]).

In the same way, it seems to me, Flinders was in the mental habit of making a statement, or thinking a thought, and then seeking the balancing idea. A scientific cast of mind might explain this automatic weighing of ideas before coming to a decision, but it also seems to me to be a sign of a well-developed moral imagination: the recognition of the other point of view, a reluctance to rush to judgement, a wariness of prejudice. Is it too far-fetched to see this as a habit which encourages balance not only in rhetoric but in moral thought?

The kind of day-to-day official writing Flinders did is not conducive to the expression of personal morality, but the journal that he maintained while detained in Mauritius and for the few remaining years of his life in London, although it too maintains a scrupulous record of weather, events and activities, allowed him more scope to express his feelings, and his thoughts about society and history, when he was inclined to do so. In this *Private Journal*, and in his personal correspondence, we discover a man who might be ambitious and determined in his efforts to make his mark as an explorer, but who was far from narcissistic. Whether writing to his wife, a family member, or a friend, he is always concerned for their welfare, and willing to give them the benefit of the doubt if he hadn't received a letter he expected. He understood very well, and shared, the grief he caused his wife, Ann, by leaving her behind in England in 1801: in 1805 he sent her a set of lyrics he had set to a song, in which he wrote from the woman's point of view about the pain she felt at being left behind 'to mourn'.[10] He even speculated in romantic fashion about the fate of the pelicans on Kangaroo Island, 'at a distance from man the great disturber of all'.[11]

This tendency to empathy had its limits. He had no problem living on Mauritius, in a society based directly on slavery. In fact, his career as a navigator began under Captain William Bligh, transporting breadfruit plants from Tahiti to Jamaica to provide food for the slaves there. He never expresses any qualms about carrying out the standard punishments for his crew – in the captain's log he often records corporal punishments for drunkenness, for 'mutinous expressions' and other breaches of discipline. The questions I want to explore in this chapter are how far his empathy extended towards the Indigenous people of Australia, in theory, and how this affected his dealings with them in the various situations when he came into contact with them.

European encounters with Australian Aboriginal people

Flinders' attitude to the Aboriginal people would have been influenced by his predecessors. In his journal kept while a midshipman under Bligh in the *Reliance*, he wrote out Bligh's instructions for dealing with the 'Natives of the South Sea Islands'. These instructions contain seventeen clauses, several of them specifically relating to the situation at Tahiti, but others more general, such as:

> 3rd. Every Person is to study to gain the good will and esteem of the Natives to treat them with all kindness and not to recover by violent means any thing that may have been stolen from them, but to acquaint me with it. ...
>
> 8th. No Canoe is to come on board after eight at Night ...
>
> 16th. No Person whatever is to take fire Arms with him on shore at Otaheite until he has my Permission.[12]

Flinders' instructions to his own crew on the *Investigator* followed in this tradition.

While he had an ambivalent relationship with Bligh, Flinders' admiration for James Cook, whose status as a national hero was confirmed by his shocking death, amounted to veneration. Cook's view of the inhabitants of New Holland was more favourable than that of the seventeenth-century visitors, whose reactions had been 'largely negative and slanderous.'[13] Cook wrote:

> From what I have said of the Natives of New-Holland they may appear to some to be the most wretched people upon Earth, but in reality they are far more happier than we Europeans; being wholly unacquainted not only with the superfluous but the necessary Conveniences so much sought after in Europe, they are happy in not knowing the use of them. They live in a Tranquillity which is not disturb'd by the Inequality of Condition.[14]

Sir Joseph Banks was Flinders' honoured patron, known to him personally. They corresponded regularly, but I have not been able to find any discussion of the Australian Aboriginal peoples in their letters. Banks' attitude was, as Anderson and Perrin have observed, 'in accordance with Enlightenment views' in which '"the human" was defined by its very capacity to rise above and to improve upon nature.'[15] Banks tended to make rather bold generalisations from the limited contact he had with them.

> We saw indeed only the sea coast; what the immense tract of inland countrey may produce is to us totaly unknown; *we may have liberty to conjecture* however that they are totaly uninhabited. The Sea has I beleive

been universaly found to be the cheif source of supplys to Indians ignorant of the arts of cultivation: the wild produce of the Land alone seems scarce able to support them at all seasons, *at least I do not remember to have read of* any inland nation who did not cultivate the ground more or less ... But should a people live inland who supported themselves by cultivation these inhabitants of the sea coast must certainly have learn'd to imitate them in some degree at least, otherwise their reason must be supposd to hold a rank little superior to that of monkies.

... That their customs were nearly the same throughout the whole length of the coast along which we saild I should think very probable. *Tho we had Connections with them only at one place* yet we saw them either with our eyes or glasses many times.[16]

This is a nice example of what Edward Said called

flexible *positional* superiority, which puts the Westerner in a whole series of possible relationships with the Orient [extended in this case to New Holland] without ever losing him the relative upper hand. ... The scientist, the scholar, the missionary, the trader, or the soldier was in, or thought about, the Orient because he *could be there*, or could think about it, with very little resistance on the Orient's part.[17]

It is worth noting, though, that Banks had been a sympathetic and active mediator with the Tahitians earlier in the *Endeavour* voyage, learning their language and living among them for some months. Holmes points out that Banks 'frequently blamed himself, rather than the Tahitians, for misunderstandings or false accusations of theft.'[18] John Gascoigne, in his book *Joseph Banks and the English Enlightenment*, discusses 'Banks's willingness to learn from other non-European societies, whether in Tahiti or elsewhere,' and points out that

this openness to non-European cultures owed much to the Enlightenment: one of the favourite devices of *philosophes* like Montesquieu or Voltaire being to contrast the practices and beliefs of Europe with the allegedly more rational characteristics of ancient, non-Christian civilisations.[19]

The Australian Aboriginal peoples whom Banks encountered – or failed to encounter – had such a different social structure from the Pacific

Islanders that it seems that he had difficulty in realising that any such social structure existed. He, like Cook, saw the advantages of what he saw as their innocent state, however:

> Thus live these I had almost said happy people, content with little nay almost nothing, Far enough removd from the anxieties attending upon riches, or even the possession of what we Europeans call common necessaries. ... From them appear how small are the real wants of human nature.[20]

These enlightened views did not prevent misunderstandings, however. There was a dispute over turtles caught by Cook's crew: without a common language and any knowledge of their customs, 'innocent gestures would be seen as forms of confrontation, by both sides.'[21] This pattern would be repeated more and more frequently as contact increased over the ensuing centuries, although as time passed it becomes less tenable to interpret many gestures as innocent, particularly when the distribution of power became much less balanced than it was in these early encounters.

Flinders and Aboriginal peoples – early encounters

Though Flinders was a generation younger than Banks, he was in many ways of like mind with his influential patron. They were both socially conservative, with a strong belief in the values of improvement and usefulness of science: 'My employments and inclinations lead to the extension of happiness and of sciences, and not to the destruction of mankind,' he wrote in his *Private Journal* (PJ 97). However, although he usually expressed the Enlightenment empirical view, especially in his official writings, Flinders' general remarks about Aboriginal peoples seem more circumspect than Banks'. He had much more personal experience than Banks, for one thing.

Before his voyage of circumnavigation, Flinders had already had close encounters with the Dharawal people on the New South Wales coast during his Tom Thumb voyages with George Bass. In March 1796, they found themselves at a disadvantage on the coast south of Sydney, their little boat full of water and all their possessions – including food, clothes and ammunition – drenched. Flinders wrote in his narrative of the expedition that 'Natives to the southward of Botany Bay were generally believed to be cannibals.'[22] However, when some Aboriginal men approached offering fish and water in 'the Port Jackson dialect',[23] which they were able to understand, Flinders and Bass cautiously allowed them to pilot their boat to a river. Despite their trepidation at being outnumbered, they engaged with the these two men and some local Dharawal men, Bass getting some of them to help him mend an oar, and Flinders trimming their hair and beards with scissors – although in his account of this incident, he makes fun of the timidity and fear some of them showed at the 'double-jawed instrument coming so near to their noses', and wrote, 'I was almost tempted to try the effect of a snip on the nose; but our situation was too critical to admit of such experiments.'[24] There was a certain amount of pretence and in the end 'a show of anger' before they could get away – Flinders fired a shot to deter them from pursuing the boat.

Guns versus spears

One way of looking at this is to see the powerful white men menacing the Aboriginal people with their superior fire-power. But Flinders and his companions were in a vulnerable position – they showed considerable nerve by engaging with them to the extent they did. Having only a few words in common and no real understanding of their society, and, no doubt, realising that they were likely to be regarded (quite justly) as intruders, firing a shot – apparently not aimed at anyone or intended to do more than frighten them away – is understandable. Perhaps they would have done so earlier, but their muskets were 'full of sand and rusty' after their mishap the previous day and had only just been 'gotten ... in order.'[25]

In July 1799, he ventured north in the sloop *Norfolk*, with Bungaree, a Guringai man from Port Jackson (now Sydney) among the crew to help him liaise with the Aboriginal peoples. In his *Voyage*, Flinders referred to Bungaree, on this trip and again on the *Investigator*, as 'my friend Bongaree' (VTA 1: cxcvii): he wrote that when making preparations for the second leg of the *Investigator* voyage in July 1802, as 'I had before experienced much advantage from the presence of a native of Port Jackson, in bringing about a friendly intercourse with the inhabitants of other parts of the coast', he was pleased that 'Bongaree, the worthy and brave fellow who had sailed with me in the *Norfolk*, now volunteered again' (VTA 1: 235). There is more than a hint of condescension in Flinders' attitude to Bungaree, but there is no doubt that they often relied on his knowledge of indigenous cultures and his willingness to act as an envoy, sometimes putting himself into potentially dangerous situations to smooth the path for the Europeans.[26]

On the 1799 *Norfolk* expedition their dealings on shore had been mixed. An exchange of gifts went badly as Flinders refused to give up his hat, and it ended with a spear being thrown and musket shots being fired. Flinders may have wounded one of the men with his musket fire. He later referred to this as 'an unfortunate occurrence' (VTA 1: cxcvi). Later on the same expedition, there was a more friendly encounter, involving dancing and singing.

These incidents are, of course, characterised by cross-cultural misunderstanding. Sutton and Veth point out that

> Aboriginal people cannot be accurately portrayed only as passive, helpless victims in these historical circumstances, in spite of great losses. ... Not all sought engagement with the strangers, but many did. Many engaged the outsiders in acts of repulsion and rejection. Many others hugged and took dance steps with them, or gave them food.[27]

And it is interesting to note, too, that the respective weaponry was not as unequal as might be assumed by those familiar with modern firearms: muskets of the day were inaccurate, heavy and useless in wet conditions, while 'spears weighed little and could be thrown on the move. Further, muzzle-loading was a time-consuming process, while a spear-thrower could be reloaded in an instant.'[28] Cook noted as much in his journal: 'by the help of these throwing sticks, as we call them, they will hit a Mark at the distance of 40 or 50 Yards, with almost, if not as much certainty as we can do with a Musquet, and much more so than with a ball.'[29] This does not obviate the fact that the Europeans were intruders, but both sides, Sutton points out, 'acted as human beings, as people of their time and place, not as timeless ideological cardboard cut-outs.'[30] Also, as Inga Clendinnen points out,

> in all first-contact situations both peoples, lacking a common language and with no accumulation of mutual cultural knowledge, are like baffled infants squinting through a keyhole: they see only actions and only some of those, and what they hear will be unintelligible babble. They will not know

what conversations and other subtler interactions are taking place before their eyes, much less offstage; they will not know where, who and what to watch.[31]

Perhaps the limits of empathy are reached not so much when the parties fail to understand each other, but when they fail to acknowledge their ignorance and act out of misguided arrogance or fear.

The *Investigator* voyage

In the captain's log of the *Investigator*, recently published by the Hakluyt Society in an edition by Kenneth Morgan, Flinders recounts several encounters during his circumnavigation of Australia 1801–1803. These accounts, which are taken from the 'fair' journals but were basically written during the voyage, can be read alongside the official account in *A Voyage to Terra Australis,* written a decade later for publication. In the *Investigator* logbook, Flinders made some remarks on the behaviour of the Aboriginal people at what is now called Port Lincoln, South Australia:

> This morning some natives were heard calling, as we supposed, to a boat which had just then landed at the tents, and two of them were seen at about half a mile from us; but they soon walked away, or perhaps retired into the woods to watch our motions. No attempts were made to follow them, as I have always found of the natives of New Holland that they avoid those that seem anxious to communicate with them, but if left entirely alone will usually come down after having watched our actions four or five days. (AC 1: 323)

This is already more considered and better informed than Banks' presumptuous statements. Moreover, Flinders added in the published *Voyage*:

> Nor does this conduct seem to be unnatural; for what, in such case, would be the conduct of any people, ourselves for instance, were we living in a state of nature, frequently at war with our neighbours, and ignorant of the existence of any other nation? (VTA 1: 146)

In what follows, I concentrate particularly on two encounters, one on the south-west coast of Australia near the present-day city of Albany, Western

Australia, and another at Morgan Island, off the coast of the Northern Territory.

The Noongar at King George Sound

The *Investigator* sighted land at Cape Leeuwin, on the south-western extremity of the Australian continent, on Sunday, 6 December 1801. They sailed eastwards along the south coast to King George Sound, named ten years earlier by George Vancouver, where they anchored on 9 December. The first meeting of the English with the Noongar people took place on 14 December.[32] Kenneth Morgan notes, 'Flinders's meetings with the Aborigines at King George Sound were notably friendly' (AC 1: 246n4). They were, however, still bedeviled by misunderstandings. Flinders noted in the *Investigator* log: 'As has usually been observed of the natives of other parts of New Holland these people did not wish for any communication, but made signs for the party to return back' (AC 1: 246). For the following week or so, however, Noongar men visited the Englishmen's camp almost every day. Flinders noted,

> We always made them presents of such things as seemed to be most agreeable, but they very rarely brought us any thing in return; nor was it uncommon to find small mirrors, and other things left about the shore; so that at length our presents were discontinued. (VTA 1: 58)

On Wednesday 23 December, Flinders set off with a party of thirteen scientists, officers and men to visit some lagoons they wanted to investigate.

> Soon after leaving the head of Princess Royal Harbour, a native was seen running before us, and an old man, who had before visited the tents, made his appearance, and was very resolute to prevent us from going into the country. He was not able to prevail, but we accommodated him by going round the part of the wood where it should seem his family were. He followed us through swamps and thick bushes, hollowing constantly for the purpose, as I suppose, of informing his friends of our movements. After we had passed some distance from the place where we had met him, he fell behind and left us. (AC 1: 248–249)

Len Collard and Dave Palmer have used a cross-cultural approach to try to reconstruct the likely reactions of the Noongar to the early explorers.

> When they first realised that the big ships carried people Nyungar thought the coastal explorers were *djanga* or returned spirits of their *noitch moort* or dead relatives coming home again. They were happy, and they welcomed the white spirit beings as members of their family.
>
> Nyungar would have known that they had important protocols to carry out. It was their responsibility to teach their ... relatives ... knowledge of the ... land, because they had obviously forgotten everything when they had 'died'. ... They stumbled about in the bush as if they were lost. Sometimes Nyungar helped the newcomers, reminding them of where they were and how to stay safe.[33]

Perhaps something of this kind was happening here: clearly there is misunderstanding on both sides. In *A Voyage to Terra Australis* Flinders' account of this incident is slightly expanded. Rather than saying baldly that 'he fell behind and left us', as in the log book entry, he wrote:

> At length, growing tired of people who persevered in keeping a bad road in opposition to his recommendation of a better, which, indeed, had nothing objectionable in it, but that it led directly contrary to where our object lay, he fell behind and left us. (VTA 1: 59)

This rather sardonic passage was written on the other side of the world a decade later, with the confidence of hindsight and distance. As Tiffany Shellam has pointed out:

> The frequent description of friendly and peaceful natives in the explorers' journals sit uneasily alongside the currents of fear and insecurity. The fear reveals how this friendship was forced or imagined by the explorers, and is telling of the uneasiness they felt in the presence of the Mineng.[34]

Flinders remarked, in both versions of the account, that 'They seemed to have no idea of any superiority we possessed over them; on the contrary, they left us, after the first interview, with some appearance of contempt for our pusillanimity' (VTA 1: 66). This statement sounds outrageous to modern ears: it seems to imply that he made a misplaced assumption of the innate superiority of himself, his companions and his civilisation. However, he uses the word 'superiority' again later in the logbook to mean nothing more than tactical advantage, and reading that meaning back on this passage, I think that he probably means the same thing here (AC 2: 186). This impression, he noted in the log, 'was probably occasioned by the comparative mildness of our manners and the desire we shewed to be friendly with them' (AC 1: 258). He added in the *Voyage* the rather menacing statement: 'This opinion, however, seemed to be corrected in their future visits' (VTA 1: 66).

One way they seem to have 'corrected' the Mineng's opinion was to exercise the marines on the beach, which Flinders noted in the log, 'raised much astonishment amongst the natives, and apparently pleasure' (AC 1: 250). In the *Voyage* this account was somewhat embellished:

> On the 30th, our wooding, and the watering of the ship were completed, the rigging was refitted, the sails repaired and bent, and the ship unmoored. *Our friends*, the natives, continued to visit us; and the old man, with several others being at the tents this morning, I ordered the party of marines on shore, to be exercised in their presence. The red coats and white crossed belts were greatly admired, having some resemblance to their own manner of ornamenting themselves; and the drum, but particularly the fife, excited their astonishment; but when they saw these *beautiful red-and-white men, with their bright muskets, drawn up in a line,* they absolutely screamed with delight; nor were their wild gestures and vociferation to be silenced, but by commencing the exercise to which they paid the most earnest and silent attention. (VTA 1: 60–61, emphasis mine)

Kenneth Morgan notes in his edition of the log that 'This military exercise by the marines appears to have been staged to assess the Aborigines' responses' (AC 1: 250n1) – or more likely, as Flinders wrote, to 'correct' their opinions. As he was getting ready to leave, Flinders wrote in the log:

> We ... parted with our new friends after the tents were struck, with good humour, and without any quarrel having taken place during our intercourse; but it is remarkable, that when the marines returned to the ship, all the sensations which had been excited in the natives went also. (AC 1: 251)

How could he know what their sensations were? Here is a limit of empathy – the belief that he could comprehend the feelings of these people. He went on,

> Such is the human mind when uncultivated; I believe, however, that they left us with higher ideas of our power than before, though from our desire to be friendly with them, which induced us to put up with little things from them which were not altogether pleasant, I suspect they took us for cowards; and had we remained longer should probably have been obliged to convince them that we were not to be insulted. (AC 1: 251)

The 'friendliness' of the encounter, as Shellam observes, is, probably on both sides, a matter of policy, rather than the result of any real cross-cultural understanding or sympathy. At one stage, some of the Noongar men – in the log there are five, but in the *Voyage* there were only two – were almost persuaded to go on board the ship. Flinders believed that 'their courage failing, they desired to be relanded' (VTA 1: 65–66). The fear he attributed to them perhaps echoed the fears he had felt back in 1796, when he and George Bass distrusted the intentions of the people they encountered and eventually fired a shot to deter them from pursuit.

The drill might have been intended as a show of power rather than a friendly display, but Morgan notes that

> The Aborigines appear to have interpreted the military drill as an appropriate contact ritual. In 1908 the anthropologist Daisy Bates met an elderly man near Albany called Nebinyan. He told her that the Nyungar Aborigines of King George Sound believed that Flinders and his party were ghosts of their own dead ancestors who had returned from Kooranup, the home of the dead across the sea. They thought the full dress parade of the marines was a Kooranup ceremony. The ritual was considered sacred, to be handed down the generations. (AC 1: 250n2)

Novelist Kim Scott talks about this ritual dance in an interview:

> The title [of my novel], 'That Deadman Dance' is a reference to the military drill, Flinders' military drill turned into a dance and kept going as a dance. When I think about that, I think ... wow, what a powerful thing to do, to turn a violent drill into a dance. Appropriating cultural products of the other.[35]

As Peter Sutton notes, 'People living far from any regular contact with other cultures showed reactions that were less hostile and more welcoming.'[36] Collard and Palmer point out that in Nyungar ontology it is inconceivable that a stranger would arrive in another person's *karleep* or homefire and assert ownership unless they had some form of relationship with the *boodjar* or land in a previous existence. Therefore many of those Nyungar who saw the mariners for the first time would have simply assumed that the mariners had enjoyed a previous connection with Nyungar *boodjar*. As a consequence, Nyungar would have been among the most obliging of Indigenous groups.[37]

The Yolŋgu at Blue Mud Bay

If there were undercurrents of violence and fear even in this 'friendly' encounter, they surfaced with tragic results a year later when the *Investigator* reached Blue Mud Bay, the land of the Djalkiripuyngu people, part of the Yolŋgu-speaking territory in what is now the Northern Territory.[38]

In the oppressive heat of late January 1803, on an island named by Flinders 'Morgan's Island', the Master's Mate, John Whitewood, was speared in what Flinders interpreted as a misunderstanding:

> Mr Whitewood put out his hand to take a spear which he supposed was offered to him: but he was fatally mistaken, for the indian was standing in his defence, and thinking an attempt was made to seize his arms, he ran the spear into the breast of his supposed enemy. (AC 2: 252)

Whitewood suffered three more spear wounds, while 'our people ... were snapping their musquets, not one of which would go off. At length two were fired and the Indians ran away' (AC 2: 252).

Flinders summarized what happened next in *A Voyage to Terra Australis*:

> I immediately despatched two armed boats to their assistance, under the direction of the master; with orders, if he met with the natives, to be friendly and give them presents, and by no means to pursue them into the wood. I suspected, indeed, that our people must have been the aggressors; but told the master, if the Indians had made a wanton attack, to bring off their canoe by way of punishment; intending myself to take such steps on the following day, as might be found expedient. (VTA 2: 196)

This is not materially different from what he wrote in the *Investigator* log, except that he omitted the phrase 'without any regard to what might have passed' after 'give them presents' (AC 2: 252).

Flinders shows little sympathy for his own men in this transaction. He says in both accounts that he suspected that they were the aggressors, although that seems to be contradicted by the account of the spearing, where apparently Whitewood acted innocently and was speared only on a misunderstanding. On reflection, however, he seems to have changed his mind:

> It does not accord with the usually timid character of the natives of Terra Australis, to suppose the Indians came over from Isle Woodah for the purpose of making an attack; yet the circumstance of their being without women or children, – their following so briskly after Mr Westall, – and advancing armed to the wooders, all imply that they rather sought than avoided a quarrel. (VTA 2: 198)

His explanation in the *Voyage* for this departure from the normally 'friendly' demeanour of the Aboriginal peoples is that 'they might have had differences with, and entertained no respectful opinion of the Asiatic visitors' – the Malay traders whom the British encountered later. In the log he had no such explanation available: this aggressive attitude was a puzzle.

Anthropologist Marcus Barber explains what might have been behind this behaviour:

> The Yolŋgu word for place, *wänga*, can mean everything from 'home' or 'hearth' to 'country'. Whilst the analogy is imperfect in some ways, there is a sense in which entering Yolŋgu country, land or sea, without following the proper protocols, is the urban Australian equivalent of walking unannounced straight into someone else's backyard or kitchen.[39]

Even this century, Barber recounts, a Yolŋgu elder from this area felt strongly enough to threaten to kill a fisherman who trespasses on this country: 'Memories of open armed indigenous resistance to colonisation are still fresh in this part of Australia and, to this day, Blue Mud Bay has a reputation in the professional fishing industry for being a hostile area.'[40]

In any event, though he did not understand the cultural background, Flinders understood the danger posed by aggressive behaviour on the part of the visitors. He records his condemnation of the Master, John Aken, for what happened next in both accounts. Instead of acting in a 'friendly' way, and offering gifts, Aken, 'forgetting the orders I had given him', sent an armed party 'with a view, I fear, of cutting them all off in revenge for the expected death of Mr Whitewood.' Three Djalkiripuyngu men managed to get to their canoe and set off. 'Thus disappointed, the wooding party commenced a sharp fire after the canoe, so that before she got out of reach, one indian fell and the other two leaped out of the canoe and dived away' (AC 2: 253). It is not clear whether one or two men died: a seaman 'who gave himself the credit of having shot the native' swam to the canoe and found a man's body in it, but he upset the canoe. The next day they found a man's body,

> lying on the shore out of the water; but not lying along the edge of it, as one would expect would be the case with a body washed up; for the head was up towards the land and the feet just touching the surf. The arms were crossed under the head, with the face downwards. It was indeed the posture of a man who was just able to crawl out of the water and die.

He speculates regretfully that this was not the same man who had been found apparently dead in the canoe: 'I very much fear that it is one of those who were thought to have escaped', he wrote, but he could not know either way (AC 2: 253).

In the *Voyage*, he wrote, 'I was much concerned at what had happened, and greatly displeased with the master for having acted so contrary to my order; but the mischief [was] unfortunately done' (VTA 2: 197). In the *Investigator* log, he added, 'if, however, there was really but one man killed, they will not have suffered more than their violence merited' (AC 2: 254).[41] He followed this up with further 'positive' orders, the next day, 'not to pursue or in any way injure the Indians should he meet with them, but to make presents and conciliate them if possible' (AC 2: 254).

So far, perhaps, this all seems an unfortunate, although perhaps predictable, result of the *Investigator*'s project of exploration, although, as Morgan points out, 'This was the first serious trouble with Aborigines that the *Investigator*'s crew encountered on the voyage,' more than a year after they made their first landfall at Cape Leeuwin (AC 2: 252n1). Flinders expresses dismay and records the displeasure he felt at the time with his Master and those under his command for disobeying his orders, with the resulting death of at least one Djalkiripuyngu man, and perhaps two.

This incident is mentioned in the anonymous 'Historical Sketch', written shortly after Flinders' death, possibly by his brother Samuel:

> His conduct on Mr Whitewood, the master's mate, being speared, his humane consideration for the lives of the natives, his mild orders, his controlled anger on their being disobeyed, and the agony of mind he is stated to have suffered on one of the poor wretches being shot by his boat's crew, speak forcibly for the benevolence of his heart.[42]

It is interesting that the author of the Sketch, which runs to 17 pages, chooses to end his account of Flinders' life with this episode to epitomise his 'benevolent' character. It clearly made an impression on those who witnessed his 'agony of mind'.

He does not, however, record that any of those involved in the attack were punished, and punishments were routinely recorded in the log on other occasions. As a Warrant Officer, John Aken would not have been liable for corporal punishment meted out to the men. Had his offense been of a more serious nature he would have had to be confined in the ship until it returned to a port where a court martial could be convened. He could have been given a reprimand or a severe reprimand or 'logged' which means the offense would have been recorded in the ship's log and the record follow him when moving to another ship. Any of these punishments could be accompanied by a loss of seniority and affect future promotion.[43]

None of this happened: the Master was a key officer in the ship's navigation, and it might be a difficult situation if the Master were at odds with the Captain, so perhaps Flinders' policy of conciliation towards the Aboriginal peoples was also extended to the Master on this occasion. Despite recording of his disapproval of Aken in both accounts of the voyage, Flinders later chose to take Aken with him on the *Cumberland*, and they were detained together on Mauritius. Aken was released in 1805 and Flinders sent letters home with him. In a letter to Ann he wrote that Aken 'is a plain man, but a good one' (PL 123).

Another consequence of the killing demonstrates another limit of empathy. The following morning, 'a boat was sent ... to search for the dead body, the painter being desirous of it to make a drawing, and the naturalist and surgeon for anatomical purposes' (VTA 2: 197). Westall's drawing of this man survives in the National Library of Australia. No mention is made of returning the body later.

This disregard for the respect due to the dead seems a flagrant breach of the rules under which Flinders usually seemed to conduct himself, and to expect those under his command to behave. It is true that many misunderstandings occurred when customs were at variance between the two cultures involved in these early contacts – matters of protocol in greeting strangers, attitudes to possessions and so on. However, respect for the dead would surely be regarded by Flinders as a universal human trait. A marine who died of sunstroke, Thomas Morgan, was 'committed to the deep with the usual ceremony; and the island was named after him' (VTA 2: 198). No such reverence or courtesy was accorded to the body of the dead Djalkiripuyngu man. Did Flinders not understand that taking away the body was likely to cause offense and distress, or did he think that the claims of science overrode such considerations? The editors of Robert Brown's diary also comment on the difference in treatment of the remains of the two men. While Brown does not mention what happened once the body had been collected, '[Peter] Good adds that the body was dissected and the head preserved in spirit. By contrast, he and Flinders report that Morgan's remains were committed to the deep, with the usual ceremony.'[44]

The manners and customs of the inhabitants

It was indeed part of the Flinders' Instructions for the voyage to 'be very diligent in your examination' of various aspects of the coast of Terra Australis, including 'the manners and customs of the inhabitants of such parts as you may be able to explore' (VTA 1: 128). There is nothing in the sailing instructions regarding the way they should behave towards the Australian Aboriginal peoples: that seems to have been left to his own discretion, and as I have mentioned, he seems to have been guided partly by the instructions he received from Bligh on the *Providence*. He registers his own discomfiture with the death of the Djalkiripuyngu man, but his duty was to gather evidence of the 'manners and customs' – and this seems to extend to the physical attributes – of the inhabitants.

That he regarded the accomplishment of the objectives of his voyage as his overriding duty is made clear in the letter he wrote to the ship's surgeon, Hugh Bell, in May 1803. Bell had clearly complained to Flinders that he had acted contrary to the welfare of 'the health of the people on board' by not making 'all possible speed to port'. Flinders' rejoinder was that the duty 'of a Commander may be either diametrically opposite to humanity, as in the case of exposing them to great danger; or it may be so in part, such as the present time to sacrifice a few days to accomplish a particular object in order to prevent the necessity of a future expedition' (PL 94).

Two weeks after the fatality on Morgan Island, they had some more dealings with Yolŋgu-speaking people. An axe was stolen, and in order to try to force its return they took a young man captive on the boat for a day. Flinders observed, 'He ate heartily, laughed, cried, & noticed everything, frequently expressing admiration' (AC 2: 269). The next day, 'he appeared a little melancholy; but upon the whole had not fared amiss, having been eating most of the morning and afternoon. He begged hard to be released, and after giving him several little presents, was set at liberty' (AC 2: 271). Flinders decided to release 'the poor indian', though he would have liked to carry him away, 'considering the circumstance only as regarding ourselves; for Woga is a spritely, good-natured and intelligent youth, whom our treatment would have soon reconciled to the ship', and he might have proved useful as an intermediary and a source of information. However, 'I was desirous to be upon good terms with the natives, lest they might do injury to other strangers that might come after us' (AC 2: 270–271).

The limits of empathy
The evidence of Flinders' feelings of empathy with the Aboriginal people he encountered is, it must be conceded, slight, coming as it does as part of the official accounts of the voyage both in the log, written during the voyage, and the published *Voyage*, written a decade later. He expresses mild though not insurmountable regret at the death of the man at Morgan's Island. He refers to Woga, the young man held captive for a day in February 1803 as 'the poor indian'. So far this is evidence more of what we would call sympathy rather than empathy. The most direct expression of empathy is in *A Voyage to Terra Australis*:

> What ... would be the conduct of any people, *ourselves for instance*, were we living in a state of nature, frequently at war with our neighbours, and ignorant of the existence of any other nation? (VTA 1: 146, emphasis mine)

This, written ten years after the voyage, after many tribulations and disappointments, and after much time for contemplation during his detention by the French, might be a unique instance of his imaginative identification with the Aboriginal people.

As for the way any feelings of sympathy or empathy might have expressed themselves in his actions during the *Investigator* voyage, I believe that they simply did not enter the equation. Though perhaps as a matter of pure humanity he would prefer not to cause pain or trouble to other human beings – and I don't think there is any evidence that he failed to recognise the Aboriginal peoples' claims to full humanity: he never likened them to 'monkeys' as Banks did – in all his dealings with them as captain of the *Investigator* his primary intention was to keep his ship's company safe, and to smooth the way for future explorations. In most cases, he deemed that humane treatment and forbearance was the best way to do this, but if a show of force, even firing at them with intent to wound, was needed 'to convince them that we were not to be insulted' (AC 1: 251), he would not shrink from doing his duty as he saw it. As Bronwen Douglas writes, 'Flinders comes across as a supreme pragmatist who took a friendly comparative interest in the particular Aboriginal people he encountered but was also quick to deploy force if threatened by their actions or demeanour.'[45] The limits of empathy are defined by duty – and Flinders' duty was in the final analysis dictated by policy rather than feelings or morality.

Part 3

Family, Friends, Patrons, Companions

7

Matthew Flinders of Donington[1]

Paul Brunton, editor of Matthew Flinders' correspondence, writes that

> For Flinders, ... friendship began with the family. He described himself to his stepsister, Hannah, in December 1806, as 'A true and very loving brother, whose greatest pleasure is to live with his relations and friends in the best understanding and to be of service to them on all occasions ... our dearest friends are naturally those to whom we are most closely tied by blood.' Such sentiments are expressed again and again in his letters to individual members of his family. (PL 19)

Matthew was the first child of Susanna, nee Ward (1752–1783), and Matthew Flinders (1751–1802) of Donington, Lincolnshire. The family originated in Nottinghamshire and moved to Donington in the late seventeenth century. Matthew Flinders senior followed family tradition by becoming an apothecary and also practised as a surgeon and man-midwife – not a physician and therefore it is not correct to call him Dr Matthew Flinders. I will refer to them as Flinders Senior and Matthew to tell them apart.

Father

The editors of Flinders Senior's diary describe him as 'a practical, methodical, perhaps even rather dour pillar of the community', and quote a contemporary account of him as 'religious, affectionate, and generous to his relatives' (GP 1: 16). He and his eldest son did not always agree: he wanted Matthew to follow in his own profession rather than going to sea, but in May 1790, at the age of 16, Matthew finally prevailed, thanks to an offer of a midshipman's berth from Captain Pasley of the *Scipio*. 'I shall heavily miss him', his father wrote in his diary (GP 2: 81).

Flinders Senior kept a good library, continually recording the purchase of new books and the sale of old ones in his journal, and reading was clearly a habit Matthew began in childhood, and not only with *Robinson Crusoe*. He came to his first ship well-prepared to profit from the education a good captain would provide to his junior officers.

Joining the navy was an expensive business and Matthew had to call on his father for loans to get himself, and later his brother Samuel, set up with uniforms, equipment and so on. In his diary and account book Flinders Senior often complains about these expenses. Matthew wrote in a letter to him in February 1801,

> It is indeed a great misfortune to want a little money, I feel as if I <u>could</u> accomplish anything if this want was not continually dragging at me. I have indeed been one of the most fortunate young men that ever was launched into the world (PL 61).

Later, when, returning to Port Jackson from his circumnavigation of New Holland in 1803, Matthew received news of his father's death the previous year, his grief is tinged with regret and guilt:

> The duty I owed him and which I had now a prospect of paying with the warmest affection and gratitude, had made me look forward to the time of our return with increased ardour. I had laid such a plan of comfort for him as would have tended to make his latter days the most delightful of his life. ... Oh, my dearest, kindest father, how much I loved and reverenced you, you cannot now know. (PL 95)

Mother

Matthew's mother Susanna died aged 31 in March 1783, a week after Matthew's ninth birthday, probably as a result of complications after his brother Samuel's birth five months earlier, having given birth to ten children since 1774, five of whom died in infancy. All this is traced in Flinders Senior's diaries, among records of his income and expenditure and his midwifery cases. In November 1776, he wrote:

> Death made his first approach in our little family, by taking from us our second son – Jackey. ... We ought to account of this a mercifull Dispensation in that Providence made choice of the Youngest: to have parted with either of the other two would have afflicted us much more. (GP 1: 41)

At this time, Matthew was two-and-a-half, his sister Betsey about fourteen months. The baby, Jackey, was about six weeks old. The next year, on 12 August 1777, he wrote:

> I have great reason to acknowledge the unmerited goodness of the Supreme, that my wife was safely delivered of two Daughters on Saturday July 19 1777. They are both dead, being two months before due time. ... How kind is the Providence of God thus to free us from the expence and care of a numerous family, for had all our young ones lived with us, we should scarce [have] known what to have done with them. The two we have living, if agreable to divine Wisdom, I would gladly keep, but by no means wish an increase. However let that happen as it may; I hope we shall always acquiesce to the good will of God. I praise God my wife is well recovered. (GP 1: 49)

It takes quite an effort of historical mental adjustment to comprehend how a professional midwife could write this: the idea that a married couple in their twenties have no way of preventing 'an increase' of their family seems extraordinary. Again, in May 1778 he wrote:

> Early in the Morn of May 28 my wife was delivered of 2 Sons John & Samuel. I thank God she seems doing very well, but as she wanted about 6 weeks of full time the Children are both dead; one the same day, and the other the next, and they were intered in one Coffin on Sunday May 30. I must not omit my humble gratitude to Divine Mercy for sparing my Partner through these perilous times and also at the same time for not burthening me with the additional Care of more Children; she has now had 4 children in about 11 Months. (GP 1: 68)

Matthew does not mention his mother in his later correspondence or his *Private Journal*. His father was beside himself when she died: 'My situation is truly deplorable and unhappy on my own account, my comfort being gone, but doubly so on account of my 5 children, two very small and out at nurse' (GP 1: 136). The five children were Matthew, Betsey, Susanna, John, and Samuel.

Stepmother

In December of the year that his wife Susanna died, Flinders Senior married Elizabeth Ellis, née Weeks (1752–1841), the sister of Hannah Franklin, mother of John (later Sir John Franklin): 'a circumstance [that] will perhaps appear somewhat odd in my records, after the real and extraordinary grief which I have manifested for my late valuable partner and whom I shall regret to my last hour' (GP 1: 143).

At the beginning of the manuscript of Flinders Senior's diary is a note reading 'This MS book given by Mrs Flinders senior to Lieutenant S.W. Flinders 30 June 1829 as containing the remainder of the events relating to his mother's life. Signed Eliz Flinders.' Perhaps Samuel, at 45, was showing increased interest in his birth mother, whom he would not have remembered, as he entered his middle years. Although of course we cannot know the circumstances of the gift, the editors of the diary speculate that the note was written by someone other than Elizabeth, perhaps Samuel himself, as the signature is in markedly different script.

In the letter Matthew wrote to his stepmother after his father's death, he wrote:

> I beg of you my dear mother to look upon me with affection and as one who means to contribute every thing in his power to your happiness. Independent of my dear fathers last wish, I am of myself desirous that the best understanding and correspondence should subsist between us; for I love and reverence you and hope to be considered by you as the most anxious and affectionate of your friends whose heart and purse will be ever ready for your service.
>
> I make no doubt, my dear mother, but you will do what is proper and right in the family affairs, and at this distance I cannot do better than leave every thing to your discretion. (PL 95)

This rather stiff note gives the impression that perhaps they were not close, although there is no suggestion of any particular friction between them.

While Matthew was detained by the French governor on Mauritius for more than six years, he worried constantly about his family. As he was the eldest son, when his father died he became head of that family. His letters home to his stepmother and siblings show his anxiety at being absent and not knowing 'the state of my affairs', or being able to ensure that his younger sisters were receiving an adequate education.[2]

Siblings

In his early letters Matthew uses 'brother' and 'sister' almost interchangeably, to refer not only to his full and half-siblings but to his cousins and step-cousins, the Franklins, and others in his close family and social circle. He had 4 sisters and 2 brothers who survived infancy.

Elizabeth (Betsey) – 1775–1799. He wrote to Ann in 1799 that since Betsey had married, 'my affection for her has run into a different channel. She wants not my protection now, – another has a just claim to even a superior share of her affection! I still love her, much; but differently. ... She is independent of me' (PL 40). Betsey died in 1799 after three years of marriage to James Harvey, leaving two children. When he found out on his return to England in 1800, Matthew wrote to Ann,

> your feeling heart will well picture my disappointment and distress, on finding my best beloved sister ... torn from my arms by that scythe-bearing villain. It is a shock to my spirits and the ardency of my hopes that will not hastily be done away ... Enough, the handkerchief has passed the eye, and sorrow shall retreat back to the heart. (PL 52)

In 1810 he mentions in his journal having met Betsey's children, James Harvey, a fine intelligent little boy of 13, and his sister Susan, during a visit to Lincolnshire after his long-delayed return to England from his travels.

Susanna 1779–1827. In the 1799 letter to Ann where he described his love of Betsey, he wrote 'have I not another sister? My Susan! I melted into tenderness, and would have taken her into the very skin with me. ... Alas, in a few years, she also will be taken from me' (PL 40). Indeed, Susanna married George Pearson in 1802, without her family's consent. Matthew wrote to his stepmother, 'I am somewhat surprised at my sisters marriage, but I think ... that rather than make any dissention we all of us ought to cultivate as much kindness as we can with every branch of the family' (PL 95).

Susanna remained close to Matthew and Ann, and Ann continued to correspond with her, and later her daughter, after Matthew's death in 1814.

John (1781–1834). John was referred to by both Matthews, senior and junior as 'unfortunate'. Flinders Senior wrote in early 1800,

> This youth is the greatest misfortune I ever met with, and what course I am to take with him I am totally at a loss. I have threatened him with the Sea – of which he seems afraid. His simplicity we might bear with but I am sorry to say that his mind is debased and vicious. (GP 2: 215)

In March 1801 he was placed in the York Lunatic Asylum, an 'excellent repository of such unfortunates' and 'the best situation we have been able to procure for him, and as to his recovery the Event must be left with Providence' (GP 2: 227). Matthew only mentions him in the *Private Journal* in relation to the annuity provided for his care. However, someone later went through the manuscript of Matthew's *Private Journal* and crossed out John's name every time it appears. Matthew also mentioned him in a letter to his father in 1801, saying he was pleased that he found the 'situation' in York.

Samuel (1782–1834) played a much larger – and certainly more publicly acknowledged – part in Matthew's life than his older brother. He was the last child of Susanna, who died a few months after his birth.

Samuel 'expressed a desire for the Sea' and his father allowed him to go with Matthew in 1794 on the *Reliance* for NSW when he was 11 (GP 2: 142). He was rated midshipman in 1798, and promoted to lieutenant in 1801. He was the second lieutenant on the *Investigator* and shared the duties of taking astronomical readings with Matthew, after the astronomer John Crossley left the voyage on the way out because of illness.

It was not an entirely easy relationship. Matthew wrote to Ann, 'my brother will tell you that I am proud, unindulgent, and hasty to take offence; but I doubt whether John Franklin will confirm it although there is more truth in the charge than I wish there was' (PL 122). Matthew's letters to Samuel betray some awkwardness. Writing from Mauritius in 1806, he says, well into a long letter,

> Excuse me, my dear Samuel, I neither mean to reproach or to lecture you. The effusions of friendship and brotherly affection, added perhaps to a desire of family distinction, will not permit me to pass over any occasion of stimulating you to bring into use those abilities and solid principles I know you to possess. In blood you are my nearest and dearest friend, and if not altogether so in reality and from the heart, it is not from a want of affection or inclination on my part. ... It cannot be supposed that I had less affection for you than for other officers on board; the desire, then, to make you excel others must have been the object proposed. Perhaps I mistook the proper means, but <u>humanum est errare</u>, with the best intentions men often tread in the path of error. (PL 163)

Samuel retired from the navy in 1808 on half pay, after being convicted (perhaps wrongfully) of disobeying orders, and demoted.

Back in London Samuel and Matthew had to work together on correcting the readings on which all Flinders' maps were based. This took them two years. In late 1811 Samuel, much to Matthew's consternation, withdrew his work and all the books he had worked on during the voyage, apparently because he felt he was not being adequately paid for his work. 'This strange conduct in a brother, affected me much,' Matthew reported (PJ 389). He managed to talk Samuel around and made some concessions. 'He promised to proceed. He was, however, hurt that I did not chuse to shake hands with him, at parting.' (PJ 389).

Samuel continued to visit Matthew in London, but after Matthew's death there was some acrimony between Ann and Samuel. Ann wrote to Thomi Pitot, Matthew's friend on Mauritius, in December 1814:

> Mr F – the brother of Capt. F – is I am sorry to observe, a character widely differing from your late friend, & one whom I find inclined to be very troublesome, he is I believe greatly mortified, at not being left Executor, but his brother had very sufficient reasons for cutting him off from all concerns in his affairs.[3]

In 1819, Ann wrote to Mr Hursthouse, cousin of Flinders Senior and executor of his will, that

> it has been deeply impressed upon my mind to fix upon another Person who might in case of <u>my own demise</u>, became with <u>you</u> a joined Guardian

> to my Child – my reason for anxiety on this head arises from the idea that, should <u>you also</u> be taken from this earthly scene of things before she comes of Age, the <u>law</u> would consign the care of her to her nearest <u>Male</u> relation, of course this is her <u>Uncle Samuel</u>–I think I need scarcely say to you, there are few things which could happen in this World, that would give me more real misery of heart to think of – the possibility of such a circumstance would embitter my dying hour, for you will know what he is, and what has long been my opinion of him.[4]

Samuel married Mary Ann Bolton in 1820 and they had four daughters and a son named Matthew. Matthew named Flinders Island, off the coast of South Australia, after Samuel. (Matthew named nothing after himself, and the Flinders Island in Bass Strait was given that name later).

Hannah (1788–1842) and Henrietta (b.1791), daughters of Elizabeth née Weeks. These two stepsisters are usually mentioned together in Matthew's letters. He wrote to his stepmother in 1805 instructing her what to do about their education.

> It will be well to keep them from reading novels, Evelina, Clarissa Harlowe and 2 or 3 others perhaps of that class excepted, at least until they are 20 years of age. Young girls often contract such romantic notions from novel reading, that their future lives are embitted (sic) by not finding that perfection which for the most part is not in human nature, and is never to be expected. (PL 138)

In 1806 he wrote to Ann from Mauritius:

> When my sister leaves school, thou wilt afford me much gratification in having her occasionally with thee: make her thy young friend, she will be grateful for the attention: read with her, reason with her upon what you read and upon the occurrences of life, be her confident (*sic*); to do which, thou must not so much attempt to make her rise to thy ideas and sentiments, but must rather descend to her: adopt her amusements, take up her own manner of thinking, and lead her on imperceptibly to the formation of just sentiments and the adoption of agreeable manners: teach her not to be too confident in the good dispositions of mankind, but to avoid shewing suspicion: not to give too much way to the sensibilities of the heart, but to

avoid misanthropy; in fine to live in charity with all men, and think well of every individual until his actions shall shew him to be undeserving of it. (PL 153)

Hannah married Joseph Dodd in 1809. Henrietta visited Matthew and Ann in London a few times before she married Mr Chambers, who is first mentioned in the *Private Journal* in April 1814.

Cousins

Our Matthew Flinders wrote in his *Private Journal*, looking back on his career from a 'romantic and interior' mountain place in Mauritius:

> I was born in the fens of Lincolnshire where a hill is not to be seen for many miles, at a distance from the sea, and my family unconnected with sea affairs or any kind of enterprise or ambition. (PJ 100–101)

However, he had a cousin in the Navy, John Flinders (1767–1793). John, seven years older that Matthew, might have been an influence on Matthew's career choice along with *Robinson Crusoe*. John, or Jackey, who had joined the navy in 1780, visited Donington in July 1792, lately promoted to Lieutenant and back from the West Indies. He died of a fever at sea the following year.

John's sister Henrietta was a governess who introduced Matthew to her boss, Captain Thomas Pasley, who got him his first posting on a Navy ship. He later (1806) wrote to Ann that Henrietta 'possesses an excellent head and a better heart: I believe, that after thee and my brother Samuel, she stands next in my affection (PL 153).

The Franklins – the children of his stepmother's sister Hannah Franklin and her husband Willingham Franklin. Mary, one of his youthful group of friends, died about the same time as Betsey Flinders. Other siblings were Ann, Hannah, Elizabeth, Sarah, James, John, Thomas and Willingham. Elizabeth (another Betsey) was a close friend of Ann Chappelle, and probably introduced her to Matthew. Willingham (born 1779) was a lawyer and Oxford graduate and Matthew initially thought he should be employed to write the *Investigator* voyage. James was in the navy and a friend of Matthew's. And John (1786–1807) became Sir John Franklin – he was a midshipman on the *Investigator* voyage. Matthew referred to him as 'my favourite midshipman' (PJ 321).

Head of the family

When his father died in 1802, Flinders was now, as the eldest son, in a responsible position in his own family. One of the frustrations of his detention on Mauritius was that he was unable to attend to his family affairs: he wrote in his *Private Journal* on the first anniversary of his detention, 'I have suffered a years imprisonment ... remain in ignorance of the state of my fortune and family both of which have suffered some late material alterations' (PL 55). He wrote to Thomi Pitot in October 1805 that he had received

> a joint letter from two of my relations. In general the accounts of my friends are satisfactory; but I have lost an uncle, to whose will, it seems, I am left an executor, with a small legacy. This is another call, which requires my presence in England, and I find that some others of my relations have suffered in their circumstances and want my assistance.[5]

He wrote to his stepmother in April 1806:

> I am at present wholly ignorant of the state of my affairs; whether the money left by my dear father is in your hands, or in those of my agent. I desired that the interest of it should be applied to the education of my two sisters, until my return.[6]

As it happened, Elizabeth Flinders and other members of the family were looking after things quite capably. However, the frustration was that he was unable to keep in touch, due to the delays and uncertainties of mail during this time of war, before the establishment of the international postal service. When he arrived back in England, he wrote that he had 'been absent from England nine years and three months, and nearly four years and a half without intelligence from any part of my connexions' (PJ 325).

The unnoticed middle order

Flinders died on 19 July 1814 and was buried in St James' Churchyard, near what is now Euston Station. His family was important to him, and he felt a deep sense of obligation to his relatives. Nevertheless, in a letter to

Sir Joseph Banks on 12 July 1804, he wrote: 'I have too much ambition to rest in the unnoticed middle order of mankind, and since neither birth nor fortune have favoured me, my actions shall speak to the world' (PL 116). He did not want to be defined by his origins.

8

Ann Chappelle of Partney

Ann and Matthew

Ann Chappelle was both fortunate and unfortunate in her choice of husband. Temperamentally and intellectually they were well suited. She wrote to a friend, after Matthew had returned from his long absence on the *Investigator* voyage and detention on Mauritius,

> I am well persuaded that very few men know how to value the regard and tender attentions of a wife who loves them. ... To make the married life as happy as this world will allow it to be, there are a thousand little amenities to be rendered on both sides, and as many little shades of comfort to be attended to. Many things must be overlooked, for we are all such imperfect beings; and to bear and forbear is essential to domestic peace. ...I have only to return kind affection and attention for uniform tenderness and regard. I have nothing unpleasant to call forth my forbearance. Day after day, month after month passes and I neither experience an angry look nor a dissatisfied word. Our domestic life is an unvaried line of peace and comfort.[1]

Matthew, for his part, had written to her, when they had been apart for six years:

> Thou will be to me not only a beloved wife, but my most dear and most intimate friend, as I hope to be to thee. If we find failings, we will look upon them with kindness and compassion, and in each other's merits we will take pride, and delight to dwell upon them. ... I think, my love, this is also thy way of thinking. (PL 182)

The family background

Ann Chappelle was born on 21 November 1770. Her father had been a mariner and died at sea when she was four, and her mother, from a Hull seafaring family, had also lost two of her brothers to the sea.[2] It is not known exactly how they met, but as Ann lived with her mother and stepfather in Partney, Lincolnshire, and Matthew's stepmother's sister's family, the Franklins, lived in nearby Spilsby, it seems more than likely that Flinders' friendship with that family introduced them. Spilsby is nearly thirty miles from Flinders' home in Donington, but Flinders Senior remarks that when Matthew was home in August 1794 'we had not much of his Company as in that time he went to Spilsby, Tidd, and other places' (GP 2: 141). Ann and Matthew were already corresponding by 1795, when Matthew's earliest surviving letters were written: he wrote a joint letter to Mary Franklin and Ann from Tenerife on 10 March of that year, thanking Miss Chappelle for her letter. Matthew was at the time on the way to New South Wales on the *Reliance* and would not return to England until 1800. Their correspondence – or at least Matthew's side of it, which is all that has survived – charts a deepening attachment to Ann which led to discussions of marriage when he returned in 1800.

Marriage and separation

By the time Flinders proposed marriage to Ann Chappelle in 1801, he had spent most of the preceding decade at sea. Ann had little enthusiasm for marrying a 'servant' of the sea. Although there was no doubting their mutual attraction, it took Matthew some persuasion, as well as some overoptimistic promises, to convince her that they had a future together. They married on 17 April 1801, to his father's surprise and displeasure:

> With concern I note that my Son Matthew came upon us suddenly & unexpectedly with a Wife. ... It is a Miss Chapple of Partney. We had known of the acquaintance, but had no Idea of Marriage taking place until the Completion of his ensuing Voyage. (GP 2: 228)

Ann's half-sister Isabella, after Ann's death in 1852, recalled their wedding day:

> Never man more happy than poor Matthew & he determined to be so, in spite of the Lords of the Admiralty & Sir Joseph Banks. – Yes of all the merry group none more merry than he. ... I can see him now, distributing his little gifts to the Bridesmaids ... pretending to tell their fortunes by the lines in their palms, promising, of course, to all good husbands & soon ... We were all fun and mirth.[3]

Matthew and Ann lived together on board ship for a few months before he left to survey the Australian coastline as commander of the HMS *Investigator*. Flinders had hoped to take his wife with him, but the Admiralty found out and offered him a stark choice. If he persisted in taking Ann with him, he would forfeit command of the expedition. He did not mince words: he wrote to Sir Joseph Banks, 'If their Lordships sentiments should continue the same, whatever may be my disappointment, I shall give up the wife for the voyage of discovery.' In the same letter, he wrote that he hoped that their Lordships 'would have shown the same indulgence to me, as to Lt. Kent of the Buffalo, and many others' (PL 69–70). It is not clear why the regulations were so rigidly enforced in the Flinders' case. These naval regulations were often disregarded, as Jane Austen's *Persuasion* shows.

In fact, Matthew had not planned to have Ann on board for his whole voyage. The plan was for her to stay in Port Jackson – Sydney – 'whilst I am employed in the most dangerous part of my duty, thou shalt be placed under some friendly roof there' (PL 65–66). So Matthew was planning to introduce Ann Flinders into a society which would (he hoped) prove hospitable and supportive. When he reached Sydney in May 1802, he wrote to her:

> The ships that sailed for this place from Spithead during the time thou wast on board, told them here of thy coming out; and there has, consequently, been many inquiries after thee, and much abuse of me for not bringing them so valuable an addition to their society. Thou wouldst have been situated as comfortably here as I hoped, and told thee. Two better or more agreeable women than M[rs] King and M[rs] Paterson are not easily found.[4]

Her new friends would have included not only the Anna Josepha King, wife of Governor Philip Gidley King, and Elizabeth Paterson, wife of Lieutenant Governor Colonel William Paterson, but Eliza Kent and

Elizabeth Macarthur. He was on friendly terms with all of these women – there are surviving letters to prove it – but his scheme might have been in trouble. As he wrote to Mrs Kent in August 1803, 'There is now Mrs King, Mrs Paterson and Mrs McArthur for all of whom I have the greatest regard, who can scarcely speak to each other; it is really a miserable thing to split a small society into such small parts. Why do you ladies meddle with politics? but I do not mean you' (PL 106).

In any case, it was not to be, and Ann stayed at home with her family for the nine years he was away. Exactly how she spent those years is not recorded, except as reflected in his replies to her letters. She destroyed her letters to Matthew, while treasuring his to her.

'Why Henry didst thou leave me?'

We know that Ann suffered deeply during their separation.[5] Stranded on Mauritius, Flinders worried constantly about his family. He also worried about his wife, realising that each year apart lessened the likelihood of their having children.[6] In March 1806 Flinders wrote to his brother Samuel about the possibility of Ann joining him on Mauritius:

> Was she with me ... I could make myself tolerably happy here ...; but the dread of the fatigue and risks she must undergo, and the difficulty of finding a proper person to accompany her, prevent me from requesting her to come, it must rest with herself and upon the turn-up of circumstances. I have however forbidden the voyage, if one of the opportunities which I have described does not offer; the honour of a woman on board a ship, is too likely to be aspersed, without proper guardianship; however circumspect her conduct might be, the tongue of slander will find some occasion to defame it, if she is not protected by a father, an uncle, or a brother, or by some respectable family. (PL 147)

In the event, Ann stayed in England with her mother and stepfather. Flinders acknowledged Ann's sorrow by writing words to a tune by Haydn and sending them to Ann in November 1805. Flinders wrote in the persona of the woman left behind: 'Why, Henry, didst thou leave me? ... Thou knew'st how much I loved thee, yet could resolve to go.' He wrote one verse, and three lines of a second, adding 'To be completed' in place of the last line. On receiving the song, Ann responded to the implied invitation to co-authorship by finishing the second verse and adding two more, ending: 'Will comforts cheering sunshine e'er beam on this sore heart? / Yes, when we meet, my Henry, never again to part.'[7] In a letter of January 1807, Matthew wrote, 'thank thee, my love, for the verses thou hast sent me. Miss Sophie D'Arifat was so pleased with them, that she has translated them into French verse.'[8] It is possible that these verses were those she wrote in response to his song lyric, the manuscript of which is now held in the Flinders Papers at Greenwich.

The story of their marriage, involving personalities now well-known, was unique in its particulars, but in its general outline was common enough during these decades of war and expansion, and many songs of the time reflect the importance of family life and fidelity in the life of men serving abroad and the women waiting for them at home. However, the use of song-writing as a form of apology, graciously accepted, is unusual.[9] Flinders' musical training and level of education meant that when he took to song to mediate in his marriage, it was in elevated poetic diction set to a melody by Haydn, one of the most celebrated composers of the eighteenth century. The words of other songs of the time, like those in the Flinders collaboration, stress the suffering of the woman waiting at home for her sea captain, but place more emphasis on her constancy. The songs that were written for publication, were (at least in part) contributing to the public conversation about the way women should behave while their men were away, while the Flinders song was a private document. Ann Flinders wrote to express her own 'misery & alarms', her 'silent agony': she had no need to convince a reader or listener of her fidelity.

Later life
After Matthew's death in 1814, only three and a half years after their reunion, Ann maintained a correspondence with his sister, Susanna Pearson, and her husband George, and later her daughter.[10] In these letters we find a woman with decided opinions – politically and socially conservative, evangelically pious and fervently anti-Catholic. From her later years we also have the watercolours she painted in the 1820s, perhaps as a result of a continuing friendship with the *Investigator*'s natural history painter, Ferdinand Bauer. Flinders University owns three of these watercolours, but many more are still in Lincolnshire.

Ann died in 1852, nearly 38 years after Matthew. She never remarried – and in 1830 she wrote to the recently widowed George Pearson,

> during the period we were permitted to live together, not a cloud cast shade over the sunshine of our affection for each other, and each day seemed but to rivet our attachment the more firmly. After such a union to seek another would be the height of folly.'[11]

At the time of her death Ann and Isabella were living in Woolwich, a few miles downriver from Greenwich, and Ann was buried at St Thomas's Church, Charlton.

Isabella Tyler

In later years, Isabella recalled seeing Matthew just before the *Investigator* set out from Portsmouth in July 1801 'in his handsome uniform, his cocked hat put slightly over one eye – his sword by his side – did he not look handsome?'[12] It seems that Flinders was on easy terms with his in-laws – perhaps easier than with some members of his own family. His letter-book includes an entry recording a letter to Ann and Isabella's mother: 'To Mrs Tyler – Partney – June 28. 1802 – Port Jackson – An affectionate jocose letter – much nonsense.'[13]

In November 1804, Flinders wrote to Ann from the 'Garden Prison' in Mauritius. At the end of a long, passionate letter, he added a teasing paragraph directed towards 'that idle thing, Belle' – Ann's teenage half-sister Isabella Tyler. 'Does she think I will bring her any pretty feathers or little fishes when she has not written me one line for these live-long three years last past?' (PL 121). In 1806 he wrote to her:

> My dear demi-sister,
> And so you scold and rant because I have not written to you; but pray who has the most time, you or me; and it is very certain, that no letter, so long even as my thumb, nor even a postscript in your sisters letters has ever come to me; and forsooth, if rights are to measured by affections, mine is certainly the greatest, for I love you infinitely more than you do me: this is a truth not to be denied, and therefore I request your writings may be regulated accordingly. (PL 167)

Isabella seems to have responded in kind. A letter of hers to Matthew survives in the National Maritime Museum Greenwich, dated 10 July 1810: they would not yet have had news of his imminent return. Her letter begins with a familiar kind of ribbing about not having had a letter from him. She goes on,

> Ann is always fidgeting & twittering about you, [not] that she says much, but I often see her eyes red, and swell'd, although I use many arguments to persuade her that she has more cause to rejoice, than to grieve, for my part, if I were ever sure my husband would be taken abroad, and confined there for nine, or ten years, I would marry tomorrow.[14]

It seems she was not keen on the married state for herself. In March 1812, shortly before the birth of his daughter Anne, Matthew wrote to Mme d'Arifat:

> Isabella comes next week, to take upon herself the office of regent of my domestic affairs, till Mrs. F. is able to re-assume the reins of government. There is no probability of an union betwixt her and my brother: she is a very decisive lady, and seems to have taken a dislike to him. (PL 218)

It was Isabella, according to Anne, who went to St James's churchyard after Ann's death to look for Matthew's grave, and 'found the churchyard remodelled, and quantities of tombstones and graves with their contents had been carted away as rubbish,' Matthew's among them.[15] Isabella never married and was buried in the same grave as Ann when she died in 1867.

Anne Flinders

Ann was pregnant when Matthew left England in 1801, but she miscarried. Matthew wrote to her in 1804, on the subject of parenthood:

> Had but my wishes been realised, of which thy last letter to me at Spithead gave hope, then should I have had an additional surety of thy health: thou wouldst have had the most delightful of all employments, and thy mind and care would have been divided between one present and one absent. ... I do indeed regret, and repine at the disappointment I may never live to see my representative enter the field as a competitor for honest fame in the cause of his country, of science, or of virtue; and as to the common midway between virtue and vice, honour and disgrace! No, I would have nobody connected

with me who has not the spirit to mend something upon the old se-saw pace. Such a vegetable state I abhor. Let him excel in something, or I would rather that my name should descend with me into the oblivious grave, as very probably it now will. (PL 123)

Young Anne (with an e) was born on 1 April 1812. Matthew's journal for the day reads: 'Occupied in correcting the bearing book, by a just proportionate variation. This afternoon Mrs Flinders was happily delivered of a daughter, to her great joy and to mine' (PJ 400).

Little Anne had some health problems, and she is only mentioned in her father's journal when she was sick or had got better. In the letters she fares a little better. On 2 April 1812, he wrote to his stepmother: 'Mrs F was happily relieved from her burthen yesterday. ... The child is a little black-eyed girl, without blemish, neither fat nor lean, and has a decent appearance enough' (PL 220). When she was about three months old, he told Louise d'Arifat, 'She is not pretty but promises to be more than commonly active and intelligent, and she occupies all her mother's thoughts by day and by night. I am now, indeed, as near to perfect happiness as is usually permitted to man' (PL 225). In November he was more forthcoming:

> My little Anne goes on very prosperously; she is fat and fresh; has cut four teeth without suffering, and seizes every thing she can catch. She is now eight months old, and supports her own weight in walking, though not yet able to go alone. This child has the most varied and expressive physiognomy, I have ever seen in one so young. Her laugh is the picture of delight, and her cry of despair. She has begun her career of coquetry already; she cannot bear strange ladies, but looks with pleasure at strange gentlemen, then hides her face, and afterwards looks again. I begin to love the child myself, now that it shows signs of intelligence; but till lately did not feel any particular attachment. (PL 228)

After Matthew's death, Ann wrote to Thomi Pitot:

> My little darling Girl grows much and is become very entertaining, she is if you can credit the word of a Mother, very active & intelligent, she often reminds me of her dear father, the upper part of her face being very like his, and I flatter myself she will inherit his noble integrity of character, & the amiability of his disposition.[16]

Anne Flinders grew up, indeed, to be active and intelligent. Her great-granddaughter, Lisette Flinders Petrie wrote:

> Anne Flinders, my great-grandmother and Matthew's daughter, was in my opinion one of the cleverer members of the family. However, being a Victorian woman, she could not develop this in the same way as either her father or her son. Among other things, she taught herself half a dozen languages, from Hebrew to Italian. ... Another of her interests was painting.[17]

She also published several books during the 1840s, under various pseudonyms. In 1851 she married William Petrie, and they had one child, William Matthew Flinders Petrie who became a celebrated archaeologist.

Matthew Flinders and Trim, at the Flinders University Railway Station, by Mark Richards, 2014. This is one of three full-sized copies of the statue: the others are on the forecourt outside Euston Station, London, and at Port Lincoln, SA.

Matthew Flinders, January 1807, at the age of 32. Painted on Mauritius by
Toussaint Antoine de Chazal de Chameral.
Art Gallery of South Australia.

Matthew Flinders c. 1800, at the age of 26.
Miniature by unknown artist. State Library of NSW (MIN 52)

Fitzroy Street, London, where Matthew, Ann and Anne Flinders lived from May 1813 to February 1814. The blue plaque affixed to the building reads 'Captain Matthew Flinders R.N. 1774–1814 Explorer and Navigator lived here.' It was erected in 1973.
The actual house where they lived is further along Fitzroy Street to the right of this photo. Image: Gillian Dooley, July 2019.

This muddy track leads to the site of Madame Louise d'Arifat's residence, Le Refuge, where Flinders lived from August 1805 to March 1810. Image: Gillian Dooley, October 2018.

The view, looking northwards, from the site of Madame Louise d'Arifat's residence, Le Refuge. Image: Gillian Dooley, October 2018.

The view from Gorges Viewpoint, Mauritius, towards Tamarind Falls. Inaccessible by vehicle, the Falls are now a well-known full-day hiking destination. Flinders wrote about his visit there in October 1805. Image: Gillian Dooley, October 2018.

Entrance to Port Lincoln, from behind Memory Cove by William Westall.
Royal Museums Greenwich PAG9778

Boongaree, chief of the Broken Bay tribe, and his wife Matora.
Drawn by Mikhailov, engraver I. Fridrits. Plate 23 from *Voyage of Captain Bellingshausen to the Antarctic Seas, 1819–1821* (Sanktpeterburg: Tip. I. Glazunova, 1831).
Courtesy State Library of NSW.

The Encounter between the *Investigator* and the *Géographe*, 1802, by John Ford.

Blue Mud Bay, body of a native shot on Morgan's Island, 1803, by William Westall. National Library of Australia.

Above: Samuel Ward Flinders. Shillinglaw Papers, La Trobe Australian Manuscripts Collection, State Library of Victoria.

Right: Statue of Matthew Flinders in Market Square, Donington, Lincolnshire

Anne L. de Chazal.
Image courtesy Marina Carter.
Library of Australia.

Headstone of Ann Flinders and Isabella Tyler
at St Thomas's Church, Charlton, London.
Image Gillian Dooley, 2019.

Portrait of Isabella Tyler, Anne Flinders and Ann Flinders, c. 1830.
Courtesy of Lisette Flinders Petrie.

William Fitzwilliam Owen, 1774–1857.
British Museum

Thomi Pitot. Shillinglaw Papers, La Trobe
Australian Manuscripts Collection, State
Library of Victoria.

Flinders' birthplace in Donington, Lincolnshire.
Shillinglaw Papers, La Trobe Australian Manuscripts Collection, State Library of Victoria.

To the memory of

Trim,

the best and most illustrious of his Race,
the most affectionate of friends,
faithful of servants,
and best of creatures.
He made the Tour of the Globe, and a voyage to

Australia,

which he circumnavigated; and was ever the
delight and pleasure of his fellow voyagers.
Returning to Europe in 1803, he was shipwrecked
in the Great Equinoxial Ocean;
This danger escaped, he sought refuge and assistance
at the Isle of France, where
he was made prisoner, contrary to the laws of
Justice, of Humanity, and of
French National Faith;
and where, alas! he terminated his useful
career, by an untimely death,
being devoured by the Catophagi of
that island.
Many a time have I beheld his little merriments with delight,
and his superior intelligence with surprise:
Never will his like be seen again!
Trim was born in the Southern Indian Ocean, in the
Year 1799, and
and perished as above at the Isle of France
in 1804.
Peace be to his shade, and
Honour to his memory

Trim's epitaph, from the *Bibligraphical Tribute to the Memory of Trim*.

Journal entry for 18 August 1805.
State Library of NSW. Mitchell Library Safe 1/58.

the happiness that a man whose desires were moderate, might enjoy in this delightful retreat with the beloved of his heart; for here the summers sun could not scorch, nor was there any dread of winters cold. Simple aliments were abundant, slaves were numerous and obedient, and a look was all the exertion that was necessary to have ones wants gratified; such wants at least as would be excited in a mind regular moderate and agreeable to simple nature. I thought such a life, well fitted for philosophical and religious contemplation, as if for love and all its train of domestic enjoyments: a delightful reverie, all these ideas passed through my mind as we walked along the sea beach back to Coupang. I inquired of Mynheer Veurtzen for how much this house with its surrounding conveniences might be bought, were it saleable, and was not a little surprised to hear him say about 900 rix dollars, or less than £200.

Pursuing my reverie farther, and considering myself in possession of this retreat, I considered well, how shall I employ and amuse myself when books weary and my plantation does not require my care? I saw no employment, of amusement, or society; — it was too warm for anything laborious. the roads were scarcely fit to walk upon, as little fit for a horse, and impassable to any kind of carriage; and moreover there was nothing but rocks, and parched-up roads. and here and there a plantation look half so beautiful as my own; there were owners indeed to these, people of property, but then they were men and women without an idea beyond Timor and chewing betel. With such I could not communicate any knowledge I might possess or acquire, and except from books could make no further acquisition. Conversation upon books is the stimulus to read, and but here could be no collision of mind upon mind; I feared that reading would under such circumstances fall with me, and that in the end I should fall a sacrifice to surrounding circumstances and become that more inactive animal, a native or rather a vegetable — a native of Timor. I energetically exclaimed No — I was not meant for this: my reverie upon Madam Van Este and her plantation house ended here; for I saw that it owed its beauty to the shade

An extract from Flinders' Journal on the *Investigator*, describing his visit to Madame Van Este's estate in Timor. UK Public Record Office ADM55/76.

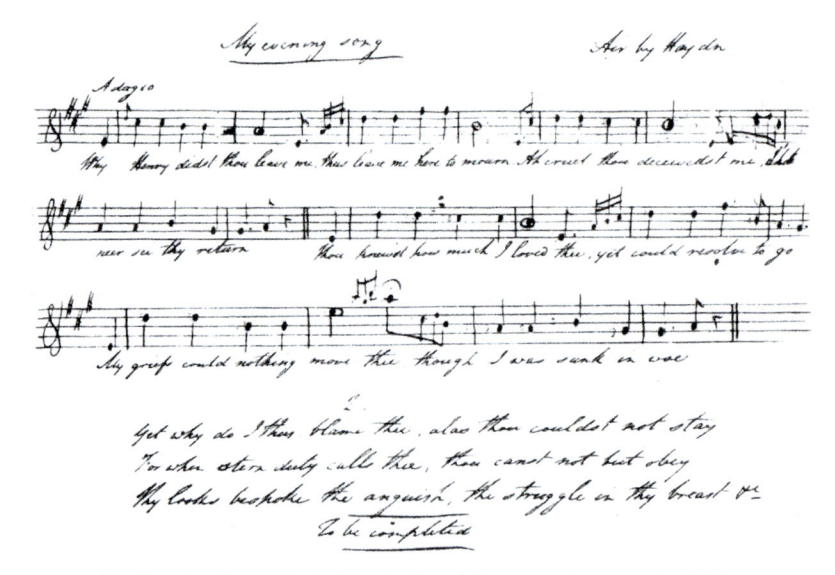

'My Evening Song', Air by Haydn. Royal Museums Greenwich. FLI25.

Sir Joseph Banks' library and herbarium at his town house in Soho Square, London, 1820, by Francis Boott. Natural History Museum, London.

Flinders family flute collection, with Matthew Flinders' flute on the left, Image courtesy Lisette Flinders Petrie.

Matthew Flinders' flute (detail), by I. Potter, c. 1788. Image courtesy Lisette Flinders Petrie.

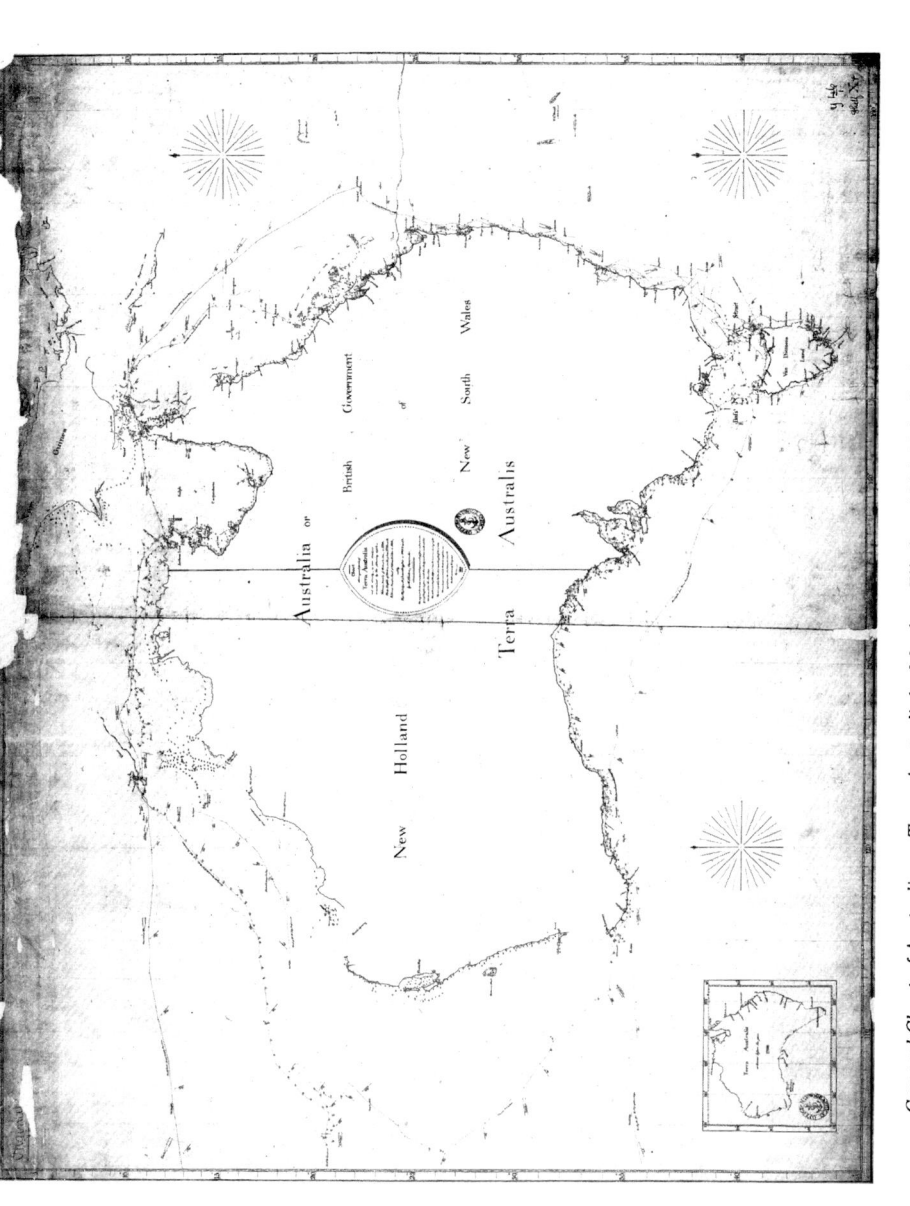

General Chart of Australia or Terra Australis by Matthew Flinders, 1804; United Kingdom Hydrographic Office. This map was drawn by Flinders during his captivity and incorporated all his charting to date.

9

Matthew Flinders and his Friends

If you have read this far, you will have noticed the many different connotations of the word 'friend' for Matthew Flinders. He wrote that he went to sea 'against the wishes of my friends',[1] which in this case means his father, who opposed his desire to join the navy. He called Sir Joseph Banks 'my greatest and best friend' (PL 73–74). Ann was 'not only a beloved wife, but my most dear and most intimate friend'.[2] In his epitaph for his cat, Trim, he called him 'the most affectionate of friends' (TCC). Even, perhaps more dubiously, the Noongar people of Western Australia were referred to as 'our friends' (VTA 1: 60–61).

The meaning of friendship to Flinders is discussed in a lengthy and fascinating article by Alecia Simmonds in *The Great Circle* (2016). She makes several interesting observations, such as that 'Flinders' tendency to characterise almost all meaningful relationships in his life as relationships of friendship meant that his list of friends was staggeringly voluminous'.[3] As she points out, we have a vast amount of evidence from his letters alone about who he regarded as his friends, and what friendship meant to him. Writing to George Bass in February 1800, he said,

> Franklin – Wiles – Smith – Bass, are names which will be ever dear to my heart; and yet how different are the men. You will know, in what sense I mean the term; – 'tis not from the coat they wear, or from the size of their breeches pockets; but the qualities first of the heart, and then of the head. (PL 48)

He wrote to Thomas Franklin on the subject of his French friends on Mauritius: 'my misfortunes have made me more friends than enemies, even here, amongst a people inimical to my country; and yet I have not sacrificed or ceased to maintain its honour or interests in order to join that friendship.'[4] He greatly valued independence and loyalty in friendship. On hearing that his friend James Wiles' son had run away from the Naval Academy, he wrote to Wiles that this act of folly had rather increased his admiration for the lad, as he had done it against his own interests, out of loyalty to a friend (PL 214).

In this chapter, I will discuss just a small selection of the many friends in Flinders' life. These particular six people have been chosen, out of many possible candidates, because there is significant documentary evidence, mostly in correspondence, of the nature of their friendships with Flinders. His letters also sometimes expound his own opinions about the nature and value of friendship.

Sir Joseph Banks[5]
As I drive southwards from my home in the western suburbs of Adelaide on the way to Flinders University, I pass the junction with Banks Avenue. Banks Avenue is a short, pleasant suburban street which crosses La Perouse Avenue and terminates at Torres Avenue. This suburb, which also includes Baudin Avenue, Westall Avenue, and Captain Cook Avenue, is called Flinders Park. One might say that his prediction, in 1804, that 'The hitherto obscure name of Flinders may thus become a light by which even the illustrious character of Sir Joseph Banks may one day receive an additional ray of glory' has come true (PL 116).

In Australia especially, there are educational institutions, major city streets and railway stations, mountain ranges, and suburbs named after Flinders, while Banks is not so well commemorated. According to the Australian Museum website,

> Joseph Banks has been honoured with many place names throughout the South Pacific, including in Australia with a group of islands (Sir Joseph Banks Group) in South Australia, Banks Strait in Tasmania and suburbs in several Australian states bear his name. He is also commemorated in the names of several plants, most notably the Australian wildflower genus *Banksia*.[6]

Geoscience Australia lists over one hundred place names including the surname Banks and its variants, many of them including *Banksia*. There are 80 plants named after Banks, and only 17 species named *Flindersia*. As the Australian National Herbarium online asserts, Sir Joseph's 'impact on the study of natural history in both Britain and Australia cannot be overestimated.'[7]

However, there are more places named Flinders, and almost all of them are directly named after Matthew Flinders. Apart from Flinders University, there are the massive Flinders Ranges in the mid north of South Australia, and, confusingly, two Flinders Islands – one on the south coast of South Australia, named by Matthew Flinders after his brother Samuel, and the other in Bass Strait, named after Matthew Flinders. There is Flinders Street, a major thoroughfare in Melbourne which gives its name to the Flinders Street Railway Station. Flinders Street is also one of Adelaide's main city streets – Flinders University's city building is on the corner of Flinders Street and Victoria Square.

If we turn the spotlight on South Australia, apart from some streets here and there, Banks is commemorated only in the group of islands Flinders named after him, located in the Spencer Gulf near Port Lincoln, and secondary denominations like Banksia Park, an Adelaide suburb. After all, Flinders spent a whole 83 days on the shores of South Australia, landing on a beach just a few miles north of modern-day Adelaide, while Banks never came around to the south coast.

Flinders had first met Banks in 1793, when on his return from Bligh's breadfruit voyage on the *Providence* his shipmate, botanist James Wiles, asked him to visit Banks twice on his behalf. The nineteen-year-old midshipman, according to Kenneth Morgan in his biography of Flinders, 'would have been well received, as someone who had sailed in the *Providence*.' Morgan goes on, 'Though he had virtually no contact with Banks for several years thereafter these initial meetings with Banks proved crucial for Flinders' later career.'[8] In fact, Morgan claims that 'Banks's greatest contribution to Australian maritime exploration came with his support for Flinders on his *Investigator* expedition and his subsequent efforts on behalf of Flinders personally and to disseminate the voyage's findings.'[9] He was 'an indispensable go-between for organizing maritime expeditions at a time when government found its administrative resources stretched', because of the war with France.[10] Flinders agreed, calling Banks 'that distinguished patron of science and useful enterprise' (VTA 1: cciv). Flinders knew no higher praise than 'useful'. In a letter of January 1801, he drew attention to their shared interest:

> Well knowing, Sir Joseph, how much you are interested in the voyage, I take the liberty of speaking at length upon the subject; and if it meets your approbation I shall continue to mention the wants we may have, and the alterations that may be necessary, hoping, for your assistance in forwarding their accomplishment.
>
> In a few days I will send up lists of the extra things that to me appear necessary for us.[11]

Thanking Banks in February 1801 for his part in obtaining his commission as commander of the *Investigator,* Flinders wrote:

> Panygeric (sic), or a long train of sentences of gratitude, would be unpleasant to a mind like that of sir Joseph Banks, I will therefore only add, that it shall be my endeavour to shew by my conduct and exertions that your good opinion has not been misplaced.(PL 60)

A little later Banks had to defend Flinders against 'many severe remarks' from the Admiralty. When he was just about to leave on the *Investigator* voyage, after the Admiralty had insisted that he leave his new wife Ann behind in England, Flinders had some trouble when bringing the ship around from the Nore to Portsmouth – a run of bad luck the Admiralty were inclined to attribute to his mismanagement. Flinders wrote a long letter to Banks, carefully explaining every circumstance and defending himself, finishing the letter thus:

> That the admiralty have thrown blame upon me, and should have represented to my greatest and best friend, that I had gotten the ship on shore, had let a prisoner escape, and three of my men run away, without adding the attendant circumstances, is most mortifying and grievous to me; but it is impossible to express so gratefully as I feel, the anxious concern with which you took the part of one who has not the least claim to such generosity; but was I to enter upon this subject, I should write to all eternity; I shall, therefore, only say, that with the highest respect, gratitude, and esteem, I am, Sir Joseph your faithful and obedient servant. (PL 73–74)

His relief is palpable in October when he writes from the Cape of Good Hope,

> I feel some satisfaction in writing to you, Sir Joseph, now that I have not to trouble you with my wants and complaints; but rather to say that we have thus far advanced prosperously in the voyage. (PL 58)

Flinders' reasons for writing to Banks always came back to the same root cause, which he expressed in a letter from the *Investigator* off Timor in March 1803:

> You have ... many anxious well-wishers, Sir Joseph, on board the Investigator; for besides the gratitude which your attention and favour to many of us has excited, we know of no one who after you will think at all of us or our labours; and truly we are somewhat ambitious of notice from those whose attention confers both information and credit. (PL 88)

Flinders knew that Banks shared his passion for exploration and for the advancement of science and knowledge, and he was a natural ally in promoting his endeavours.

The 'wants and complaints' did return in later correspondence, of course, redoubled when Flinders was detained on Mauritius by the French colonial governor there, between December 1803 and July 1810. Banks did what he could to help Flinders, by pleading his cause with the Admiralty and his French colleagues and connections, but the obdurate General Decaen was not to be moved. Banks also corresponded sympathetically with Flinders' wife Ann and keeping her informed of his efforts on Flinders' behalf. In 1807 he wrote to her:

> It Greives me to hear that Capt. Flinders, after having for so long supported with manly fortitude the very disgracefull treatment he has met with from those Enemies to humanity, the French, has at last given way to oppression, & Sufferd his Spirits to Flag. I can not, however, have a doubt from the well Known Energies of his mind that his Low Spirits are only a temporary Attack of depression, which will not be Lasting.[12]

Finally released from detention on Mauritius in 1810, and back in London, Flinders threw himself with all those 'well known energies of his mind' into the completion of his *Voyage*. Banks' town house in Soho

Square was a hub of Flinders' activity. He visited there every two or three days, borrowing books, but more importantly consulting Sir Joseph about the writing of his voyage.[13] Mr Yorke, the first Lord of the Admiralty, had appointed Sir Joseph and Flinders, along with John Barrow, the second secretary to the Admiralty, as the committee to undertake the writing of the *Investigator*'s voyage, so the three of them had much business to take care of at this early stage of the project.

But Flinders also frequently asked his advice about his own affairs, such as the vexed question of his promotion to Post Captain. Banks had been advocating on Flinders' behalf since before his return: in a letter of October 1810 he wrote to John Barrow, 'I am Gratefull for Mr Yorke's kindness to Flinders as far as it goes, & Shall always feel for his kindness a proportionate degree of Gratitude,' but protested at the 'harsh rule which interdicts the Promotion of a Brave man, however well he has fought, if the fortune of war has placed him in the hands of his Enemies till his Enemies are Pleasd on their own mere motions to Restore his Liberty. Surely this Rule is more like a French one than and English one.'[14] Other letters concerned the question of Flinders' remuneration while writing the voyage – he was kept on half pay, and estimated that it would therefore put him about £500 out of pocket to write the voyage – and the affairs of his brother Samuel and other members of the *Investigator*'s company. Banks tried to help as much as possible, but even his influence was not unlimited.

In March 1811, Sir Joseph invited Flinders to attend his Sunday evening 'conversations' and the meetings of the Royal Society. It seems that Banks had been wondering why he had not been coming: a few days earlier Flinders had noted a conversation with Robert Brown where the subject had arisen. In his *Private Journal*, Flinders writes,

> I had indeed thought it somewhat strange, that Sir Jos. had never invited me to these conversations, as he had done in 1800 on my return from N.S. Wales; but as I do not wish to intrude myself into societies where I am not certain of being welcome, I did not chuse to go without an invitation, or some hint that I was expected to go. (PJ 351)

From this time on, Flinders attended Banks' weekly gatherings, where he met many like-minded people and made many useful connections. Their close association continued, and Flinders was keen to return the many favours Banks had done him whenever he could. In July 1812 he arranged to get a book from his French friends in Paris 'which Sir J.B. wished to obtain. I am very glad to seize any opportunity of being useful to Sir Joseph, from his having done so much (though not every thing) for me' (PJ 416). Their only significant disagreement was over the naming of Australia. Banks did not give 'Australia' his imprimatur and consequently the publication was named *A Voyage to Terra Australis* not 'A Voyage to Australia', which Flinders would have preferred. It was not long before Flinders' preference for the name Australia won out, as it was adopted by Governor Macquarie in NSW in 1817 and approved by the Admiralty in 1824.

Banks' influence was ubiquitous in the founding of the colony at New South Wales, in botanical research in Australia and the Pacific, and in the geographical exploration of Australia's coasts and islands. He was clearly a brilliant and well-informed man, and I think Flinders was lucky that he had also possessed practical kindness, generosity and compassion. From Banks' letters about Flinders, it is clear that Flinders was not mistaken in regarding him as his 'greatest and best friend.'

George Bass[15]

When I was at school in the eastern states of Australia, Bass and Flinders came as a package, like Gilbert and Sullivan or Laurel and Hardy. I barely knew them as separate entities until I came to South Australia, where Flinders has a much higher profile. Times have changed, too, I suspect. In recent years, too, there has been much more published on Flinders than on Bass. Josephine Bastian, whose joint biography of the two explorers was published in 2016, says that she has written this book because she feels that 'although Flinders and Bass are well known by name and reputation, that is, as public figures, they are not known well so far as the details of their individual lives – their private faces – are concerned.'[16] I would say that is more true of Bass than Flinders – there are now many biographies of Flinders, and there is a huge amount of primary material available.

Bass and Flinders become jointly famous for their 'Tom Thumb' voyages and their circumnavigation of Tasmania in 1798–1799, finally proving that it was an island. There are, as Bastian points out, some personal parallels between them. Their activities together lasted something short of four years and the Tasmanian voyage was their last together.

Their association began with their meeting on board the *Reliance, en route* to Port Jackson in 1795, and ended with the eighteenth century, when Bass left the Navy and set off on high-risk ventures – risking not only his own and other people's money but the lives of himself and his shipmates, all of which were lost in early 1803 when he left Port Jackson for South America.

Nothing I have read, including Bastian's book, makes me like George Bass. He was brilliant – or so we are always told. One of the documents Bastian has consulted is a list of the 84 books he left behind in Sydney. 'The collection looks typical of the library of a man with a good grammar school education, who happens to have an inquiring mind and an unusually broad range of interests', including 'a solid core of philosophers of the Enlightenment'.[17] At this stage he was probably better read than Flinders – he was three years older and had joined the Navy slightly later in life – and perhaps that was why Flinders, as Bastian claims, 'could not match wits with his friend'.[18] It seems to me more likely that it was a matter of personality.

Flinders was proud, reserved and sensitive. Quick repartee was not his style. In Flinders' letter to him, quoted earlier, he wrote 'often have I been determined to deny you my respect and esteem, when your treatment has been such as said to me, "You are unworthy of being my friend"; but I have been forced to wince and depart from my resolution' (PL 48). I have the impression that Bass was attractive to Flinders, as to others, because he didn't really care about other people. Flinders also wrote, 'Perhaps it is not in human nature, to preserve an entire friendship for another, that one knows to be so superior. Is this pride, or a proper independence of spirit?' (PL 49). Flinders was proud, or spirited, enough to let the association lapse when he finally understood Bass's character.

Bass abandoned his subsequent business partner, Charles Bishop, when he became ill: he 'wanted nothing more to do with him'.[19] Bastian writes that the books in his library 'are the best evidence we have that George Bass was a man of mature intellect and feeling – indeed the only evidence for no sign of it emerges in his letters or his intimate relationships'.[20] His letters to his wife, Elizabeth, are occasionally affectionate in a patronising way, but nothing like the passionate, confiding and trusting letters of Matthew to Ann.

Flinders wrote the long and revealing letter to Bass that I have been quoting from Sydney in February 1800. Though it was despatched three years before Bass disappeared, he never received it, which is surely for the best. It may have afforded Flinders some relief to express the hurt his friend had caused him, but it would have done him no good with someone like Bass, who I suspect would have despised his expressions of vulnerability

There is a mystery about this letter. The outside of it is annotated by Elizabeth Bass: 'This George is written by a Man that bears a bad Character no one has seen this letter but I could tell you many things that makes me dislike him rest assured he is no friend of yours or any ones farther than his own interest is concerned' (PL 49). I have never seen a satisfactory explanation of this note and its seemingly unfair though vague allegations. If anyone is characterised by overweening selfishness in this story, I do not believe it is Flinders: ambitious, yes, but loyal to a fault to his friends and those to whom he felt he owed favours.

I have seen no convincing evidence that he was Bass's intellectual inferior, and he was certainly a better friend, a better husband, and went on to make a major contribution to Australian history and science, while Bass sailed off on a disastrous private voyage which destroyed many lives.

Eliza Kent

In August 1805, Flinders wrote in his journal that he had 'been little accustomed to female society' (PJ 79). It is true that there were no women on board the *Investigator* or the *Cumberland*, and that he had perhaps not been in female company very often during his detention in Port Louis. However, he would soon be in the largely female company of the d'Arifat household on Mauritius, and he had many female friends, both in England and Australia.

One friend he corresponded with was Eliza Kent, the wife of his fellow naval officer William Kent (1760–1812). They married in 1791, and although her date of birth is not known, she would presumably have been a little older than Flinders. She was one of the women to whom he was hoping to introduce Ann when he brought her to Sydney. In his letter to Banks in 1801, after he had been told that he must leave Ann behind, he wrote that he hoped that their Lordships 'would have shown the same indulgence to me, as to Lt. Kent of the *Buffalo*, and many others' (PL 69).

A letter to Mrs Kent, written in mid-1803, was left with governor King to be passed on to her when she returned to Sydney:

> My dear Madam
>
> Your two friendly letters I have received, and for which I thank you almost more than for the one you were kind enough to bring out for me. Fortune seems determined to give me disappointment – when I come into Port Jackson two of the most esteemed of my friends are absent, and are not to return until we are gone: in the case of Bass I have been twice served this way. (PL 105)

Eliza Kent's letters to Flinders do not survive, but this reply implies that in them she had given her husband's excuses for not writing to Flinders, to which he responds with a kind of extravagant and humorous courtliness:

> If captain Kent has any dislike to have me find fault with him, it is a lucky circumstance that he has an advocate whose eloquence almost prevents one from observing that he has said nothing. I should indeed have been gratified by a letter from him, though it had been a short one, but since his silence has produced me a higher banquet, I kiss the kind hand that bestows it and be even pleased at his omission.
>
> ...Wishing you and all yours, much health, and all the happiness that your wanderings will permit, I remain my dear Madam, your very sincere and obliged friend. (PL 105–106)

Back in England from his travels and his long detention, in June 1812, he records that he 'walked in the evening with Mrs F. to Paddington, and examined the church yard for Mrs Kents tomb, but could not find it; probably from its being within the church, which was shut' (PL 411). This sad errand is explained in a letter from William Kent of September 1811:

> May you long enjoy that happiness, the Almighty, in his wisdom, has thought proper to retire from me. ... If you walk into the Church on Paddington Green you will see the Monument of my ever-to-be lamented Eliza, who loved you with the Affection of a Sister.[21]

William Kent died soon after, in August 1812.

Louise d'Arifat

The d'Arifat family was Flinders' constant support and resource during the last four and a half years of his detention. In November 1805 he wrote to Ann with the news that his situation had improved, and he had been permitted to move to the country. His new abode

> was offered me by Madame D'Arifat an elderly widow lady, of an excellent understanding and disposition, and respectable character. Her family consists of three sons and three daughters four of whom are grown up and compose one of the most amiable families this island can boast; but it is with the eldest son [Labauve], of about 27 years, and the eldest daughter [Delphine] of about 20 that I have more particularly attached myself. Thou canst not conceive how anxious they are to see and be acquainted with thee. (PL 135)

Louise d'Arifat does indeed seem to have been a very sensible and kind woman. She dissuaded him from his plan to withdraw and live a solitary life in late 1806 with practical good sense – 'the soothing consolations and reasonings of Madam D. induced me to abandon my ill-omened project', he wrote in his Journal (PJ 138). In October 1807 he wrote to his friend Charles Desbassayns, now the husband of Lise, the youngest of the d'Arifat daughters:

> I am much obliged by your kind remembrances transmitted me by our dear friend Madame D. I know not when I may be permitted to quit the island, but ... enough of this subject, it makes me sick at heart; let me talk to you [of] this charming, this excellent family. Madame D. is as she has always been; neither sick nor yet enjoying strong health. Her godlike disposition is also, and ever will be, the same.[22]

Flinders corresponded with Madame d'Arifat regularly on his return to England, until in April 1813, in the middle of a writing her a letter, he broke off and continued:

> Thus far, my dear Labauve, I had written, when your letter of Dec. 25th. announced to me the melancholy and greatly regretted event of your most worthy mother's decease. The shock was to me as if I had lost my own mother, and most sincerely do I sympathise in the affliction of the family;

and deep it must be, for the loss of so excellent a parent and member of society.[23]

Thomi Pitot

Charles Desbassayns and Labauve d'Arifat were two of his particular friends on Mauritius, but there were several more. He often visited M. and Mme Chazal, the neighbours of the d'Arifats, where he played chess with Monsieur and music for flute and harpsichord with Madame. Charles Baudin, a French naval officer who had been on Nicolas Baudin's expedition, was a close friend despite his active participation in the war with Britain. And one of the earliest, and most enduring, of his Mauritius friends was Thomi Pitot.

They first met in Port Louis in August 1804, when Thomi and his brother Edouard dined in the mess at the Maison Despaux. 'They were very agreeable and seemed interested to do him and me service. They have lent us books and music and behaved more liberally than is customary to any strangers' (PJ 40). Within ten days, Flinders reported that Pitot had become 'one of my best friends' (PJ 41). Pitot introduced him to many other French settlers, including Louise d'Arifat. He played music with Flinders, lent him books, and kept him informed of any developments which might affect him.

In September 1805, Flinders wrote a long letter to Pitot, a meditation on the nature of friendship, which expands upon what he had written to Philip Gidley King (quoted in Chapter One) two years earlier:

> Upon the subject of friendship and obligation, I foresee we shall continue to have some difference so long as our relative situations continue the same. It will always be in your power to vanquish me, by reducing me to the dilemma which this question must produce 'Would you not have done the same for me in similar circumstances?' If I was to answer, no; I show myself unworthy of your friendship; and if yes, my own argument is defeated. It is to your generosity, I believe, that I am indebted for your forbearance of it. In most points, I fully agree with your sentiments upon the subject of friendship, so far as you have developed them; but I think you may be assured, that the conferring of benefits, so far as they form a part of friendship, ought to be mutual; observe, I do not mean that they must be exactly balanced, for that friendship which is served out by weight is unworthy of the name; but there

ought to be a degree of reciprocity between them, to ease the conscience of the receiver; to prevent the sting of dependence from entering too deeply into his soul. If I do not make myself clearly understood, you will probably comprehend what I mean in framing an answer to the following question, which I put to you. Suppose yourself to have acquired two new friends, for whom you have an equal esteem and respect, and between whom there is no other difference than this, that your friend A has conferred numberless obligations upon you, but it has never been in your power to do him any service, though you have anxiously sought for opportunities: A is complete within himself, and in some measure beyond the reach of your services; but your friend B, on the contrary, has been unfortunate, his situation has seemed to require your assistance and you have given it gladly, being satisfied of his worth, and from your friendship for him; he is grateful to you for what you have done, so that his eyes swim in tears, but he has no means of serving you. Now, my friend, let me ask you which of these two, A or B, you love best: to whom does your heart give the preference? I doubt not on which side your answer will be, but I beg of you to examine your feelings, and account reasonably to yourself for the preference. In so doing, I think you will fully understand my sentiments upon the subject of friendship, and why I say there ought to be some degree of reciprocity.

I do not, however, place the criterion of friendship either in the conferring or receiving of benefits, though I admit them to be good accessories. It is in the almost indescribable communion of mind, the similarity of sentiments and of taste, and that jumping together of the heart upon occasions that call forth the feelings of humanity, which combined with a sincere esteem for the virtue and ability of our friend, and a wakeful anxiety for his welfare and happiness; – these are the foundations of ardent genuine friendship, and before which, benefits and obligations have scarcely a name. I do not hesitate to avow, that I loved you more for giving me the early intelligence of the arrival of the Bellona in the Grand Port, which you thought was a frigate from France, than for the greatest of those benefits you have conferred upon me; there I saw the heart of the friend; and though it was not, like your letters to Fleurieu and others, a full-length portrait of friendship, it was a sketch, done in such an artless though masterly stile, that it will never be erased from my memory. – But you will think me a visionary, leaving the solid for the artificial enjoyments of life; and if you do, I must forgive you; for you are not the first person nor is this the only subject upon which I have been so accused. (PL 129–130)

In July 1806, he gave Thomi a letter to be given 'to the captain or commander of any of His Majestys ships', in the event that in his travels his ship might be captured by the British:

Sir – I have taken the liberty of recommending my very particular friend Mr. Thomas Pitot to your notice and good offices, and I further request of you, should circumstances render a sum of money to him necessary ...

Should I, Sir, have the honour of your acquaintance, this request will not appear strange, and depending upon the liberal sentiments that almost uniformly characterise the commanders of His Majestys ships, where a brother officer in misfortune is concerned I have ventured to address this to you at a hazard; and in complying with it you will most sensibly oblige your most obedient humble servant Mattw. Flinders[24]

He had often written such recommendations for his Mauritius friends but he was particularly warm in his recommendation in this case. He wrote to Pitot in 1807,

I inclose you the letter for my countrimen, hoping at the same time that the application of it may never be necessary, but should it be otherwise, I have little doubt that the obligations you have conferred upon me and others of my countrimen will meet with their reward; at all events, they will ever live in the breast of your most affectionate and sincere friend.[25]

This would have been one way he could relieve his anxiety at being on the receiving end of so many favours that he was unable to return.

Finally allowed to leave in June 1810, after many false hopes, he wrote to Charles Desbassayns, 'Now that I am certain of going, the pleasure I had in contemplating this event in perspective, is vanished. My heart is oppressed at the idea of quitting my friends here, perhaps forever' (PL 199).

Flinders retained investments in Mauritius and Bourbon that required his friends' help, and in turn he carried out several commissions for them and helped mutual friends in captivity in England. Like all the landowners of Mauritius, Pitot owned slaves and was having legal problems with transporting them from Mauritius to Bourbon or the Cape of Good Hope, now that Mauritius was an English possession, since the slave trade had been abolished in the British Empire in 1807. Flinders helped Pitot by trying to fathom the legal intricacies of the case, consulting lawyers, obtaining documents and legal opinions for him.

Flinders looked forward to a time when he could return to Mauritius, now a British possession. He wrote affectionate letters to his French friends there for the rest of his short life, imagining plans for bringing his wife with him to meet his island companions.

Ann continued corresponding with Pitot after Matthew's death, and in December 1814 wrote that little Anne, then not yet three years old, was 'perfectly familiar with your name & very often talks of writing to Mr. Thomy Pitot.'[26] Pitot died in 1821, at the age of 41.

William Fitzwilliam Owen[27]

William Fitzwilliam Owen first appears in Flinders' *Private Journal* in mid-1809 as the Commander of the *Seaflower*, which had been captured by the French. Although Flinders was by now on parole at the d'Arifat family's plantation at Plaines Wilhems, his friends in Port Louis liked to keep him informed about any developments which might have a bearing on his chances of being released from detention, and a new British officer in town was always of interest.

They began corresponding in June 1809. A midshipman from the *Seaflower* had attempted to impose on Flinders, pretending to be a relative, and Flinders, while not being taken in, had lent him some money out of kindness. Owen wrote to him apologising for the young man's behaviour and offering to repay the money. This disposed Flinders favourably to Owen, though they don't seem to have met until Flinders was finally allowed to leave: Owen was leaving on the same cartel. They boarded on 8 May 1810, but it was several weeks before they sailed, and they got to know each other well during this time. On 15 May, Flinders reported that he was 'Perusing a treatise upon telegraphic and naval signals' by Lt. Owen, 'who appears to have paid much attention to this subject' (PJ 31). This would have been another mark in his favour – Flinders appreciated careful attention to detail, and had himself written on naval and scientific subjects. It seems likely that during these three weeks they shared their knowledge of navigation.

They didn't sail until mid-June, and Flinders transferred to another ship soon after they left Port Louis and made his way home to England via the Cape of Good Hope, while Owen stayed with the cartel.

There are three letters from Owen to Flinders in the Flinders Archive at the National Maritime Museum, Greenwich. On 1 August 1810, Owen wrote to Flinders from Madras, where he had arrived on 7 July. It is a chatty and affectionate letter:

> With a Man of your Science and precision My Dear Captain Flinders, I may perhaps risk my credit a little by writing to you in my common negligent style ... When we parted we had little time to say much to each other. Events passed too rapidly, we had both much to do in the time, and both had too long been out of the habit of such rapid changes.

Owen goes on to tell Flinders how much they missed him on board the cartel. 'We toasted you, Sir, like Englishmen. ... Few men know better how to appreciate Sentiment than yourself. I will therefore offer you no reflections of mine on the Satisfaction you must derive from the unanimous concurrence of Esteem.' He also assures Flinders that 'All the World in India had taken so much Interest in your fate, that your liberation caused general Satisfaction.'

He fills Flinders in with the gossip from the short voyage from Mauritius to Madras, among 'a heterogeneous lot', including his own flirtation with 'one Young lady': 'I could have worshipped the little witch for life, but Fate, or in your Philosophic language, The General laws by which the universe is governed, seem to have denied me this indulgence.' Owen goes on to tell him that 'On my Arrival here, Adm[ira]l Drury was glad to see me ... and proposed to turn me to Account against the Isle of France, where I yet hope to Justify both you and me.'[28]

He wrote again on 10 September, 'Just three months have Elapsed since our happy happy Separation from that diabolical hell hole and from each other.' Owen has lots of news, and not much time. He explains the advice he has given to those in command, that 'Mauritius will be attacked w[ith] a force little Short of twenty Thousand – I wrote on the principle of saving blood ...; this Principle I know you wou'd have admired.' He tells Flinders that he had been put in charge of the transport of the 'Troops who shall avenge your wrongs.'[29]

In 1811, Flinders had cause to correspond with Captain Owen's brother Commodore Edward Owen of the *Inconstant* about his own brother Samuel, and his letters included friendly comments about Captain W. Owen. Edward Owen's letters are also in the Flinders Archive at Greenwich.

In September 1811, Flinders wrote to Hugh Hope, the captain of the cartel, 'I have had two letters from Owen, who, I find, is posted. I should have written to him long ago had I not expected him home, by every fleet that has arrived. Should you see him, pray tell him this; give my kind remembrances, and say I have been in correspondence with his brother the commodore, but that we have not yet met' (PL 212–213).

Owen wrote to him once more on 7 January 1812 from the coast of Malabar, giving Flinders his news of promotions and postings. 'Scribbling this as I have done, the chance is that you will not make ten following words of sense out of it – but by Jove I will not read it over again, to correct.'[30]

Flinders finally got around to writing to Owen in February 1813. 'Will it believed, that after the pleasure those letters gave me, I have not once written to you since I arrived in England? Yet such is the fact; and the cause was, that I fully expected your promotion would bring you home; but such, it seems, is not likely to be the case.' Flinders explains what has happened in his career and his work since he arrived back in England in October 1810, particularly writing his voyage and doing experiments on the science of navigation. He tells Owen about the birth of his daughter Anne in April 1812, and goes on to give him some advice about the difficulties he will face if he marries a 'foreigner', mentioning a Miss Foisy who he hopes not to have offended by his remarks. He signs off 'very faithfully and affectionately'.[31]

They did meet again – Flinders' journal mentions three visits from him in London in the second half of 1813, but he gives scant details, except that Owen lent him his brother Edward Owen's 'paper on Double Altitudes'. The last reference we find to Owen in Flinders' papers is in a letter addressed to him by Ann Flinders in late July 1814, ten days after her husband died. She thanks him for his for 'his friendly letter, & the kind offer of service which it contains. ... She feels assured that ... Capt. O – in some degree knew the excellency & exalted worth of the Treasure she has lost.'[32]

The correspondence between Flinders and Owen is remarkable not only because letters survive in both directions, from each to the other, but also because they met on an equal footing and formed a friendship based on mutual respect and shared interests. From their letters, it seems that their acquaintance, though lasting only for the few weeks they were thrown together on the cartel, was intense: they seem to have had spirited debates on philosophy and religion as well as sharing ideas about science and navigation. They were the same age and clearly shared personal confidences – rather like the young French men who Flinders had criticised in his journal, who discussed their *amours* while 'I never make [them] a topick of conversation' (PJ 108).

Owen went on to have a distinguished career in the British Navy, charting parts of the African coast and the Canadian Great Lakes. He died in 1857.

10

'The sporting, affectionate, and useful companion of my voyages': Matthew Flinders and Trim[1]

The History of my cat Trim

On 11 January 1807 Matthew Flinders was at Plaines Wilhems on the island of Mauritius in the Indian Ocean, where he had already been detained by the French governor, General Charles-Mathieu-Isodore Decaen, on suspicion of being a spy for more than three years. Although he was very frustrated at his detention, he kept himself busy. He wrote in his journal:

> When not otherwise occupied, I have lately employed myself, either in correcting my narrative, ... – in reading Grants history of the Isle of France and making notes upon it, – or in translating into French the history of my cat Trim, which I *wrote out* for the purpose. (PJ 150, emphasis mine)

In the previous days he had been visiting his friend, the artist Toussaint Antoine de Chazal de Chamarel, who was painting his portrait. The portrait M. Chazal was painting in December 1806 and January 1807 gives us the best idea we have of what Matthew looked like. Unsmiling, he fixes the viewer with a sombre, slightly stern gaze. His mouth is set in a determined line: he looks as if he hasn't had a shave for a day or two. Matthew described what M. Chazal was doing as 'tak[ing] a copy of my face, of the natural size' (PJ 149).

It seems odd to us these days to describe the creative process in this way – to describe painting a portrait as if it were merely 'taking a copy' of someone's face, or 'writing out' a story as if no art were involved in the telling of it. But in the eighteenth and nineteenth centuries it was common enough for writers to claim to be 'copying Nature'[2] or presenting 'a definite and substantial reality'.[3]

M. Chazal could have decided to paint Matthew as he was when he was laughing at one of his jokes, or arguing with him over a card game, or playing the flute to Mme Chazal's harpsichord accompaniment. But for him the 'reality' of Matthew was to be captured with the use of measuring instruments. And for Matthew the story of his cat Trim was just a matter of sitting down to write 'a history' that he could then use for French translation practice.

Was the 'history' he wrote in January 1807 the *Biographical Tribute to the Memory of Trim*? On the surviving manuscript he added 'Isle de France 1809' to the title. Maybe what he wrote in 1807 was a simpler version that he elaborated over the next two or three years. In any case, what we have is far from a simple 'history'.

There can't be many cats in history who have been described in such affectionate detail, and who have become so famous. Trim now has his share of portraits and statues – it seems hardly proper nowadays to depict Matthew without his faithful Trim somewhere nearby. How lucky we are that somehow the manuscript of *Trim* survived among Matthew's papers, to be rediscovered in 1971 by Stephen Murray-Smith.[4] It has been published several times since then, most lately in *Trim: The Cartographer's Cat* edited by Philippa Sandall and me.

Flinders the writer

Flinders wrote hundreds of letters, several journals, and many reports, as well as his published books, *A Voyage to Terra Australis* being the major work. All his prose has a certain classic eighteenth-century poise and flexibility, but these qualities are allowed more room to play in his 'Biographical Tribute'. T.M. Perry sees the Tribute as 'evidence that, despite imprisonment, the human qualities of the man endured.'[5] They may even have developed. The weary 36-year-old returned wanderer of 1810 must have been different in many ways from the determined 27-year-old who set out on his great exploration in 1801: it is easy to believe that in 1801, when he left on his expedition to chart the Australian coast, he would have had neither the inclination nor the time to write a *jeu d'esprit* like this.

Some of the editions of the *Tribute* are abridged. They leave out an important clue to Flinders' literary influences, in the name of the hero of this tale, taken from Laurence Sterne's *Tristram Shandy*: 'From his gentleness and the innate goodness of his heart,' Flinders writes, 'I gave him the name of my uncle Toby's honest, kind-hearted, humble companion' (TCC 16). This is fitting: the gentle whimsy of the whole piece is utterly Sternian.

Jane Austen complained that her naval brothers 'write so even, so clear, both in style and penmanship, so much to the point, and give so much intelligence, that it is enough to kill one.'[6] In Flinders' case, at least, this long discipline of economy and pertinence combined with the example of the best prose writing of the eighteenth century, of which he had read at least the major works, to give his writing by this time a feline elegance and aplomb perfect for this little essay. He allows his sentences room to develop: Perry cautions that we have to remember 'that it was written in the age of grand-scale verbosity'.[7] But it is the most delicious verbosity:

> Trim, though vain as we have seen, was not like those young men who, being assured of an independence, spend their youth in idle trifling, and consider all serious application as pedantic and derogatory, or at least to be useless: He was, on the contrary, animated with a noble zeal for the improvement of his faculties. ... He was taught to lie flat upon the deck on his back, with his four feet stretched out like one dead; and in this posture he would remain until a signal was given him to rise, whilst his preceptor resumed his walk backwards and forwards: if, however, he was kept in this position, which it must be confessed was not very agreeable to a quadruped, a slight motion of the end of his tail denoted the commencement of impatience, and his friends never pushed their lesson further. (TCC 20)

Trim on board ship

Trim was not the only cat on board Flinders' various vessels, and he was of course not the first ships' cat in history. The importance of taking cats on long sea voyages has been recognised for centuries. Philippa Sandall's book *Seafurrers* is a mine of information about the feline role in seafaring. In 1494 a Spanish publication recorded an item of maritime law about rodent control:

> If goods laden on board of a ship are devoured by rats, and the owners consequently suffer considerable damage, the master must repair the injury

sustained by the owners, for he is considered in fault. But if the master kept cats on board, he is excused from that liability.[8]

Trim, though now known as 'Matthew Flinders' cat', was a valued member of the crew, 'a favourite with everybody on board' (TCC 17). Flinders describes the friendship between Trim and the Aboriginal interpreter, Bungaree, on board the *Norfolk* in 1799:

> In an expedition made to examine the northern parts of the coast of New South Wales, Trim presented a request to be of the party, promising to take upon himself the defence of our bread bags, and his services were accepted. Bongaree,[9] an intelligent native of Port Jackson, was also on board our little sloop; and with Trim formed an intimate acquaintance. If he had occasion to drink, he mewed to Bongaree and leaped up to the water cask; if to eat, he called him down below and went strait to his kid,[10] where there was generally a remnant of black swan. In short, Bongaree was his great resource, and his kindness was repaid with caresses. (TCC 32)

Trim climbed aloft with the seamen, and was welcomed at the tables of officers and men alike. At the wreck of the *Porpoise* in August 1803, Flinders writes, 'The imagination can scarcely attain to what Trim had to suffer during this dreadful night, but his courage was not beat down' (TCC 44).

Trim ashore

One feels in this essay the full force of Flinders' longing for everything he had been denied, all embodied in this delightful animal. Trim may even have been an idealised version of himself, or how he would like to think of himself: brave, daring, useful, affectionate, and courteous, but not accustomed to living in houses ashore:

> Your delicat town-bred cats go mincing in amongst cup and sawcers without touching them; but Trim! If he spied a mouse there he dashed at it like a man of war, through thick and thin: the splinters flew in all directions. (TCC 38)

Perhaps this might reflect something of his own impatience with the genteel confinement to which he was subjected on Mauritius. Reading his journal from the years between 1805 and 1810 when he was staying with Madame d'Arifat, we can see that he was living among people whom he could regard as friends – some remained friends for the rest of his life – and that in many ways his life was not unpleasant, except for the obdurate fact that he could not leave. The history of his imprisonment is narrated here with Trim as a central character:

> The Minikin [otherwise, the Cumberland – a very small ship] being very leaky, was obliged to stop at the Isle of France; and there poor Trim, his master and few followers were all made prisoners; under the pretext that they had come to spy out the nakedness of the land; though it was clear as day, that they knew nothing of the war that had taken place a few months before. (TCC 46)

When Flinders was moved to the Garden Prison in 1804, 'a French lady offered to be Trim's security, in order to have him for a companion to her little daughter; and the fear of some clandestine proceedings on the part of the soldiers of the guard' induced Flinders to agree, thinking that he would be safer there. But Trim escaped and was never seen again: Flinders suspected he had been caught and 'eaten by some hungry black slave' (TCC 49). Of course there's no way of knowing what actually happened. Perhaps Trim made his way to the waterfront and boarded another ship: after all, he was ship's cat by birth and training.

The real Trim
But outside this manuscript, what do we know about the real Trim? In all the 235,000 words of his *Private Journal* Flinders only mentions him that one time, to say he was 'writing out' his history, and then once, a few weeks later, to say that among 'varied amusements' he was 'translating into French the History of my cat, Trim' (PJ 155). He didn't figure in the journal during the dark days when, according to the *Tribute*, 'confined in a room with his master and another officer, ... he contributed by his gay humour to soften our straight captivity' (TCC 46).

Matthew's correspondence gives us a few more hints. He mentioned him twice in letters to his wife Ann. Ann would have known Trim from her short and ill-fated sojourn on board the *Investigator* between her marriage to Matthew on 17 April 1801, and the middle of June that year, when she was sent back to her family, sternly banished from the voyage by the Lords of the Admiralty. He was allowed to take his cat with him, but not his wife. Matthew wrote news of Trim from Sydney in June 1803 as one among several shipmates: 'Trim, like his master is becoming grey; he is at present fat and frisky, and takes meat from ones forks with his former dexterity: he is commonly my bedfellow' (PL 100).

In November 1804, he wrote to Ann from the Garden Prison in Mauritius. At the end of the letter, he added a message to Ann's teenage half-sister Isabella Tyler complaining that he had not had a letter from her, and listed a whole lot of presents that he wouldn't give her if she didn't write to him. One of them was 'a set of Trim's finger nails which he shed in the Gulph of Carpentaria' (PL 121).

Trim is mentioned in one more letter, to Governor Philip Gidley King, written in September 1803 at sea in the tiny schooner *Cumberland*, which Matthew had decided to sail all the way to England even though nobody had ever been so far in such a small vessel. He didn't make it – as we know, when he stopped at the French colony of Île de France to repair the ship he, Trim, and the rest of the dozen crew were taken prisoner.

But when he wrote to Governor King he didn't know what awaited him and he was in a jovial mood. He wrote, 'of all the filthy little things I ever saw, this schooner, for bugs, lice, fleas, weavels, mosquitos, cockroaches large and small, and mice, rises superior to them all.' He described the measures they were taking against the various insects, with the bugs being the most persistent: he suggested that 'before this vile bug-like smell will leave me, [I] must, I believe, as well as my clothes, undergo a good boiling in the large kettle.'

The rodents, however, were easily dealt with: 'I shall set my old friend Trim to work upon the mice' (PL 109–110). He knew he could rely on his 'faithful, intelligent ... sporting, affectionate and useful' feline friend.

Statues and memorials

There are now memorials to Flinders and Trim in Australia, Britain and Mauritius. The first one, by John Cornwell, was erected in 1996 on a window-sill of the State Library of New South Wales, behind the 1925 state of Matthew. Trim was included in a Flinders memorial plaque erected in Baie du Cap on Mauritius, where he first landed on that ill-fated day in December 1803. There is a statue of Matthew in the town square of his home town of Donington, Lincolnshire, with Trim winding around his left leg. It was erected in 2006.

The most recent major statue of Trim and Matthew is in the concourse outside Euston Station in London, not far from St James's Churchyard, where Matthew was buried (and has recently been rediscovered). It was designed and created by Mark Richards for an international committee determined to erect a permanent memorial in the city where Matthew spent his last few years. Prince William unveiled the statue on the bicentenary of his death, 19 July 2014.

In 1911, Australian writer George Gordon McCrae – who somehow had come across the manuscript of Trim and drew some amusing sketches to illustrate the story – described his ideal for a statue of Matthew, as quoted in the Introduction: 'In a working undress of the period, the pose easy and natural ...'[11] McCrae's notion for a statue of a working chartmaker rather than a uniformed hero had to wait for nearly a century – and Mark Richards went one better, by adding Trim sitting patiently behind Flinders while he works. 'Richards was struck not so much by his representing the grand ambitions of king and country as by the day-to-day reality of his seafaring life; the discipline, organisation, unimaginable privations and determination. ... With all this in mind, Mark Richards presents Matthew not as a distant heroic figure, but as a man among us.'[12]

Two full-sized copies of this statue of Flinders and Trim have now been installed in South Australia, and there are dozens of miniature versions (maquettes) around the world, bought by Flinders' enthusiasts, local councils, educational institutions and historical societies. When Barack and Michelle Obama visited the Duke and Duchess of Cambridge in London in June 2015, the publicity photo shows Trim and Matthew just over Michelle's shoulder.

Trim's Epitaph
At the end of his Biographical Tribute, Flinders composed an Epitaph for Trim:

To the memory of
Trim
The best and most illustrious of his Race, —
The most affectionate of friends, —
Faithful of servants,

> And best of creatures.
> He made the Tour of the Globe, and a voyage to Australia,
> Which he circumnavigated, and was ever the
> Delight and pleasure of his fellow voyagers.
> Returning to Europe in 1803, he was shipwrecked in the
> Great Equinoxial Ocean;
> This danger escaped, he sought refuge and assistance
> At the Isle of France, where
> He was made prisoner, contrary to the laws of
> Justice, of Humanity and of
> French National Faith;
> And where, alas! He terminated his useful
> Career, by an untimely death,
> Being devoured by the Catophagi of
> That island.
> Many a time have I beheld his little merriments with delight,
> And his superior intelligence with surprise:
> Never will his like be seen again!
> Trim was born in the Southern Indian Ocean, in the
> Year 1799, and
> Perished as above at the Isle of France
> In 1804.
> Peace be to his shade, and
> Honour to his memory. (TCC 50)

I can scarcely read Trim's epitaph dry-eyed, and this is, I am sure, partly the result of Flinders' embodiment of all his own disappointed hopes and thwarted ambitions in this 'best of creatures'. In hindsight, it is impossible to resist carrying the comparison even further. After all, Flinders himself was within a few short years to 'terminate his useful career by an untimely death'.

Through all his trials and tribulations, Matthew was always dreaming about retiring to the English countryside to live quietly with Ann. And, 'if ever he shall have the happiness to enjoy repose in his native country', there would be a place for Trim: 'under a thatched cottage surrounded by half an acre of land … in a retired corner, a monument to perpetuate thy memory and record thy uncommon merits' (TCC 49).

Sadly, that never happened. But Trim's memory has now been restored and perpetuated until he is one of history's most famous cats. His affectionate master and friend did him proud. At the same time, as Stephen Murray-Smith writes, *Trim* 'tells us as much about [Flinders'] personality and humanity as, perhaps, the rest of his published work does in total.'[13] In writing this loving, witty, moving tribute to Trim, he revealed a side of himself that we wouldn't otherwise suspect had ever existed, and at the same time shows us the value of a feline companion: as a pest controller on board, entertainment for the ship's company, and companion for the lonely commander.

Part 4

Writing,
Reading,
Music

11

Matthew Flinders, Life-writer[1]

Matthew Flinders never wrote an autobiography, but he was constantly reflecting on his life in the written word – sometimes explaining himself to those who would read his published work, or his letters, and sometimes just explaining himself to himself. He wrote to understand his place in the history of exploration and navigation, he wrote to justify his actions and decisions, both personal and professional, he wrote to express his frustrations, and sometimes he wrote to imagine a different life – to try it on for size. His one explicit excursion into life-writing was his 'Biographical Tribute to the Memory of Trim', which as well as being the story of his cat, I believe can be read as vicarious autobiography, as discussed in Chapter Ten. In this chapter I have chosen just a few examples from countless possibilities – touching only very briefly on the rich vein of material in his letters – to explore the self-construction of this young explorer's biography, and the way he used words to discover himself and reveal himself to his readers.

Flinders, like other explorers of the time, and indeed perhaps like all ambitious people born in relatively humble circumstances, was driven by a mixture of pride, humility, competitiveness and fear of failure. He knew about the imposter syndrome long before the term was invented, and he was always measuring himself against his predecessors and rivals, and wondering about his own legacy.

Memoir
He actually wrote at least one 'Memoir', to accompany his journals and charts. It is dated 'Isle of France 14 May 1805', and the full title is '*A Memoir*

explaining the marks used in the charts of Australia constructed on board His Majesty's ship Investigator; *and the manner in which the latitude, longitude, and variation of the compass were obtained, corrected, and applied in their construction; With some new facts and additional observations upon these and other nautical subjects connected with Australia; by Mattw Flinders, Late commander of the* Investigator: *a prisoner in the Isle of France.*' (AC 2: 402)

This title, though purporting to be scientific and business-like, has a sting in the tail: he cannot resist the opportunity to point out his unfair imprisonment by the French, and the Preface to the Memoir gives a short history of all the mishaps that led to his detention on Mauritius and prevented him finishing the charting of the Australian coast to the level of precision he expected of himself. And delving more deeply, we can understand that in explaining these technical matters he has an agenda. During the *Investigator* surveying voyage, he writes:

> The original rough charts were always made on the same day in which the land they described had been seen, and most commonly whilst the different parts were in sight: ... On coming into harbour, or when the distance of the land gave me leisure time, I placed these rough sheets before me, and with the assistance of my log book, my astronomical observation and bearing book, the whole was afresh laid down with great exactness. (AC 2: 407)

Implied in this explanation, perhaps, is a criticism of other chart-makers who took the readings and then only completed the charts when they got back to civilisation. This invites us to visualise the proud perfectionist, straining his eyes, working into the night at his drafting table in his cabin – Trim perhaps sitting at his feet: I'd like to think that he wasn't one of those helpful cats who insist on sitting on exactly the most inconvenient spot when his human was trying to get something done.

In the Memoir, Flinders explains in great detail his choices for the scale of the various maps he drew, depending on what would be most useful, but when it came to drawing the first chart of the complete outline of Australia, his explanation betrays the precarity of this enterprise and its very physical limitations: 'the general chart ... is drawn upon the scale that suited the only sheet of paper that I had remaining' (AC 2: 408).

The criticism implied earlier soon becomes explicit:

I have been careful not to insert my own conjectures in the place of actual observation, as has been too much the case with some navigators, to the detriment of true geography and the hindrance of further investigation. (AC 2: 407–408).

It is always frustrating to find conjectures leading to inaccuracy and error in any kind of research, but it could be disastrous for navigators entering uncharted waters, hence the soapbox style. He begins to get defensive when describing some of the markings he had used on the charts to denote various geographic and climatic features, and also the degree of certainty with which he has made observations: 'It will be seen that these marks are, amongst other uses, intended to be my apologists ... I ought not be blamed for the omission', he says, if the weather, or the time of night, or some other circumstance would have prevented him from noticing some significant feature (AC 2: 413).

His anxiety reaches its peak when he has to explain the corrections he has made to Captain Cook's charts of the east coast of Australia:

> Those who reflect ... and consider that captain Cook was liable to all the errors of a first examination and was without a time-keeper, will readily understand why I have ventured to take such great liberties with the works of so greatly and so justly distinguished a navigator; and these circumstances shall be my apology: If the corrections shall be found to approximate to the truth I shall be excused; if it should prove otherwise, I shall never excuse myself. (AC 2: 455)

Cook was his idol, and the idea that he might be setting himself up as his critic, and correcting his work, was deeply intimidating. In a letter to Sir Joseph Banks, written from Mauritius in 1804, this complicated young man wrote:

> In the regular service of the navy there are too many competitors for fame: I have therefore chosen a branch which, though less rewarded by rank and fortune, is yet little less in celebrity ... . If adverse fortune does not oppose me, I will succeed; and although I cannot rival the immortalized name of Cook, yet if persevering industry joined to what ability I may possess, can accomplish it, then I will secure the second place. (PL 118)

I knew not how to accomplish the task

In both his Log, written at the time, and *A Voyage to Terra Australis*, written ten years later, he wrote of his feelings when the master and carpenter gave him the news that the *Investigator* was rotting and would not survive rough seas. This is the later account:

> I cannot express the surprise and sorrow which this statement gave me. According to it, a return to Port Jackson was almost immediately necessary; as well to secure the journals and charts of the examinations already made, as to preserve the lives of the ship's company; ... My leading object had hitherto been, to make so accurate an investigation of the shores of Terra Australis that no future voyage to this country should be necessary; ...; but with a ship incapable of encountering bad weather – ..., I knew not how to accomplish the task. (VTA 2: 143)

He agonised over the decision, and in the Log he wrote out the arguments for and against continuing the survey, setting 'the possible loss of the whole produce of our risks and labours as well as the loss of our lives' (think of that one last remaining piece of paper on which he drew his chart of the Australian coast – no way of scanning and backing it up to the cloud) versus the 'genuine spirit of discovery which contains all danger and inconvenience when put in competition with its gratification. Upon the score of duty I might (it may be said) be forgiven, but must never boast of a single spark of that ethereal fire with which the souls of Columbus and of Cook were wont to burn!' Only then does he bring up the sorry 'state of health of me and the crew' as another factor in deciding to discontinue the work and head for Sydney (AC 2: 311–312). Looking back on this decision, when writing the *Voyage*, he had this to say:

> The accomplishment of the survey was, in fact, an object so near to my heart, that could I have foreseen the train of ills that were to follow the decay of the Investigator and prevent the survey being resumed – and had my existence depended upon the expression of a wish, I do not know that it would have received utterance; but Infinite Wisdom has, in infinite mercy, reserved the knowledge of futurity to itself. (VTA 2: 248)

Not quite suicidal ideation, perhaps, but retrospective despair, and written for publication.

Reverie on Timor

Just after making this difficult but inevitable decision, they put in at Timor to take on fresh food and water – bad move, since it brought dysentery with it. But while he was there, Flinders visited a plantation, with shady trees and fish ponds:

> I thought this to be a little paradise, ... and I could not prevent my ideas from dwelling upon the happiness that a man whose desires were moderate might enjoy in this delightful retreat with the beloved of his heart. ... I thought such a life as well fitted for philosophical and religious contemplation, as it was for love and all its train of domestic enjoyments. (AC 2: 337)

But as he pursues his 'reverie', he starts to see the drawbacks – no amusement, or society, and the weather too hot for exertion and the roads impassable, no one to discuss his books with. 'I energetically exclaimed – No – I was not meant for this; my reverie ended here' (AC 2: 338). This passage, discussed in detail in Chapter 3, is an example of his writing a parallel self, possibly with the sole intention of rejecting it and asserting the real self, the one whose desires are not moderate, the one who was not meant for vegetating in an island paradise. And this, as far as I can tell, was written just for himself. It has only recently been published: it appears out of order at the beginning of a volume of the fair copy of his log book, probably because that was the only blank paper he had available and the notebook later had to be used for official purposes.

The *Private Journal*

Another construction of self appears in the *Private Journal*. During his years in Mauritius, Flinders quite often confided in his journal, apparently for himself alone. He would begin entries with expressions like 'It is some time since I have expressed the state of my sentiments and feelings ...' (PF 129). Some of these entries are profoundly moving, detailing his isolation and struggles with depression. But in October 1805, he was in quite good spirits. He had been allowed to live in the countryside after nearly two years in confinement, and was out walking with his French friends. Exploring the spectacular Tamarind Falls, he found a cavern behind the waterfall, and, presumably back in his room, wrote about the 'reflexions' he had made, firstly on the geophysics of the area, then proceeding to draw an analogy with politics: 'The greater the inequalities are, (the higher the mountains are above the valleys, or that kings are above other men) the more is a sudden fall or revolution to be apprehended' (PJ 100).

Then his thoughts turn towards 'the vicissitudes of my own life':

> I was born in the fens of Lincolnshire where a hill is not to be seen for many miles, at a distance from the sea, and my family unconnected with sea affairs or any kind of enterprise or ambition. (PJ 100–101).

This is fudging things a bit. He had a cousin in the Navy, John Flinders, who told him what he needed to read if he wanted to be a sailor; and John's sister Henrietta was a governess who introduced him to her boss, Captain Thomas Pasley, who got him his first posting on a Navy ship. But it's true his father, a surgeon and man-midwife, didn't want him to go to sea: he was to be apprenticed and follow the same profession. Anyway, his account of his life continues:

> After many incidents of fortune and adventure, I found myself a commander in the Royal Navy, having been charged with an arduous expedition on discovery; have visited a great variety of countries, made three times the tour of the world; find my name known in more kingdoms than that where I was born, with some degree of credit; and this moment a prisoner in a mountainous island in the Indian Ocean, lying under a cascade in a situation very romantic and interior, meditating upon the progress which nature is continually making towards a moderate degree of equality in the physical and moral worlds; and in company with a foreigner, a Frenchman, whom I call, and believe to be, my friend. (PJ 101)

The 'romantic and interior' situation are reminiscent of the 'little paradise' he encountered on Timor, but here on Mauritius he had achieved a kind of accommodation with the restrictions of his life, and befriended some of the 'foreigners' amongst whom he had found himself. He knits his life together with his environment – the observations he makes on the 'physical and moral worlds' are linked to his origins in the fens of Lincolnshire – surely one of the flattest places on earth, and perhaps, thus, in his mind, one of the least romantic – and his current picturesque situation in a 'mountainous island' far from home.

18 August 1805[2]
Another kind of life-writing that Flinders had experimented with a few months earlier was a 'day-in-the-life'. One particular journal entry is set out differently from all the others. There is a solid line drawn across the page, followed by a centred heading: 'Journal of Sunday Aug[t] 18th.' He follows himself through one of his last days in the 'Garden Prison' or Maison Despaux, before he was allowed to go and live in the country on parole. Activities, thoughts, memories, speculations, complaints, commentary on what he's reading – all these jostle together into a kind of stream of consciousness experiment.

Flinders' *Private Journal* fascinates me. For whom was he writing? Was it for us – for posterity: did he realise that 200 years later we would be poring over his innermost thoughts? Was the habit of journal-writing inculcated by the Navy so ingrained that he continued in it as a matter of discipline, whether he thought anyone would read it or not? Or was he filling in time, or recording his thoughts and activities for his own later reference? American essayist Joan Didion, writing in 1966, speculated that

> The impulse to write things down is a peculiarly compulsive one, inexplicable to those who do not share it, useful only accidentally, only secondarily, in the way that any compulsion tries to justify itself. ... Keepers of private notebooks are a different breed ..., lonely and resistant rearrangers of things, anxious malcontents, children afflicted apparently at birth with some presentiment of loss.[3]

Although she explicitly differentiates keepers of notebooks from keepers of diaries, which requires 'an instinct for reality which I sometimes envy but do not possess',[4] this passage struck a chord for me. I feel as though Flinders, while assiduously keeping a diary to record facts, sometimes, especially during this period, emerges one of those 'keepers of private notebooks' that Didion identifies with.

The entry for 18 August 1805 is particularly long – over 2,000 words. He is about to be moved from his confinement to the house and grounds at the Maison Despaux in Port Louis to a more civilised arrangement. He will be staying in the country with the respectable Madame d'Arifat and her family. However, he is not yet certain of this – he has been disappointed so many times in the last two years that he will believe it only when it happens.

It is hard to know whether he wrote it as the day went on, or whether it was written in retrospect. The writing is very neat and even and there is no evidence of stopping and starting in the manuscript – different shades of ink, for example – but I gather he had a habit of making fair copies of things later so it is hard to know what he did on the actual day.

This journal entry has the entertaining inconsequentiality which often characterises such writing, but it is more than telegraphic in this case. It is a 'day in the life' done in slightly self-conscious stream-of-consciousness:

> Rose at half past six. Slipped on my shoes and morning gown, and went down to walk in the garden. Met the serjeant and bid him bonjour. Think the old man looks a little melancholy at the prospect of his last prisoner leaving the house, for he will lose his situation. The dogs came running after me, and seemed more attentive than when there were more prisoners in the house: suppose they are a little pinched for food. The grass being wet with a shower that had fallen at daybreak, confined myself to the walk at the head of the garden, where the gentlemen had cut it down. Meditated during my walk upon the extreme folly of general De Caën keeping me a prisoner here, for it can answer no one good purpose either to him or the French government; and some expense, and probably odium, must be incurred by it. The injury that it is to me is almost incalculable: – but this will not bear to be dwelt upon, it leads almost to madness. Got up into the tall almond tree to see if there was any ship off: none to be seen. (PJ 75)

And so it continues – angst, tree-climbing, General DeCaen, the weather, his ablutions and the activities of his servants all jostling together. Disarmingly he describes stripping himself naked and washing 'from head to foot in the little tub'. He originally continued 'Called Smith to bring me', but crossed that out, and wrote 'Put on my clothes. Called Smith to bring me …' (PJ 75). Mustn't let the diary think he let the servants see him naked.

Next he describes the book he's reading. It is an account of a voyage down the Amazon. He makes some acute hydrological comments, which he interrupts with 'Elder not returned from the Bazar yet. Can't think what keeps him.' This must surely have been written as the day went on. It's not a summary of a day, it's an account as it proceeds. 'Took three pinches of snuff, whilst I sat thinking of my wife and friends in England.' What a desolate, romantic picture! but he goes on, 'Mem. Must not take so much snuff when I return for it makes me spit about the rooms' (PJ 76). This is an observation worthy of Leopold Bloom, and almost convinces me that this diary wasn't intended for publication, but was a way of talking to himself in his isolation. It almost seems as if, on this day at any rate, he is writing to keep himself occupied and sane, and perhaps out of a solitary habit built up over the years.

The Matthew Flinders who manifests himself to me through his writing is capable of strong friendships but is not particularly easy in the company of strangers. He had been befriended by Thomas Pitot, a Mauritius merchant, but he writes, 'Do not wish my friend Pitot to give me introductions to more than two or three families when I go into the country. In applying myself to the French language then, must not wholly neglect the continuation of the accounts of my voyage' (PJ 78). He doesn't want an active social life interfering with his life's work, which he gets on with as well as he can under the circumstances. His career is always on his mind, even though he knows dwelling upon the interruption to his ambitions will lead to madness. He wonders if he might get a promotion to Post Captain in his absence, considers whether he would go out as governor to a settlement in north-west Australia if he were offered the post, asserts his wish to finish his exploration of the whole coast before he does anything else, and to explore inland as well. It is no wonder that he felt ill – he had headaches, which he mentions several times on this day – better at first, then growing worse during the day as his worries prey upon him. For a man who had been so untrammelled in many ways – taking risks, directing the fortunes of nearly 100 people on board ship, naming islands and capes by the dozen, getting things done in spectacular fashion – but who was also so definite about what he wanted to achieve, this abrupt confinement, however pleasant the surroundings, would have caused untold stress, on top of any physical malady he might have had. He wrote to Ann, 'I shall learn patience in this island, which will perhaps counteract the insolence acquired by having had unlimited command over my fellow men' (PL 122). A salutary lesson no doubt, but not conducive to either mental or physical health.

Finally, after a day of frustrated pottering, he goes to bed and lies awake thinking about 'the causes of the trade and westwardly winds, especially upon the earths revolution round its axis ... Must have some kind of trap sent for that rat, which comes disturbing me every night.' Finally he sleeps and dreams 'that general De Caen was setting a lion upon me to devour me, and that he eat me up. Was surprised to find devouring so easy to be borne, and that after death I had the consciousness of existence' (PJ 78).

The literary gift that Flinders shows in this journal entry is that of detachment – of considering his experience and make rational observations on it. His habit of mind was scientific: just on this one day he records having given thought to the currents of the Amazon, and the likelihood of a 'great opening' on the north-west coast of Australia that he missed on his circumnavigation; having read and commented on the articles on Meteorology, Weather and Wind in the Encyclopedia Britannica; and having criticised a theory of the effect of the moon on the weather. Even in his dream he describes detached surprise, rather than terror, at the experience of being eaten by a lion. He cannot help dwelling on that dreadful incident with Decaen which resulted in his captivity. Nearly two years later, he is still explaining to himself that his 'conduct must have originated in unjust suspicion, been prosecuted in revenge, his dignity being injured at my refusing to dine with him, and continued from obstinacy and pride.' How many times must he have repeated that little formula to himself over the years – but nevertheless he doesn't indulge in self-pity, he makes what use he can of his time, and writes down this narrative to try to soothe and control his feelings of frustration. I believe that this journal was an exercise in what we might today call 'narrative therapy', as well as a memorandum to his future self, full of things to remember on that happy day when his life could resume.

My Evening Song: verses set to music
One form he used that was certainly not original was the song lyric. As far as I know he only wrote one. It forms part of the dialogue that he maintained with his wife during his nine-year absence. Only his side of their correspondence remains – Ann destroyed her own letters – but in this single case there is a precious example of her response to his communication.

In November 1805, he sent her a letter:

Comparatively with my situation in this island for the first 20 months I am now very happy; and yet I often retire to the little pavilion which is my study and bed room, and with my flute in my hand and sometimes tears in my eyes I warble over the little evening song of which I sent thee a copy. Ah my beloved, then my heart overleaps the distance of half a world and wholly embraces thee.

The 'evening song' was presumably enclosed with this or an earlier letter. He wrote out the words and music, attributing the melody to Haydn,[5] but the words were his own:

Why Henry didst thou leave me, thus leave me here to mourn?
Ah cruel! Thou deceivedst me, I'll ne'er see thy return.
Thou knew'st how much I loved thee, yet could resolve to go,
My griefs could nothing move thee, though I was sunk in woe.

'Henry', being addressed here in the second person, is obviously Matthew himself, and he is imagining what Ann would say to him – or perhaps what she had said to him in the letters that don't survive. The way I read this first verse is that it is his apology to Ann – implied by writing the words from her point of view – although this, with its strong rhetoric of the implacable demands of duty, is a rationalisation of his actions which he knew were deep source of anguish to his wife.

In the second verse he makes his excuses and enacts her forgiving him because *she* understands *his* point of view:

But why do I thus blame thee, alas thou couldst not stay
For when stern duty calls thee, thou canst not but obey
Thy looks bespoke the anguish, the struggle in thy breast &c.
To be completed[6]

He wrote 'to be completed' in place of the last line of the second verse, perhaps, as I surmised in a short essay written in 2002, because he did not know how to bring it to a conclusion: 'Even his rational mind would superstitiously shy away from anticipating a happy ending for his life's romance.'[7] However, at the time of writing this I was not aware that, with the manuscript, held in the National Maritime Museum at Greenwich, is a scrap of paper with a last line for the second verse plus two more verses, in what has been verified as Ann Flinders' writing.

His attempt at self-justification doesn't seem to have backfired, perhaps helped by his gesture of incompleteness, which could have been a suggestion that she co-author their future together. Ann Flinders' manuscript continues the song in these yearning words:

> *... While pangs of bitter sorrow. thy inmost Soul oppress'd —*
>
> *Sad was the fatal moment which tore thee from my arms,*
> *What hours since then I've counted of misery & alarms —*
> *Ah hast thou in this absence let Fancy dwell as me?*
> *Or sigh with ardent wishes, thy faithful Love to see?*
>
> *My soul with deep felt anguish, incessant mourns for thee*
> *In pining grief I languish & silent agony,*
> *Will comforts cheering sunshine e'er beam on this sore heart?*
> *Yes, when we meet, my Henry, never again to part.*

What I imagine happened was that she received the song some time in 1806 and accepted his implied invitation to complete it, probably writing these words during the years before he returned in 1810. Maybe she even sent him the completed version, though there is no definite record of his receiving it and, because of the war with France, communication was becoming increasingly difficult.[8] When he returned in October 1810, he wrote that he had been 'nearly four years and a half without intelligence from any part of my connexions' (PJ 235).

The Romantic Scientist

While Flinders prided himself on being scientific and scrupulously accurate in his professional activities, he was constantly spilling over into parenthetical speculation and what seem like quite private ruminations in the margins of his scientific work, as it were. The demarcation between the official and scientific, and the personal and imaginative, was not at all clear. In a letter to Ann from December 1800, when it seemed that they would not be able to marry, he wrote:

> The search after knowledge – the contemplation of nature in the barren wild, the overhanging crags of utmost height and the open field decked with the spicy attire of the tropical climes, may – nay must prevent me from casting one thought on England, – on my home ...

Although in this case he was suggesting that the search for knowledge might distract him from his personal troubles, he was certainly thoroughly initiated in the heady spirit of Romantic Science described by Richard Holmes in *The Age of Wonder*. It is not surprising that his *Private Journal* includes much very personal and revealing writing, but we also find extraordinary passages like that one written in Timor in the official Captain's log of the *Investigator* – which he would have had to hand into the Admiralty when he got back to London. And even when he seemed to be sticking to the 'facts', he seemed to understand instinctively the importance of acknowledging his subjective point of view and circumstances when describing his methodology. But for his one foray into actual biographical writing, he did not write about himself or another human being, but concentrated his energies on his beloved cat Trim, whose short life, significantly, coincided with his own short active career.

12

'Well it is for me that I have books': Books in Matthew Flinders' Life[1]

I suppose most people would not think of Matthew Flinders as a bookish man, but reading his *Private Journal* one might think again. Books were important to him not only in his work – he was, as an explorer, continuing the work of his predecessors, most of whom had published not only maps but also accounts of their voyages – but also as recreation and sometimes solace.

The books on board *Investigator*
On the 22 May 1801, Flinders reports in *A Voyage to Terra Australis*, various items were sent on board the *Investigator* by the Navy Board. 'Amongst the [articles ... for our own use and convenience] were most of the books of voyages to the South Seas, which, with our own individual collections, and the *Encyclopedia Britannica*, presented by the Right Hon. Sir Joseph Banks, formed a library in my cabin for the use of all the officers' (VTA 1: 5–6).

That *Encyclopedia* was to play its part in one of the dramas of his career. In 1803, when approaching Mauritius for emergency repairs to the *Cumberland*, the map of Mauritius in the *Encyclopedia* was all he had to navigate by. It would have been the third edition, published in 1797, which Sir Joseph Banks had provided. This must have seemed an almost miraculous work at the time. The first edition of 1771 had three volumes, the second, in 1783, had ten, and the third edition was increased to eighteen.

In a long journal entry of 18 August 1805 Flinders mentions that he read the articles on Wind, Weather and Meteorology. Comparing the first edition's short, bemused and uninformative paragraph on Weather to the nearly fifteen pages on the same subject in the third edition gives an idea of the rapid increase in knowledge of the natural world during the last quarter of the eighteenth century, a development of which Flinders himself was part. His major achievement was the mapping of large tracts of the Australian coastline, written up in *A Voyage to Terra Australis*, and in 1801 he had published his *Observations on the Coasts of Van Diemens Land, On Bass's Strait and its Islands, and on Part of the Coasts of New South Wales*. But he made two other significant contributions to the science of navigation. While on Mauritius he wrote a paper on the uses of the marine barometer based on his observations at sea, which was published in the *Philosophical Transactions* of the Royal Society in 1806, and back in England in 1812 he conducted experiments on the interference with compass readings caused by a ship's iron, a subject which had been on his mind, understandably, throughout his career as a navigator. His experiments were written up in the *Naval Chronicle* in 1812 and eventually led to the invention of the Flinders bar, a device to correct the errors caused by magnetism.

Among the other books he had in his cabin on the *Investigator* was Milton's *Paradise Lost*. Nearly two years after their painful separation so soon after their marriage, he wrote to his wife Ann of the effect it had upon him:

> In the evenings I oft take a book, then reclining on my little couch, and running oer some pleasant tale or sentiment, perhaps of love, my mind retraces with delight, our joys, our conversation, our looks, our everything of love. The loves, and alas! the fall of our first parents, told with such majesty by him whose eyes lacked all of what he threw with hand so masterly o'er this great subject, dark before and intricate; – these with delight I last perused; not knowing which to admire most, the poets daring, the subject, or the success with which his bold attempt was crowned. Eve in innocence, shewed me the excellence of my beloved wife. (PL 88)

This was written in March 1803, at a time when things were just beginning to go wrong for Flinders. Having left Sydney in July 1802 and spent a good eight months charting Australia's eastern and northern coasts, he now found that the *Investigator* was rotting beneath them. His work could not continue, and he knew they would have to return to Port Jackson without too much delay. Thus began the series of disasters which led to his detention on the Indian Ocean island of Mauritius in December 1803 on the suspicion of being a spy.

Reclaiming his books
During his captivity on Mauritius, which stretched to an interminable six and a half years, books were of great importance to Flinders. For some time many of his books were kept from him by General Decaen, the Governor of the island, and his pleas for their return accompanied every communication he had with the General. When he talks of his books, he is referring to both his logbooks, essential to the work of finishing his charts and writing his *Voyage*, and also his printed books, such as the *Encyclopaedia*. Eventually, after repeated requests, he was allowed all his books except one, vital, logbook, which, incidentally, was never returned to him, even after his release. He found that some of the books, which had been sealed up in a trunk, had been damaged, probably in the humidity of Mauritius, and back in London he had to have several repaired.

Understandably, the fact of being detained and, at first, imprisoned, made him profoundly depressed. In his darkest hours, he was able to distract himself with reading and work. 'Well it is for me that I have books and charts and employment,' he wrote while still under close arrest two months after his arrival at Mauritius (PJ 24). A little later, threatened with the removal of his books, he wrote, 'to lose my charts and books would be a more dreadful blow than even being made prisoner was at first' (PJ 45). In October 1805, released on parole to live on the estate of Madame Louise d'Arifat in the south-east of the island, he wrote 'I cannot say that, at present, I am very unhappy. Time has softened my disappointments. I have my books, am making acquisitions in knowledge, enjoy good health, and innocent amusements for which I have still a relish' (PJ 95–96).

Books and friendship
But it was not only his own books that were important to him during his captivity. The Pitot brothers, merchants on Mauritius who befriended Flinders and other English prisoners, endeared themselves to him by lending him books and music while he was still quite closely confined at the Maison Despaux. Their friendship, and the provision of literature, continued during the whole of Flinders' stay on Mauritius. He was always

keen to read the latest newspapers available, and Thomi Pitot, in Port Louis, would obtain English papers and the navy lists, with news of promotions and so on, from any visiting Englishmen and get them to Flinders in his country retreat.

Flinders knew no French when he arrived at Mauritius in December 1803, but by the time he left he had read dozens of French books. He read history – Lacretelle and Voltaire on the French Revolution, and philosophy. Rousseau's *Emile* had a strong effect on him: 'For these three or four days I have enjoyed a tranquillity of mind beyond what I have been accustomed to. The *Emile* of Rousseau is partly the cause of it; in looking into myself I find more reason to be satisfied with myself than when making a comparison with the general manners of the world,' he reported in January 1807 (PJ 152). He read biographies of Louis XV and Potemkin, books on chess, which his neighbour Chazal taught him to play, scientific books and, of course, voyages.

Trifling novels

As discussed in Chapter Two, Voltaire was something of a moral barometer, and he was surprised to find that the French ladies read his work. One assumes, then, that he would not approve of his wife reading Voltaire. Back in 1800, when their marriage seemed an impossible prospect, he advised Ann to distract herself by 'read[ing] every book that comes in thy way, save trifling novels' (PL 89). It seems that he did not regard all novels as 'trifling', since he read many himself. In a letter to Ann from Port Jackson in 1799, he wrote:

> My reading this morning, has called up a train of recollections; which in my present situation at least, ought to be suppressed. I read the first volume of Mrs Radcliff's *Udolpho*, which I had not seen before. Thou, I think, hast; for from the specimens of poetry in this, it will surprise me not to find thy beautiful lines on Autumn in a future volume.
>
> The parting description at the end, recalled to my remembrance what my feelings were, on something like a similar situation. Fatal, enervating, moment! (PL 39)

He read several novels on Mauritius, including Le Sage's *Gil Blas*, Madame de Staël's *Corinne* and Chateaubriand's *Atala*, the story of a young

American Indian couple. He was clearly taken with *Atala*: Delphine d'Arifat, his hostess's daughter, made a translation of it for him to take back to London for Ann.

The explorer as critic

In the *Private Journal* he rarely comments on the books he is reading, just mentioning the titles. Two exceptions are René Just Haüy's *Traité elementaire de physique*, which he read at least twice, and declared to be 'a favourite work with me' (PJ 230), and St Pierre's *Etudes de la Nature*, 'the most superficial work that I have ever read; more false systems supported by disguised facts were perhaps never before hazarded in public: his style is said to be very attractive, and to have seduced many to the adoption of his opinions' (PJ 180). Perhaps Flinders missed his vocation: he would have made a fine literary critic.

Books for research

Arriving back in England finally in late 1810, books still played their part in shaping his life. To write up his voyage, he had to consult a wide variety of sources: his lengthy introduction was a thorough survey of previous works on the exploration of the south Pacific and Australia. This meant that he had to live in London, where the libraries were. He used the British Museum library, but his principal source was the library of Sir Joseph Banks, presided over by his former colleague Robert Brown, the naturalist from the *Investigator* voyage. I discuss these books in detail in Chapter 14.

London life was expensive and he was living on half pay. At the end of 1812 he calculated that his expenses for the year outstripped his income of £275 by about £156. However, one of his first purchases on arriving home was a French dictionary at the cost of £1.5 – quite an investment, comparable to roughly $200, based on today's average incomes.

Books were still part of his social currency. He repaid Thomi Pitot's kindness by sending English books out to him in Mauritius, and he used his contacts in France, people he had met on Mauritius, to obtain 'Cuvier and Brognard's geology of the vicinity of Paris, which Sir J[oseph] B[anks] wished to obtain. I am very glad to seize any opportunity of being useful to Sir Joseph, from his having done so much (though not every thing) for me' (PJ 416).

Every time he and Ann changed lodgings – six times in three-and-a-half years – he spent a day setting up his bookcase, cleaning his books, and occasionally reviewing and rationalising. On 26 September 1811 he bought George Dixon's *Voyage Round the World* and volume one of James Burney's *Chronological History of the Discoveries in the South Seas* for 6 shillings each, and a few days later, in preparation for moving house, returned ten borrowed books to Sir Joseph Banks and sold the six volumes of Dr Isaac Watts' works to a bookseller for £3.10 (PJ 378). Watts was the author of 'Divine Songs for Children' and several popular hymns, and it is interesting to speculate on the reason for the presence of these volumes in the library of the rational, scientifically-minded Flinders. Several of Flinders' favourite books, like Rousseau's *Emile*, concerned the subject of education, and Watts wrote educational manuals as well as Christian doctrinal treatises. On the other hand, Ann Flinders was a devout Christian: perhaps they belonged to her.

Robinson Crusoe

When all is said and done, however, perhaps the most influential book in Flinders' life was *Robinson Crusoe*. In 1812, in answer to a questionnaire from the *Naval Chronicle*, Flinders wrote that he was 'induced to go to sea against the wishes of friends, from reading *Robinson Crusoe*.'[2] And his last letter, written two weeks before his death, reads, 'Captain Flinders' compliments to the Hydrographer of the *Naval Chronicle*, and will thank him to insert his name in the list of subscribers to his new edition of *Robinson Crusoe*; he wishes also that the volume, on delivery, should have a neat common binding, and be lettered.'[3] Thus his career began and ended with thoughts of this most influential of adventure stories.

13

'When tired of writing, I apply to music': Music in Matthew Flinders' Life[1]

Musical ability is not the best-known attribute of Matthew Flinders, the explorer and navigator who had captained the *Investigator* on the first circumnavigation of the Australian continent 1801–1803. But in his cabin, through all his adventures and mishaps at sea, Flinders kept his wooden flute, bought for him when he was a young teenager. Arriving at Mauritius in December 1803, Flinders was detained indefinitely, kept first under close guard in a single room in the Café Marengo with John Aken, the Master from the *Investigator*, and then moved to the Maison Despaux, known as 'The Garden Prison', in March 1804, where he joined some eight English prisoners of war.

Music in the Garden Prison

It was in the Maison Despaux that Flinders first wrote in his *Private Journal* about the place of music in his daily life:

> My time is now employed as follows. Before breakfast my time is devoted to the latin language, to bring up what I formerly learned. After breakfast I am employed making out a fair copy of the *Investigators* log in lieu of my own which was spoiled at the shipwreck. When tired of writing, I apply to music, and when my fingers are tired with the flute, I write again until dinner. After dinner we amuse ourselves with billiards until tea, and afterwards walk in the garden till dusk. From thence till supper I make one at Pleyels quartettes. … [M]y time does not pass wearily or uselessly run. (PJ 33)

Musical education

It is not known when Flinders learned music, though his father recorded in his accounts that he spent 8 shillings on buying him a German flute in November 1788, when he was 14 (GP 2: 50). Flinders' flute, a wooden instrument of the latest design made by Potter of Fleet Street, London, survives in a private collection.

His father intended young Matthew to follow him into the profession of surgeon and apothecary, which entailed lessons in reading, writing and Latin at the local free school in Donington, Lincolnshire, until he was twelve, followed by Greek and literature at a boarding school in Horbling for eighteen months, but some attention to the arts was clearly not to be despised. In 1785 Flinders Senior notes that he has 'put Matthew ... to a dancing master ... as a little address seems to be a necessary addition in this age' (GP 2: 22). Music lessons are not specifically mentioned – although, as Geoffrey Ingleton points out, neither is mathematics, in which 'presumably the young scholar received some tuition' as it was 'a subject in which he became most proficient later in life' (MFNC 1). The same could be said of music: he could read music and it is most likely this is a skill he learned when young. As we know, Matthew did not follow in his father's profession but left Lincolnshire in 1790 to go to sea, presumably taking his flute with him.

Music at sea

The National Maritime Museum points out that 'music has played a central part in life at sea providing not only entertainment and contributing to the health and morale of seamen but also providing rhythm and cohesion to the everyday tasks of sailors and fishermen.'[2] Sea shanties and hornpipes are the natural associations one makes between music and the sea. Flinders reported in *A Voyage to Terra Australis* that, on crossing the Equator,

> It was a part of my plan for preserving the health of the people, to promote active amusements amongst them, so long as it did not interfere with the duties of the ship; and therefore the ancient ceremonies used on this occasion, were allowed to be performed this evening; and the ship being

previously put under snug sail, the seamen were furnished with the means, and the permission, to conclude the day with merriment. (VTA 1: 29)

The means for merriment no doubt involved alcohol, but it is hard to imagine this scene without musical accompaniment. Among the officers, too, the ability to amuse oneself and perhaps one's shipmates with music during the long journey would have been valuable, and the flute, unlike larger instruments, is eminently portable. According to *The Harvard Dictionary of Music*, 'flute playing became one of the marks of a cultivated gentleman' in the eighteenth century.[3] Flinders' German flute is one of the four-keyed flutes which became available in the last quarter of the century, a great improvement on the earlier one-keyed instruments: Charles Burney noted that it was 'natural to those instruments to be out of tune'.[4]

The violin was also popular among male amateurs. The naturalist on the *Investigator*, Robert Brown, played the violin. The fact that a quartet (typically consisting of two treble instruments such as violins or flutes, a tenor instrument, such as a viola, and a bass, such as a cello) could be recruited from among a group of nine English military officers in the Maison Despaux attests to the fact that some degree of musical accomplishment was not unusual in the English officers of the period. Indeed, Captain John Hunter, under whom Flinders sailed as a midshipman on the *Reliance* on his first journey to Australia in 1795, was musically inclined. He had not been permitted to pursue music as a profession, as he had wished, but had been allowed to learn music from Dr Charles Burney, organist and composer as well as music historian, in his early teens.[5]

The musical Pitots

Thomi Pitot and his brother Edouard first met Flinders in August 1804 when they dined with another prisoner in the mess at the Maison Despaux:

> They were very agreeable and seemed interested to do him and me service. They have lent us books and music and behaved more liberally than is customary to any strangers, but especially to prisoners and Englishmen. (PJ 40)

Pitot remained a friend for the rest of Flinders' life, and while he was detained made every effort to help him, by advocating on his behalf with the authorities as well as by providing books, music and friendship. Pitot played the violin and their friendship involved playing music together. It was to Pitot that Flinders wrote his first letter in French in September 1805: he had no knowledge of the language before arriving on Mauritius. Flinders soon became fluent in French: an aptitude for languages is frequently associated with an ear for music, and perhaps this was true in Flinders' case.

Solace and recreation

Music continued to provide Flinders with solace and recreation throughout his long detention. In the last days before leaving Maison Despaux to take up residence with Madame d'Arifat on her plantation in the south-west of the island, he wrote a long account of his activities on one day. Among the reading, conversation, walking and contemplation, he devotes a paragraph to music:

> Took up my flute and played the 1st and 5th Duo of Pleyel's opera 9. Note, the first commences in a grand stile, and is sweetly plaintive in some parts of it. The Andante of the 5 is marked for minuet time, whereas the time is 2/4. Must have all Pleyels musick when I return to England, that is set for the flute, and Mozarts, and Haydns, and some of Hoffmeisters and Deviennes, but the whole will be too expensive, musick is so very dear in England; and indeed so is almost everything else. (PJ 76)

These are the words of a musical literate, if not an expert, who is aware that a minuet should be in triple rather than duple time, and who knows the principal composers of flute music of the age. Austrian-born French composer Ignaz Pleyel (1757–1831) was as famous as Haydn and Mozart during his lifetime. His music was typically easy enough for the amateur to attempt, which added to his popularity at the time, although it has perhaps contributed to his music's failure to maintain a high reputation since his death. His Opera (or opus) 9, which Flinders mentions, seems to have been 'A Second set of three quintetts for two violins, two tenors and a violoncello', published in London in 1787, although this does not tally with the description Flinders gives of a set of at least five duos. There is a set of six duets for violin, opus 8, which is a possible alternative candidate. But Pleyel was an extremely prolific composer and his music was published in many editions and arrangements, and sometimes the same opus number was assigned by a different publisher to the same piece. It may be impossible to be absolutely sure which piece Flinders means.

Musical women

Young ladies of the eighteenth and nineteenth centuries were unlikely to learn the flute or violin, and were more often steered towards the more sedentary pursuits of harp and keyboard playing:

> No lady considering herself worthy of that title would blow into anything – this might result in a reddening of the face or unseemly heaving of the bosom. Equally, the violin was not suitable ... This left our would-be heroines with the principal choices of singing, the harpsichord/pianoforte or, if they had the financial means, the harp.[6]

Flinders met several female keyboard and harp players on Mauritius. When he moved to the d'Arifat's estate, he was almost immediately introduced to Madame Couve, a neighbour who had two teenage daughters:

> She invited me kindly to come frequently, every day if I pleased, to dine and sup, and spend the morning or evening, in a neighbourly way, without ceremony. ... the invitation was not the less agreeable for that the two young ladies were musicians and had good voices. (PJ 84)

Music remained part of his everyday life, both in solitude and society. He did visit the Couve family often, but he soon met another musician in the neighbourhood. On 27 November 1805 he records, 'The afternoon was occupied with music, in accompanying Mad. Chazals harpsichord with the flute. This lady is indeed an excellent performer, and is besides one of the most agreeable women I have ever met with' (PJ 106). Her husband, Toussaint Antoine de Chazal, was a cultivated man, a trained artist, who in 1807 painted the only life-size portrait of Flinders made during his lifetime, which now hangs in the Art Gallery of South Australia. Over the ensuing years, as his detention dragged on, he often described being entertained by music, sometimes as a listener, and more often as a player, most frequently accompanied by Madame Chazal. On 21 January 1807, he records that he 'passed the evening in accompanying Madame in Steibelt's Sonatas' (PJ 151). As most amateur musicians did at the time, he also copied music from printed scores to share it. In March 1809 he reported that he was 'copying music for Mad. D['Arifat] to take to Bourbon for Mad. Desbasns.', her married daughter (PJ 249).

My Evening Song

We can see that his music script was clear and competent from the manuscript song he sent to Ann in November 1805. He attributes the music to Haydn, and it is adapted from the second movement of the Imperial Symphony (Hob. 1/53). It is, however, different enough from the Haydn melody that it took some ingenuity to identify it: Flinders was possibly working from memory, having played a chamber version of the work, for example the arrangement for harp and violin (ad lib) by J.B. Krumpholtz. A more interesting possibility is that he knew the music well but adapted the outline of the melody to suit his own purpose. Haydn's original composition, although formally the symphony's 'slow movement', is a cheerful Andante, while Flinders' song is plaintive and marked Adagio.

The words he wrote himself: though couched in the conventional sentimental language of the age, they are nevertheless heartfelt and expressive:

> *Why Henry didst thou leave me, thus leave me here to mourn?*
> *Ah, cruel, thou deceivedst me, I'll ne'er see thy return.*[7]

Flinders' verses show a musical sensitivity to accommodating words to the simple and unaffected melody, allowing the rhythm of the words to fit the tune without any unnatural or misplaced stresses. As I discuss in Chapter 11, there is a manuscript held in the National Maritime Museum at Greenwich in which Ann Flinders adds more verses to her husband's song, probably before he returned. It is touching to think that, even over the distance that separated them, they were able to collaborate on this small creative project.

London: no time for music

Once Flinders was back in England, music occupied little of his time. He was busy working on his voyage and had many other anxieties and distractions, as the *Private Journal* shows. And, despite his exhortation to Ann in a letter of 18 December 1800 to '[l]earn music' as one of many ways of keeping herself busy during their separation (PL 55), she was not musical: her talents lay in the visual arts: after Flinders' death she painted a series of very attractive botanical watercolours. He does say that on 19 October 1811 he 'went out ... and bought music' (PJ 380). There is, however, no indication that he ever found the time to play it, and the social side of musicianship, so important a pastime and distraction from his worries on Mauritius, seems to have vanished from his busy life in London. After his death, Ann sent his flute music to Thomi Pitot in Mauritius, as she presumably had no use for it.[8]

Reading the *Private Journal*, it is tempting to see the later years on Mauritius, even with all their frustrations, as a happier, more relaxed period, spent with congenial friends in leisurely pursuits such as reading for pleasure, walking in the country and playing music, than the three years that followed, which were crammed with close, gruelling work with little official acknowledgement from the Admiralty, on half pay, with a wife and later a child who were often unwell, and followed by six months of agonising illness. Even before he left Mauritius, he wrote to his friend Charles Desbassayns, 'Now that I am certain of going, the pleasure I had in contemplating this event in perspective, is vanished. My heart is oppressed at the idea of quitting my friends here, perhaps forever' (PL 199). One cannot but wonder whether, in the middle of July 1813 when almost all his journal entries consisted of variations on 'Worked all day at the charts, and writing in the evening,' he sometimes looked back with fond nostalgia at the days when he would spend the afternoon at the Chazals' playing tric-trac, followed by an evening accompanying Madame in Steibelt's sonatas for flute and harpsichord.

14

The Library at Soho Square: Matthew Flinders, Sir Joseph Banks and the Publication of *A Voyage to Terra Australis* (1814)[1]

A Voyage to Terra Australis

Matthew Flinders' major work, *A Voyage to Terra Australis: Undertaken for the Purpose of Completing the Discovery of that Vast Country, and Prosecuted in the Years 1801, 1802, and 1803, in His Majesty's Ship the Investigator*, appeared in 1814, eleven years after the voyage it describes finished, and just days before he died. Although it has now become a canonical work in Australian history and a copy of the first edition is a highly-prized and expensive investment, at the time it was published it did not sell well.[2] The moment had passed – during the intervening decade Napoleon had crowned himself Emperor and made a battleground of the whole of Europe, and the distant activities of a surveying expedition must have seemed irrelevant to many who had been confronted with these more urgent and proximate events. As Ingleton points out, in respect of Flinders' prospects of promotion and financial support while writing the *Voyage*, 'the war had been long and relentless, and promotion came when vacancies occurred ... Possibly the lords commissioners of the Admiralty were beginning to consider that Flinders had been rewarded sufficiently for the explorations and surveys he had made so long ago' (MFNC 384).

Voyage narratives: delays and difficulties

It was usual for an official account of a major government-funded voyage (like the outcomes of present-day scientific research) to be made available to the public, but the path to publication was rarely smooth for voyage narratives at this time. The publication process was often beset by difficulties and disagreements: none of the accounts of Captain James

Cook's voyages proceeded smoothly to publication, for example, and in the case of the contemporary French voyages, as Danielle Clode and Carol E. Harrison have shown, 'the concept of a national venture in knowledge generation broke down completely over publication, which was a bone of contention for all of France's Old Regime and revolutionary expeditions to the Pacific,' in part because 'expeditionary scientists ... were not always willing to subsume their own individual ambitions for national aspirations'.[3]

However, the problem was somewhat different in Flinders' case: the delay was caused mainly by his detention on Mauritius by the French from December 1803 to June 1810. He had done much work towards the preparation of his publication while detained by the French: he wrote to his patron Sir Joseph Banks in July 1804 that 'General De Caën still keeps me closely confined, but he has lately given me the greater part of my books and papers, and therefore I shall again be able to proceed in preparing the accounts of our discoveries' (PL 115). In his *Private Journal* entries for the years on Mauritius, he regularly mentions working on these accounts, and he sent charts and written accounts back to Banks and to the Admiralty whenever he had the chance to circumvent the French authorities or the British blockade. Nevertheless, there were several factors preventing him from completing the work before he returned to England.

One reason was that Flinders was not expecting to write up the voyage himself. In 1801, on the voyage out, he had even written to his step-cousin Willingham Franklin (Sir John's brother), an Oxford scholar, to ask if he would write the account for him when the time came, as 'authorship sits awkward upon me' (PL 79). Back in London in November 1810, he wrote to his friend James Wiles,

> The original plan was, that all my charts and accounts, and those of the men of science, should be put into the hands of some literary man, to be employed by the admiralty to write the account from our documents; and this plan I should suppose Sir J[oseph Banks] would still wish to be pursued; but I find an opinion prevailing at the admiralty that it would be better done by me, so that I know not yet what plan will be adopted. (PL 205)

Unknown to Flinders, however, Banks had already been recommending him to William Marsden, the first secretary of the Admiralty, as the person most 'Capable of Stating the Particulars of his discoveries in a manner Creditable to his Employers & honourable to his Country.'[4] This recommendation carried weight: as Joppien and Chambers write,

> Banks was one of the most influential private citizens of late-eighteenth-century European learning and empire. He had at his disposal leisure, wealth, social prestige and unfailing enthusiasm. It was these things that enabled him to act as a patron of science *par excellence* before that role was increasingly assumed by state-run institutions in the course of the nineteenth century.[5]

Flinders would have found Banks's recommendation very gratifying, but he was not so impressed with the practicalities. He found out the news on 12 January 1811, when the Admiralty appointed him to a committee along with Banks and John Barrow, the second secretary of the Admiralty, to undertake the preparation of the Voyage and the Atlas (PJ 340). Because he was not on active service, Flinders was to be on half pay while doing this work. He asked

> if, during the time I was employed writing the voyage, I could not be put on full pay, which would make up the difference of expense I should be at betwixt living in the town and privately in the country, but Mr B[arrow] thought the Admiralty would object from want of a precedent. Thus, in all appearance, my time and labour must be given in, – it will cost me £500 or 600, and I cannot be employed during the time in any way that might be advantageous to my fortune. (PJ 341)

His dismay at this development is implicit in the irritable last sentence of this journal entry: 'We dined today, stupidly, with Mrs Major and a small party of Goths' (PJ 341).

Another reason for the delay in publishing the voyage related to revisions that had to be made because 'while the *Investigator* expedition was in progress, the Royal Observatory had undertaken astronomical observations showing that some of the predicted figures in the *Nautical Almanac*, which Flinders was using, were in error to a significant degree.'[6] This work took those undertaking it two years, delaying the reconstruction of Flinders' Australian maps: he was not willing to base them on incorrect data.

London libraries

Constant meetings and discussions with Banks and others relating to this work, to the artwork and to other aspects of the publication partly explained the necessity for Flinders staying in London. However, another significant reason why he could not retire to the country to write the Voyage – and why he had not been able to finish it while he was on Mauritius – was that he needed access to the accounts of previous voyages. In his introduction, he methodically documented all the 'Prior discoveries in Terra Australis', dividing his chronological account into four parts of the coastline, proceeding anticlockwise around the continent.[7] Despite his disappointment over being underpaid and kept from promotion, he was clearly determined to do a thorough job.

For the first few months of 1811 Flinders worked on his charts, but on 1 May 1811 he 'determined to wait awhile' before continuing that work, 'and begin writing the introduction to my voyage. Went out after dinner and bought paper and quills' (PJ 358).

Writing the Introduction

Flinders was engaged in as serious a literature review as any present-day scholar. It was obviously important to him to understand, and to convey, his own place in the history of exploration; duly acknowledging his predecessors and basing his own claims on firm ground. He commented on the accounts of his predecessors at the beginning of the Introduction to the *Voyage:*

> The various discoveries which had been made upon the coasts of Terra Australis, antecedently to the present voyage, are of dates as widely distant, as are the degrees of confidence to which they are respectively entitled; the accounts, also, lie scattered through various books in different languages; and many are still in manuscript. It has, therefore, been judged, that a succinct history of these discoveries would be acceptable to the public; and would form an appropriate introduction to a voyage, whose principal object was to complete what they had left unfinished. (VTA 1: iv)

This 'succinct history' is more than 200 pages long, and the first draft took him more than six months to write.

Previous voyage publications

There were several comprehensive reference works available at this time summarising the history of exploration of various parts of the world, including works by James Burney and John Harris that Flinders consulted. However, the introductions to previous voyage publications tended to be quite brief. The introduction to Hawkesworth's account of Cook's first voyage (1773) is 21 pages long; Thomas Forrest's *A Voyage to New Guinea, and the Moluccas, from Balambangan* (1780) has a 12-page introduction. Cook's introduction to his second voyage is about 3000 words – about 10 pages. However, James King, who edited Cook's journals and completed the account of his fatal third voyage for publication, wrote an introduction that extends to 86 pages and gives a detailed account of previous voyages.

King began by celebrating the revived 'spirit of discovery'[8] in the middle of the eighteenth century, and explained his intention in writing 'a short, though comprehensive, abstract of the principal objects that had been previously accomplished, arranged in such a manner, as may serve to unite, into one point of view, the various articles which lie scattered' in previous accounts.[9] As Cook did not visit Australia on the third voyage, Flinders did not mention King's publication in his introduction, or in his *Private Journal*, but he would certainly have been familiar with all the accounts of Cook's voyages. He may well have found a model for his 'succinct history' in King's 'short, though comprehensive, abstract'. King describes the 'imperfection' of earlier accounts, leading to 'an endless variety of plausible conjectures, suggested by ingenious speculation; of idle tales, handed down by obscure tradition; or of bold fictions, invented by deliberate falsehood.'[10] Flinders remarks likewise on the inaccuracies of several earlier publications, and promises to stick with the evidence and not waste his readers' time with 'such as depend upon conjecture and probability':

> Conformably to this plan, no attempt will be made to investigate the claims of the *Chinese* to the earliest knowledge of Terra Australis; which some, from the chart of *Marco Polo*, have thought they possessed. Nor yet will much be said upon the plea advanced by the Abbé PRÉVOST and after him by the President DEBROSSES, in favour of *Paulmier de Gonneville*, a French captain; for whom they claim the honour of having discovered Terra Australis, in 1504. It is evident from the proofs they adduce, that it was not

to any part of this country, but to Madagascar, that Gonneville was driven. (VTA 1: v)

'The limits of an introduction'

Flinders explains that he will summarise accounts that are already published, 'abridged to their leading heads', providing references to the original works,

> but in such articles as have either not appeared before, or but very imperfectly, in an English dress, as also in those extracted from unpublished manuscripts, a wider range will be taken: in these, so far as the documents go, on the one hand, and the limits of an introduction can allow, on the other, no interesting fact will be omitted. (VTA 1: v)

It is not absolutely clear what Flinders regarded as 'the limits of an introduction', given that no previous voyage seems to have contained such a long one, or whether any such limits were discussed with Banks and Barrow. In November 1811 he was negotiating as diplomatically as he could with William Bligh over the account of his second passage through Torres Strait in 1792 on the *Providence*. Flinders had served on this voyage as a midshipman, and he wrote in the *Voyage*:

> No account of this voyage having yet been published; it is conceived, that the following brief relation of the passage through the strait, will be acceptable to the nautical reader; and, having had the honour to serve in the expedition, I am enabled to give it from my own journal, with the sanction of captain Bligh. (VTA 1: xix)

His letter to Bligh in November 1811 reveals something of the efforts he put into obtaining Bligh's 'sanction':

> Such corrections and omissions as you may wish to be made, shall be adopted; and I would add such additions also, did not the limits of an introduction, and the number of articles it will contain, necessarily restrain the extent of each article to narrow bounds. ... My ... desire in this, is to do what is agreeable to your wishes, as fully as the limits of my plan will allow. (PL 215)

From this it is tempting to infer that Bligh believed his account deserved more space than the eleven pages Flinders eventually devoted to it.

'My work grows upon me'

Flinders realised from the start that writing the *Voyage* was going to take a long time. In February 1811 he wrote to his friend Charles Desbassayns that 'I shall probably so remain employed for two years' (PL 207). The deadline was moveable: in September of the same year, he wrote to another friend, 'as is usually the case in such like undertakings, my work grows upon me; and I do not think it can be ready for the press before two years from this time' (PL 212). By November 1812, he was still postponing the completion of the work, but this time he predicted correctly 'that it will be the middle of 1814 before my labour will terminate' (PL 228).

Flinders sought out and read all the previous accounts of voyages to the coasts of Australia. In all he referenced more than 20 books, and he needed access to good libraries such as were only to be found in London. The best of these libraries was at Banks's town house at 32 Soho Square, where he obtained at least half of the books he consulted. During the six months while he was writing the introduction, Flinders records in his journal all the visits he had to make (on foot) to borrow or consult the previous publications and accounts on which he was basing his summary. These books are listed in the Appendix to this chapter.

He is likely to have had the first five of the publications on the list in his possession already, as he cites them in the introduction but does not mention them in his *Private Journal*. Some or all of them were probably books he took with him on the *Investigator* and which had been with him on his travels and sojourns since then. They included Bligh's ill-fated *Bounty* voyage; William Dampier's influential 1699 voyage to the west coast of 'Terra Australis'; George Vancouver's voyage around the world in the 1790s, during which he had explored further eastwards along the south coast of Australia than any earlier European; La Billardière's account of D'Entrecasteaux's voyage in search of La Pérouse; and Hawkesworth's controversial 1773 account of Cook's *Endeavour* voyage.

The Library at Soho Square

So although Flinders had been able to do significant work on the charts and the narrative of his own expedition from his own journals, logbooks, and other material that he had with him on Mauritius, including the books just mentioned, many of the major works of his predecessors were not available there. He became a regular visitor at Banks's Library, where Robert Brown, who had been the naturalist on Flinders' *Investigator* expedition, was now Banks's librarian.

According to Rüdiger Joppien and Neil Chambers, 'while he lived, Banks's collections were made freely available to the many scholars who visited London. Indeed, his main base at Soho Square became a social and scientific hub in the London scene for over four decades.'[11] Banks's library, when transferred to the British Museum in 1827, contained about 14,000 titles.[12]

In Harold B. Carter's bibliography of Banks, published in 1987, he says 'The Banks Library has remained more or less intact as a collection as far as can be judged without a detailed check of the surviving items against the inventory … of 1823.'[13] However, I understand that when the British Library moved to its new location in 1997 (or perhaps earlier, when the new British Museum building was built in the middle of the nineteenth century) the Banks library was split up and interfiled with the rest of the collection, and although provenance information is probably to be found on the individual physical items, it is unfortunately impossible to search by provenance. Edwin Rose, a doctoral student at Cambridge who is working on the Banks Library, has told me that the only way of locating books from Banks's collection in the current British Library is to order up every copy of the edition and to check it for Banks's very distinctive ownership marks.[14]

Banks's Library, according to Carter, was unique:

> As a library system it was developed jointly, by Banks and Dryander [Banks's first librarian], apparently from the first occupation of 32 Soho Square in 1777, a partnership of some 33 years, during which the library's benefits were freely open and during which, it is said, no book was lost. This is a tribute not only to the careful surveillance of Dryander, but also to the respect in which its contents were held by those who were privileged to use it, for it was not a mere collection for its own sake. It was a working tool for Banks the scholar, those who worked with him and all those whom

he accepted as fellow labourers in 'the vineyard of natural history' or the evolving sciences in other ways. ...

As a reference library for the rising generation of young nineteenth-century scientists, of whom [Robert] Brown is a prime example, there was no other such facility so freely available, so well organised nor so comprehensive in the fields it purported to cover and gathered in one place – certainly not in Great Britain, perhaps not in all western Europe at that time.[15]

Flinders was another prime example of this 'rising generation', and he relied heavily on Banks's library. Like many other researchers of the period, he acknowledged Banks and his library, specifically, in a footnote:

I am proud to take this opportunity of publicly expressing my obligations to the Right Hon. President of the Royal Society; and of thus adding my voice to the many who, in the pursuit of science, have found in him a friend and patron. Such he proved in the commencement of my voyage, and in the whole course of its duration; in the distresses which tyranny heaped upon those of accident; and after they were overcome. His extensive and valuable library has been laid open; and has furnished much that no time or expense, within my reach, could otherwise have procured. (VTA 1: lxxvi)[16]

He did visit the British Museum; he borrowed James Burney's book from the author himself, and obtained some manuscripts from the Admiralty, but there are a dozen or so books he definitely either borrowed from Banks's library, or located through contacts he made there. A few are not mentioned in the *Private Journal*, so it is not known where he found them. In any case, it was via Banks that he gained access to a large proportion of the books he used in his research.

Rarities

Some of the items Banks was able to provide were rare, if not unique. On the first page of Section 1 of his introduction, 'Prior Discoveries in Terra Australis: North Coast', he was already acknowledging a publication 'procured by the Right Hon. Sir Joseph Banks':

a copy of the instructions to commodore Abel Jansz Tasman, for his second voyage of discovery. ... the instructions are prefaced with a recital, in chronological order, of the previous discoveries of the Dutch, whether made by accident or design, in Nova Guinea, and the *Great* South Land. (VTA 1: vii)

Flinders was of course also interested in Tasman's voyage to Van Diemen's Land. He wrote, 'It was not, however, the policy of the Dutch government to make discoveries for the benefit of general knowledge' and so this voyage was never published in its entirety. However, Flinders was lucky enough to find an account, again with Banks's help:

> It is taken from a journal containing, besides the daily transactions and observations throughout the whole voyage, a series of thirty-eight manuscript charts, views, and figures. The expression *by me*, which often occurs in it, and followed by the signature *Abel Jansz Tasman*, shows that if this were not his original journal, it is a copy from it: probably one made on board for the governor and council of Batavia. With this interesting document, and a translation made in 1776, by Mr. C. G. Woide, chaplain of His Majesty's Dutch chapel at St. James's, I was favoured by the Right Hon. SIR JOSEPH BANKS. (VTA 1: lxxvi)

One book he was unable to obtain was Willem De Vlaming's 1696 voyage to New Holland [1696] published at Amsterdam in 1701. However, he was able to find a workable substitute by means of Banks's library and librarians:

> I have had recourse to *Valentyn*, who, in his *Description of Banda*, has given what appears to be an abridgment of the relation. What follows is conformable to the sense of the translation which Dr. L. Tiarks [Assistant librarian to Joseph Banks] had the goodness to make for me; and the reasons for entering more into the particulars of this voyage than usual are, the apparent correctness of the observations, and that no account of them seems to have been published in the English language. (VTA 1: lviii)

'No pretension to authorship'

Flinders provided some more background about this source in his *Private Journal*. Having got the translation from Tiarks, he says he had to spend the rest of the day 'writing this translation into proper English' (PJ 367).

Nevertheless, he was still modest about his claims to be regarded as a writer. In the Preface to the *Voyage*, he wrote

> From the general tenour of the explanations here given, it will perhaps be inferred that the perfection of the Atlas has been the principal object of concern; in fact, having no pretension to authorship, the writing of the narrative, though by much the most troublesome part of my labour, was not that upon which any hope of reputation was founded; a polished style was therefore not attempted, but some pains have been taken to render it clearly intelligible. (VTA 1: ix)

At the end of his literature review, Flinders wrote:

> On a general review of the various objects in Terra Australis, to which investigation might be usefully directed at the commencement of the nineteenth century, and in which natural history, geography, navigation, and commerce were so much interested, the question, Why it should have been thought necessary to send out another expedition? will no longer be asked. But rather it will be allowed that, instead of one, there was ample room for two or three ships; each to be employed for years, and to be conducted with a zeal and perseverance not inferior to the examples given by the best navigators. (VTA 1: cciv)

Finishing the *Voyage*

Flinders worked on his voyage from the beginning of 1811 to just before his death in 1814. Once the introduction was finished, he turned to writing his account of the *Investigator*'s voyage and completing the charts. Then there were proofs to be corrected. Months of 1813 go by in the *Private Journal* with almost identical entries, recording his unremitting work on the voyage: close work on charts requiring good light during the day, and checking proofs at night. On 11 September 1813 he wrote to Captain Farquarson Stuart, who had been a regular weekly visitor and an increasingly unwelcome distraction, with the most exquisite courtesy, to ask him to 'do away his regular Monday visits' (PJ 453):

> The conversation we had last Monday evening has induced me to state to you, how much I am pressed to get out my voyage by next spring, for which

it is advertised for publication. I have, in fact, so little time, that I never go out but on pressing business, and am closely occupied every day and hour in the week, from breakfast until going to bed. It pains me to forego the pleasure of seeing you as usual, but the frankness and consideration which you have shewn have explained to me, that I should do an injustice to your character in longer witholding (sic) the truth. After this next winter is passed, when the extreme pressure of occupation will have ceased, I hope to see our communications renewed ...[17]

On 13 October 1813, he '[w]orked all day at the chart of the Gulph. Examining the second quire in the evening, and the last proof sheet of the Introduction, making 204 pages' (PJ 455). He was finding that he had to check the charts from the engravers 'rather closely' in order 'to have them done satisfactorily' (PJ 454). There was no break for Christmas or New Year festivities, and as 1814 proceeds the daily chronicle of his increasing illness becomes harrowing, while much close work on the publication remains to be completed. In a journal entry from 26 May 1814, he wrote:

Finished the examination of the proof sheet of the G. of Carpentaria, and examined a little for Errata; but sitting down is now the most painful posture though on a hollow cushion, and after half an hour I am obliged to lie down on the sofa. (VTA 479)

Last months

Whether or not Flinders was correct, as he claimed in a letter to Charles Desbassayns, that his illness was 'brought on first by my imprisonment, and increased by sitting so closely to my work for three years as not to allow of proper exercise' (PL 236), the journal entries for his last months depict the extreme suffering and the grim dedication it took to see the work through, surely an unusually detailed record of the physical cost of completing a work for publication. The last time he mentioned the voyage was in his *Private Journal* on Wednesday 29 June 1814: 'Mr Arrowsmith brought me a set of proof of all the charts of the atlas, and I gave him a note to sir joseph expressing my approbation of the engraving' (PJ 484). By this time he was very ill and had only three weeks to live.

Robert Brown visited him often in these last few months. Brown's position as Banks's Librarian, replacing Jonas Dryander who had died in

October 1810, meant that Flinders would have had regular dealings with him. Though they had known each other well since the *Investigator* days, this rather gruff Scotsman seems to have grown closer to Flinders in these last years in London. In June 1803, Flinders had not been so sure about Brown: in a draft letter to his wife Ann he wrote from Sydney, 'we are not altogether cordial, but our mutual anxiety to forward the voyage is a bond of union: he is a man of abilities and knowledge, but wants kindness' (PL 99n3). This passage, though crossed out in his letter book, is still legible. However, Brown's regular visits in this difficult time showed his practical kindness. He brought proofs for Flinders to correct, articles from the *Philosophical Transactions* containing the latest medical knowledge about his particular malady, and friendship – 'Mr Brown called upon me today, and he has been very kind in doing so several times lately,' Flinders wrote on 16 June 1814 (PJ 482).

An important date for the voyage publication was Sunday 26 June: 'Mr Brown called in the evening to say that he had obtained from Mr Nicol a copy of the voyage and atlas to put on Sir Jos. Banks' table this evening, which is the last meeting for sometime' (PJ 483). This was three days before Arrowsmith had brought the proofs of the atlas for him to check, so could not have been the final, definitive version, and was probably not bound. But nevertheless, Sir Joseph Banks, his 'greatest and best friend' (PL 73–74), his trusted mentor and patron, had been presented with the result of Flinders' life's work. Whether he himself saw a finished copy is not certain. He recorded the last entry in his journal on Sunday 10 July, and he died on 19 July 1814.

Afterlife

John Franklin wrote to Robert Brown that, in *A Voyage to Terra Australis*,

> [Flinders'] observations are reduced with the greatest nicety and precision; they together with his charts which certainly are very superior, will gain for him what he most desired, the character of a good navigator a man of perseverance and science and procure that respect for his memory which I think he deserves.[18]

The *Voyage* was not a popular success: the qualities which made it an indispensable reference for 'Men of Science and Navigators'[19] and modern historians, were not calculated to sell books in large numbers. Ann Flinders, who was left in a parlous financial situation after Flinders' death, wrote to the publisher, George Nicol, in September 1815:

> I fear there is but little to expect from the sale of that <u>unfortunate</u> Work which cost the <u>life</u> of one of the best of human Beings, one infinitely & deservedly dear, whose loss is an irremediable calamity to his Widow & Child.[20]

Banks himself was frequently ill during this time. He did what he could to help Ann but 'in old age he was no longer as influential as he had been and nothing further was done to help Ann Flinders financially.'[21] In 1837, Nicol sent a final account for £51.9.1 to Ann for the *Voyage*: Geoffrey Ingleton believes that 'it is not entirely clear' whether Nicol was expecting her to pay them that sum, or whether she did, and points out that she had already received £190 income from the publication (MFNC). In any case, it seems that they had been on good terms and knew each other well in the years after Flinders' death. In 1815, Nicol wrote to Ann:

> I dreamt I was sent for to the Admiralty, where the names of Astronomers, Draughtsmen, Naturalists &c were given me, who they said were to have a share of the Profits of Capt Flinders's Voyage. This I most strenuously opposed, and said, that I was employed by Capt Flinders to publish his Voyage, and would be accountable to Nobody but his Family for the Profits – This is so near my waking Sentiments, that I very much approve of my Dream.[22]

Banks's health declined and he died six years after Flinders in 1820, at the age of 77. Morgan claims that 'Banks's greatest contribution to Australian maritime exploration came with his support for Flinders on his *Investigator* expedition and his subsequent efforts on behalf of Flinders personally and to disseminate the voyage's findings.'[23] The library at Soho Square was a part of this support, and a part of the larger enterprise which Banks made his life's work, of supporting science: 'I am a bird of peace ... I am no politician,' he told Governor John Hunter.[24] In this, he had a disciple and admirer in Flinders, who wrote in his *Private Journal*, 'My employments and inclinations lead to the extension of happiness and of sciences, and not to the destruction of mankind' (PJ 97). The conjunction of these two personalities during a time when Great Britain was at war enabled the preparation and publication of the *Investigator* Voyage, a major work of scholarship, broad in its scope and meticulous in its detail, which remains as a monument to Flinders' intelligence, industry and tenacity, and to his friendship with Joseph Banks.

Matthew Flinders and Sir Joseph Banks: The Library at Soho Square

Chapter Fourteen: Appendix 1
List of books mentioned in Flinders' Introduction to
A Voyage to Terra Australis (1814)

Abbreviations
   VTA: Flinders, Matthew. *Voyage to Terra Australis* ... Vol. I. (1814)
   PJ: Matthew Flinders. *Private Journal 1803–1814*, edited by Anthony J. Brown and Gillian Dooley (Adelaide: Friends of the State Library of SA, 2005)
   JB: Sir Joseph Banks's library at 32 Soho Square.
   Note: The books are listed in each section in the order in which they first appear in Flinders' *Voyage*.

Books (some possibly donated by Sir Joseph Banks) and taken on the *Investigator* voyage

   Dampier, William. *A voyage to New Holland, &c. in the year, 1699 : wherein are described, the Canary-Islands, the isles of Mayo and St. Jago : the Bay of All Saints, with the forts and town of* ... (1703)
   PJ p77; VTA intr. lxiii

   Vancouver, George. *A voyage of discovery to the North Pacific Ocean, and round the world; in which the coast of north-west America has been carefully examined and accurately surveyed.* (1798)
   VTA intr. lxix

   Hawkesworth, John. *An account of the voyages undertaken by the order of His present Majesty, for making discoveries in the southern hemisphere, and successively performed by Commodore Byron, Captain Wallis, Captain Carteret, and Captain Cook, in the Dolphin, the Swallow, and the Endeavour: drawn up from the journals which were kept by the several commanders and from the papers of Joseph Banks, Esq.* Vol. 111. (1773)
   VTA Intr. lxxxii

   Bligh, William. *A voyage to the South Sea, undertaken by command of His*

Majesty, for the purpose of conveying the bread-fruit tree to the West Indies, in His Majesty's ship the Bounty,... (1792)
VTA intr. xc

La Billardière, Jacques-Julien Houtou de. *Voyage in search of La Pérouse, : performed by order of the Constituent Assembly, during the years 1791, 1792, 1793 and 1794.* [D'Entrecasteaux's expedition] (1800)
VTA intr. xciii

Other books mentioned in the Introduction to *A Voyage to Terra Australis*

Opening remarks

James Cook's *Endeavour* MS journal/log book (Unpublished, 1770)
Flinders' source: Admiralty
PJ p377; VTA preface viii.

Thévenot, Jean de. *Relations de divers voyages curieux,: qui n'ont point esté publiées, et qu'on a traduit ou tiré des originaux des voyageurs françois, espagnols, allemands, portugais ...* (1696)
Flinders' source: JB
PJ p362; VTA intr. ii

Section 1 North coast

Prevost, Abbé. *Histoire generale des Voyages* (Paris, 1746–1759; 15 volumes) Tome xvi
Flinders' source: JB
PJ p363; VTA intr. v

Dalrymple, Alexander. 'Collection concerning Papua' – probably *Considerations on M. Buache's memoir concerning New Britain and the north coast of the New Guinea* (1790)
Flinders' source: uncertain – JB? – 'This interesting paper was procured by ... Sir Joseph Banks.' VTA intr. vii
PJ pp358/366-7

Purchas, Samuel. *Purchas his Pilgrimage, or, Relations of the world and the religions oberued in all ages and places discouered, from the Creation vnto this present : contayning a theologicall ...* (1626)
Flinders' source: uncertain
VTA intr. vii

Struyck, Nicolaas. *Vervolg van de beschrijving der staartsterren en nadere ontdekkingen omtrent den staat van't menselyk geslagt* ... (1753)
Flinders' source: uncertain
PJ p363; VTA intr. xiii

Forrest, Thomas. *A voyage to New Guinea, and the Moluccas, from Balambangan : including an account of Magindano, Sooloo, and other islands; and illustrated with thirty copperplates* (1780)
Flinders' source: uncertain
VTA: intr. xxii

Bampton, William. MS journal of survey of Torres Strait in the ship *Hormuzeer* (1793)
Flinders' source: copy of journal furnished by Arrowsmith at JB
PJ p362; intr. xxx-xlv

Section II: West Coast

Burney, James. *A chronological history of the discoveries in the South Sea or Pacific Ocean* ... vol. 1 (1803–1817)
Flinders' source: James Burney
PJ pp366/368; VTA intr. v

Valentijn, Francois. *Oud en Nieuw Oost-Indiën, vervattende een naaukeurige en uitvoerige verhandelinge van Nederlands mogentheyd in die gewesten* (1724–26)
Flinders' source: translation of abridgement by Mr Tiarks, assistant librarian to JB
PJ p363; VTA intr. lviii

Section III: South Coast

Brosses, Charles de. *Terra Australis cognita: or, voyages to the Terra Australis : , or Southern Hemisphere, during the sixteenth, seventeenth, and eighteenth centuries. Containing an account of the manners of the people, and the productions of the countries, hitherto found in the Southern latitudes; the advantages that may result from further discoveries on this great continent, and the methods of establishing colonies there, to the advantage of Great Britain.* (1766–1768)
Flinders' source: JB
PJ 361; VTA intr. v, lxviii

Péron, Francois. *Voyage de découvertes aux terres australes, exécuté par ordre de sa Majesté, l'Empereur et Roi, sur les corvettes le Géographe, le Naturaliste et la Goëlette le Casuarina.* (1807–1816)
Flinders' source: JB
PJ 241, 271, 339; VTA intr. lvi

Rossel, E.P.E. *Voyage de Dentrecasteaux, envoyé à la recherche de La Pérouse* (1808)
Flinders' source: From Arrowsmith at JB
PJ 342; VTA intr. lxxi, xci

Section IV: East Coast

Harris, John, ed. Campbell. *Navigantium atque itinerantium bibliotheca, or, A complete collection of voyages and travels : consisting of above six hundred of the most authentic writers* (1764)
Flinders' source: JB
PJ p361; VTA intr. lxxvi

Crozet, Julien Marie. *Nouveau voyage a la mer du Sud, commencé sous les ordres de M. Marion ... & achevé, après la mort de cet officier, sous ceux de M. le Chevalier Duclesmeur ... Cette relation a été redigée d'après les plans & journaux de M. Crozet. On a joint a ce voyage un extrait de celui de M. de Surville dans les mêmes parages.* (1783)
Flinders' source: uncertain
VTA intr. lxxxiii-lxxxvi

Mortimer, George. *Observations &c made during a voyage in the brig Mercury (Capt. Cox)* (1791)
Flinders' source: JB
PJ p369; VTA intr. xci

Hunter, John. *An historical journal of the transactions at Port Jackson and Norfolk Island : with the discoveries which have been made in New South Wales and in the Southern Ocean since the ...* (1793)
Flinders' source: JB
PJ p352; VTA xcvi

Part 5

Occasional Pieces

Address for the bicentenary of Matthew Flinders' death, 19 July 2014

Flinders University, Victoria Square, Adelaide, South Australia

The Vice-chancellor recently encouraged us to be 'risk aware but not risk averse,' and I immediately thought of Matthew Flinders. Flinders knew that anything worth doing involves risk. How do I know that? He may never have said so, but it was borne out in his whole career.

I believe that we have a truly inspiring model in our namesake, so I decided today that I would measure Matthew Flinders against the graduate qualities Flinders University aims to develop in its students:

> We expect our students to develop an intellectual and cultural curiosity, both within academic and professional disciplines and across discipline boundaries. We expect them to develop the problem-solving work-ready skills required in our dynamic and changing world. We expect them to demonstrate cultural awareness, to develop a global perspective and to cultivate a respect and tolerance for others.
>
> We hope to produce graduates ...

1. who are knowledgeable
Flinders had an inquisitive mind and read widely – we know this from his letters and his *Private Journal*. His father kept a good library, and reading was a habit Flinders began in childhood, and not only with *Robinson Crusoe*. 'Tradition holds that on his own Matthew mastered John Robertson's *The Elements of Navigation* and John Hamilton Moore's *The New Practical Navigator*' at the age of 15.[1]

2. who can apply their knowledge
Flinders came to his first ship well-prepared to profit from the education

a good captain would give his junior officers. Captain William Bligh taught Flinders the navigation and charting skills he in turn had learned from James Cook. 'Flinders drew at least seven plans and one chart while on board the Providence' (MFNC 15).

He then went on to apply this knowledge. In New South Wales as Master's Mate of the *Reliance*, he offered to explore the rivers around Sydney in his spare time, with his friend George Bass, in an eight-foot boat which they called the *Tom Thumb*. He and Bass continued their exploring whenever they could, eventually circumnavigating Tasmania in 1798–99. As he wrote, 'the furor of discovery, upon whatever scale it is, is perhaps as strong, and can overlook obstacles, as well as most other kinds of mania.'[2] This experience gave him confidence, so back in London in 1800, he wrote to the influential scientist Sir Joseph Banks to suggest himself as leader of an expedition to complete the exploration of the island continent.

3. who communicate effectively

He communicated very effectively with Sir Joseph Banks, because Banks quickly agreed.

Hundreds of Flinders' letters survive, as well as his *Voyage to Terra Australis* – published 200 years ago, his *Private Journal*, and several articles – and his tribute to his cat Trim, which became a hit 150 years after it was written. His prose is a model of balance and clarity.

Finding himself stranded among the French inhabitants of Mauritius, he learned French from the daughters of his host. He was soon quite fluent and able to participate in the Francophone society and to read the French books his new friends lent him.

4. who can work independently

Flinders was a leader and was constantly making decisions. When the *Porpoise* was wrecked on the way back to England from Sydney, it was Flinders who took charge and acted promptly to save lives, even though he wasn't the captain of the wrecked ship.

When detained on Mauritius for six and half years, didn't waste his time. He accomplished as much as he could, absent from the libraries in London, towards the task that awaited him on his return: completing his charts and the account of his voyage. He sent papers on the science of navigation to the Royal Society. He studied the geology and geophysics of the island, and wrote detailed observations in his journal on the local methods of processing products like indigo and maize. His mind was never unoccupied.

5. who are collaborative

Collaboration is essential on a ship – the phrase 'we're all in the same boat' has a literal meaning. The charting of the Australian coastline was collaborative work, requiring the participation of several officers, taking readings and maintaining the instruments. Flinders' sailing directions also included the collection of natural history specimens. The naturalist on the voyage was Robert Brown, who did intensive botanic research in Australia, collecting about 3400 species, 2000 previously unknown, and published the first systematic account of the Australian flora. In addition to Brown's descriptions, landscapes and coastal views were painted by William Westall, and natural history artist Ferdinand Bauer returned to England with exquisite illustrations of more than 1700 plants and over 300 animals. So a major contribution to the knowledge of Australian natural history was made which would not have been possible without Flinders' active collaboration in allowing the 'scientific gentlemen' time ashore to collect and explore.

Flinders also loved to play chamber music with his friends, one of the most pleasant forms of collaboration that exists.

6. who value ethical behaviour

Flinders was a man of honour. He thought very carefully whenever there was a possible conflict between his duty to his country and a promise he had made. On a personal level, when he regarded himself under obligation, he was very generous with his time and attention. An outstanding example of this is the help he gave French prisoners in England, after his release from detention. He saw this as repayment for the kindness of various French inhabitants of Mauritius during his detention.

7. Who connect across boundaries.

The famous encounter between Flinders and Baudin in April 1802 demonstrates Flinders' willingness to connect across boundaries, even with members of an enemy nation. He showed his respect to Captain Baudin by taking off his hat, which, 'set the scene for the meeting that was about to take place between these explorers from two rival nations.'[3] Detained on Mauritius a couple of years later, he soon found that many members of the French community in Port Louis were inclined to befriend him, and he responded by making of some of them friends for life, even though their countries were at war.

All in all, I think our namesake is the very embodiment of our graduate qualities, and we can be very proud to be part of Flinders University.

Gillian Dooley
July 2014

Book reviews

Miriam Estensen. *The Life of Matthew Flinders* and Klaus Toft. *The Navigators: The Great Race between Matthew Flinders and Nicolas Baudin for the North-South Passage through Australia.*[4]

In the fever of bicentennial celebrations of Flinders' circumnavigation of Australia, thousands of words have been written and dozens of new books have appeared. The South Australian events and publications alone celebrating the Encounter between Flinders and Baudin, many titled 'Encounters', have practically reached plague proportions.

However, Miriam Estensen's *Life of Matthew Flinders* (Allen and Unwin) is the first full-blown biography of Flinders since Geoffrey Ingleton's *Matthew Flinders: Navigator and Chartmaker* in 1986, a deluxe volume not intended for the mass market. A paperback edition of Ernest Scott's 1914 biography has recently appeared, but new sources have become available since then and it is certainly time for a new assessment of Flinders' achievements and character based on the evidence we now have.

Estensen's book is a work of painstaking scholarship, borne lightly. I find it hard to fault in any significant way. Her style is easy to read, her judgments are shrewd and well-informed, her use of background information is adequate but not intrusive. There are no rhetorical tricks: Flinders' birth is related in the second paragraph of the first chapter, and the narrative proceeds in an orderly fashion to the end of his life. A small amount of family history is given but we are not burdened with an extensive genealogy.

A figure like Flinders is particularly susceptible to historical gossip-mongering. He himself remarked,

> Let the conduct of a woman on board a ship without her husband, be ever so prudent and circumspect, the tongue of slander will almost certainly find occasion, or it will create one, to embitter the future peace of her husband and family.

The same, it seems, applies to a man without his wife. Recent commentators have pounced gleefully on the evidence that Flinders contracted venereal disease during his teenage voyage with Bligh in the early 1790s, and have regarded this as evidence of a later promiscuity which seems to have no basis either in the historical record or in what is known of Flinders' character and personality. Rumours abound about his relationship with Delphine d'Arifat, the daughter of the family with whom he lived for four years while detained on Mauritius. There are certainly intriguing references to Delphine in Flinders' journal, and a letter he drafted but never sent her showed how disturbingly attractive he found her, but it is impossible to believe that his close friendship with the d'Arifat family, including Delphine's mother and older brothers, would have survived an affair. It is far more likely that the coolness which sprang up between Delphine and Flinders resulted, as Estensen surmises, from her disappointed hopes, perhaps at first indiscreetly encouraged by Flinders but soon quenched.

It is I suppose hard to believe that he remained chaste for nine whole years away from his wife. Estensen, however, wisely wastes little speculation on such matters. 'He loved his wife,' she says, 'with, on the evidence, absolute devotion.' Their love story is the stuff of legends, and legends have a way of inviting deconstruction in our cynical times. Estensen is quite right to rise above the gossip, but I do wonder whether she idealises Ann a little, perhaps failing to read between the lines. Upon Flinders' return in 1810, 'Ann no doubt watched with overflowing pride and happiness' while Flinders related the stories of his adventures 'over and over to fascinated listeners'. Yes, perhaps; but the strains of the past nine years, the shock of being confronted with a physically altered husband, and the stress of adjusting to her new life as a married woman, can be readily imagined.

There was a possible source of tension, too, in their different attitudes to religion. Estensen observes that Flinders, although following religious forms, was not especially devout — 'religion was an area of belief and abstractions that Flinders generally avoided'. Ann, on the other hand, was deeply religious. Her own letters written to Flinders were almost all destroyed, but letters written to family members after his death survive and show a woman of strong and somewhat intolerant religious beliefs. The one remaining letter from Ann to Matthew was never delivered: it was written before the birth of her daughter, to be read in the event of her death in childbirth (which she survived by forty years while he died two years later). It is a deeply moving document testifying to a deep and satisfied love, but it is significant that she earnestly pleads with him to pray. It can be assumed from this that she felt he was disinclined to do so without encouragement, and this might well have been a source of some friction in the marriage.

The fashionable belief is that Flinders died from complications related to his youthful sexual indiscretions. Estensen explains this away plausibly, saying that he died 'insofar as a modern diagnosis can be made, from renal failure' and that it is unlikely 'that his early venereal infections had any direct bearing on it.' Unfortunately she gives no authority for this medical opinion which would help discredit the gossips.

These are minor quibbles, and do not detract from my hearty recommendation of this biography. Estensen obviously admires Flinders but does not adulate him. She deals fairly with his captor Decaen, seeing fault on both sides, and she assesses his achievements with a cool eye, explaining, for example, his failure to discover any major rivers by a discussion of Australia's geographical differences from Europe. I am not aware of any important sources she has failed to consult, and her bibliography and references are extensive. There is a good collection of illustrations, some in colour: most available portraits of significant people are included. Above all, this book is a pleasure to read without ever falling below an exalted standard of scholarship, and will be an enduring contribution to Australian history.

Klaus Toft's *The Navigators* does not aspire to the same level of scholarship. A tie-in to an ABC mini-series, it is a book written with a mission. Originally engaged to produce a documentary on Flinders, Toft became convinced that Baudin's story was as vital and interesting as Flinders', and the material for his program spilled over into this book. As he acknowledges, much of this ground has been covered already in Anthony Brown's *Ill-Starred Captains*, and Toft's work relies heavily on this and other sometimes less reliable secondary sources as well as journals and letters. Written in a breezy but inoffensive and very readable style, it manages to convey very well the difficulties faced by both captains, and the immense injustice Baudin's reputation suffered, both personally and professionally, after his death. He emerges as an intelligent, able commander beset by jealous and ignorant enemies among his officers and the scientists he was lumbered with on his voyage. The sub-title of this book, 'The Great Race between Matthew Flinders and Nicolas Baudin for the north-south passage through Australia', is quite misleading. Flinders was in a hurry, it is true; but the non-existence of the north-south passage was established at the famous encounter in April 1802, and is therefore irrelevant to nearly two-thirds of the book. For both captains, the race was more against disease and weather than each other. However, it makes a highly entertaining adventure story with a fairly solid basis in fact, and should do much to popularise this passage of Australia's early history.

Miriam Estensen. *The Life of George Bass: Surgeon and Sailor of the Enlightenment.* Allen & Unwin.[5]

The only surviving image of George Bass is surrounded by as much mystery as his death. It is a photograph of a painting that has now disappeared, thought to have been painted in about 1800. A handsome young man looks straight out at the viewer, with a faintly supercilious smirk. His hair is tied back and perhaps powdered — old-fashioned, I would have thought, for a young man in 1800, when Bass was only 29.

Bass is known to every eastern-states school child as half of Bass and Flinders, famous for their exploits in *Tom Thumb*, actually two different small open boats in which they explored the south coast of New South Wales at different times. Matthew Flinders proposed that Bass Strait be so named because it was Bass's 1797–98 voyage in a whaleboat that had convinced him that it must be a strait rather than a bay, and led to their circumnavigation of Tasmania in the *Norfolk* in 1798–99.

Miriam Estensen, having produced a landmark biography of Flinders in 2002, has now tackled the rather more enigmatic Bass. With less to work on, *The Life of George Bass* is a smaller and less satisfying book.

Flinders, of course, went on to greater things — and greater lasting fame — while Bass found exploration, though fun, unrewarding. A navy surgeon's pay was 5 pounds per month, before deductions, and all Bass received for his extraordinary efforts was a grant of land at Banks Town which, though worth many millions today, was no use to him. It eventually reverted to the Crown. Bass arranged to take an extended 'sickie' from the Navy and set out to be a trader. Modern employers would be less willing to allow a patently healthy and active individual like Bass to stay on sick leave (on half pay) for three years, but the Navy seemed to be willing to go along with it. Perhaps it was after all some kind of reward for his services.

In 1800, during a brief stay in England, he met and married Elizabeth Waterhouse. After a three-month honeymoon, he sailed for Port Jackson again to earn enough to become 'clear of the world' — an expression Flinders also used — so that they would never have to part again. Neither he nor Flinders succeeded in this modest enough ambition: to be able to live for long with their wives in reasonable comfort was, it seems, too much for either of them to expect.

But then, the call of the sea was strong. It seems that Bass only became a surgeon with the intention of joining the Navy, and he always saw himself as having 'two professions, I am a sailor as well as a surgeon'. In 1798 he announced to his mother that he was capable 'of navigating and conducting a ship to any part of the world.' A naval surgeon had no need to learn navigation, and Bass first went to sea at the late age of eighteen, so he was self-taught in this as in many of his other accomplishments. He was good at languages, studying them whenever he judged they could be of use. He dabbled in the infant science of geology, and in natural history: he was the first to scientifically describe the wombat. His letters show him to possess wit and supreme self-confidence.

Along with this keen intelligence, however, Bass could be hurtful and contemptuous even towards his closest friends. Flinders, younger, shorter and less well-educated, though far from stupid, hero-worshipped Bass and, in a letter he wrote in 1800, complained of the 'unpleasant manner you took to point out my failings.' Estensen, while extolling his intellectual qualities and personal courage, never claims that Bass was kind or thoughtful. 'He was devoted to his mother and in love with his wife,' but 'impatient of ignorance and sharply critical of what he called "insipidity".' He tended to overawe people, and then despised them for their admiration. In a letter to his wife in 1802, he wrote that he was 'getting smoothened down with a drenching of P. Pinders <u>Oil of fool</u> administered by the hand of M Baudin the French Commodore who is collecting curiosities for the national Museum & has threatened me with a niche in the Glass Case.'

Although Estensen followed up every rumour, there is no trace of Bass, his crew, and his brig *Venus* after they left Sydney to trade in the Pacific on 5 February 1803. A collection of letters from Elizabeth's family is in the

Mitchell Library, but other sources for Bass's biography are frustratingly scarce, and Estensen's text is peppered with modifiers like 'evidently', 'probably', and 'it seems likely that'. Scrupulously researched and ably written, *The Life of George Bass*, though not a compulsive read, is a solid contribution to Australian history.

Miriam Estensen. *The Letters of George & Elizabeth Bass*. Allen & Unwin.[6]

In the shadow of the famous romance of Ann and Matthew Flinders lies another, even sadder love story, between Flinders' partner in exploration George Bass and his wife Elizabeth.

Bass and Flinders are so firmly bracketed in the Australian historical imagination that it comes as a surprise to find that the only references to Flinders in this collection of the Bass letters come from Elizabeth. Flinders does not even merit an entry in the biographical notes at the beginning of the book. The parallels between the two men are many. Both were born in Lincolnshire, and were destined by their parents for a medical career, while being fascinated by the sea. Flinders managed to convince his father to let him join the Navy at 15, while Bass was apprenticed by his widowed mother to an apothecary-surgeon. His apprenticeship completed, he joined the navy as a naval surgeon's first mate at 18. The two met when they joined the *Reliance* under John Hunter, bound for New South Wales. The coincidences continue. Back in England in 1800–1801, they both married and sailed away from their respective wives three months after the weddings. Flinders returned nine years later, but Bass never came back.

Bass and Flinders both excused their absence from their wives by pleading stern economic necessity: once this first long separation had passed, they promised they would never be apart again. That George Bass did really long to be back with his 'Bess Bass' is clear from these letters. However, one could not imagine him sitting alone with his flute playing a little song he wrote for his wife as Flinders did when detained on Mauritius. Intelligent, impatient and not at all sentimental, George chivvies his wife, laughs at her for her atrocious spelling and even makes the occasional blue joke.

For her part, Elizabeth Bass is revealed in her letters as a woman of spirit. In George's absence she had to deal with his London agents in matters of his career and his pay. 'Young Mr Sykes has behaved very kind to me each time I have gone. I never wish to see his Father again, as I consider him a compleate Bear,' she reported in December 1801. In her early letters she is obviously extremely anxious and worried for George's safety. Some charts which had arrived too late for him to take with him on his journey preyed on her mind:

> The Day after you left me I received a parcel of Charts from Mr Delrumple [i.e. Alexander Dalrymple] you so much wished for, and another the following Day. O I would have given Thousands if I had them to have got them conveyed to you as it constantly dwelt on my mind that having them might save your dear Life.

These charts recur in later letters—perhaps not just because they are a focus of Elizabeth's anxiety but because there was such uncertainty about whether any one letter would arrive at its destination that anything important needed to be mentioned at every opportunity. In the second of her letters to survive, written in April 1801, she says, 'this is either the 6 or 7 Letter I have written the first by the Nutwell either two or three by the Hindostane to the Cape one by the Venus to New South Wales one by C't Flinders and this to China. perhaps you may never get any of them. I hope your mind is too employed to feel the want of them as I do.' Elizabeth had the eternal malady of the sailor's wife: too much time to worry. Although of the 22 surviving letters between them (all included in this book) only eight are from Elizabeth to George, they are on the whole much longer than George's letters, which were often written in a hurry whenever an opportunity arose: in November 1802 he wrote, 'Two minutes must suffice to tell thee I love thee; and that I am yet alive as thou mayest perhaps surmise by my writing to thee.'

Estensen is keen to point out that George's 'expectations of his wife's very proper conduct were typical of the time,' but it is a little disconcerting to read, 'Remember my Bess you have a husband who will not forsake you nor ever cease to love you as long as my Bess remains deserving of it.' Just before he left on his final voyage in 1803, to disappear mysteriously into the Pacific, he wrote a confused and possibly drunken letter:

> In all my walks, at every beautiful prospect in every pleasantly situated house—but hold Bess I am going to give thee proofs I love thee when I ought to give thee only words. In short Bess they all bring thee into my mind. Thou shalt one day or other admire them with me—that is if thou are good—old woman.—for I thou art bad thou mayest 'een stay in England, we have enough of that sort here. Again.
>
> Thou shalt not breed. & fill my cabin full of squallers, there's no room for such gentry.

Cruelly, this was the last direct word she seems to have had from her husband. She would never accept that he had died, although she lived for another 21 years.

Estensen's editing is thorough and helpful, though there is no index—just names and places would suffice. The book design is elegant and clear, once one gets accustomed to the odd arrangement whereby each entire left-hand page is left free for footnotes. There is a map and a few colour plates, though sadly no picture of Elizabeth survives. The publication of the *Letters* makes a valuable companion volume to Estensen's *Life of George Bass* (2005).

Peter Ashley. *The Indomitable Captain Matthew Flinders, Royal Navy*. Pierhead Press, 2006 and Marion Body. *The Fever of Discovery: The Story of Matthew Flinders Who Gave Australia Her Name*. New European Publications, 2006.[7]

Scratch an Australian and you'll usually find a Matthew Flinders fan – certainly most of us have at least heard of him and a surprising number of people will claim him as a personal hero. The situation is quite different in his native country, and both these books have been written with the aim of correcting this deplorable state of affairs.

Peter Ashley is a retired British naval officer who has become a self-confessed 'Flindersphile'. *The Indomitable Captain Matthew* is Ashley's masters thesis, and in it he is, as is required by the genre, concerned to present an argument and prove a point. His hypothesis is that Flinders' actions at three critical times of his life amounted to a 'courtship with failure', though he finally acknowledges that this is a little too neat to fit the facts. Much is made of the gonorrhoea Flinders contracted in Tahiti. In fact, his behaviour was typical of a healthy eighteen-year-old, and anyway it was the primitive treatment rather than the disease itself that was likely to have caused his long-term illness and early death. The unsoundness of the *Investigator* is described with convincing naval knowhow, but all the legends of the famous meeting with Decaen are treated as established facts even though no unbiased account survives. However, Ashley the naval officer gives a compelling assessment of Flinders' 'superb' ability as a navigator.

Marion Body's interest in Flinders sprang from a friendship with his great-grand-daughter Ann Flinders Petrie. *The Fever of Discovery* is a straightforward biography, shorter and less detailed than Miriam Estensen's *Life*, aimed at introducing him to an English audience. She writes sympathetically, covering all the major phases of his short, eventful life, and including for good measure the full text of his tribute to his cat Trim, without mentioning that it has been published already.

Both books would benefit from some editorial assistance, to shape and sharpen the prose and to correct errors: particularly distracting is Body's repetition of *Bellepheron* for *Bellerophon*. Ashley's book is replete with supporting matter – notes, appendices and illustrations occupy nearly half the 86 pages – while Body's has no bibliographical references at all, either to her sources or to further reading. It's not intended as a scholarly work, but some guidance for readers whose interest has been aroused would surely be in the spirit of her undertaking.

Australia Circumnavigated: The Voyage of Matthew Flinders in HMS Investigator, 1801–1803 edited by Kenneth Morgan. Hakluyt Society, 2015.[8]

Kenneth Morgan of Brunel University has done Australian exploration history a great service in editing for publication the official journals kept by Matthew Flinders on board the *Investigator*. These documents are in the National Archives at Kew and a digitised facsimile is available online – interestingly, as a dataset for the British Atmospheric Data Centre – but a scholarly edition is long overdue.

Morgan has provided a detailed and well-researched introduction, concentrating on Flinders' professional achievements. He concludes,

With his passion for precision and the deployment of new knowledge, Flinders had used a methodology that synthesized all that could then be known, from practical fieldwork and scholarly research, about the shape of the Australian continent and the details of its coastal geography. (AC 1: 86)

He writes of Flinders with measured praise, defending him occasionally from previous writers who have judged him severely with the benefit of hindsight. This journal shows how decisions often had to be made quickly and without full knowledge of all the circumstances: yes, some turned out to be mistakes but without that decisiveness nothing would have been achieved to begin with. At other times, inaction or delay would have been disastrous.

The main text of *Australia Navigated* is in some ways a first draft of Flinders' *Voyage to Terra Australis* (1814). The difference is that this journal was written day by day at the time the events were happening. The *Voyage* does not contain the detailed quantitative data reproduced here. On the other hand, Flinders' Introduction to the *Voyage* is a comprehensive essay on the history of the exploration of Australia, written in London a decade later with reference to all available sources and charts.

Morgan has rounded out his edition with Flinders' 'Memoir', ostensibly an account of 'the marks used in the charts' and 'the manner in which the latitude, longitude, and variation of the compass were obtained'. When he wrote this, Flinders had been imprisoned on Mauritius for seventeen months, and his preface is an account of how this came about. His grief and frustration cannot help showing through. The Memoir also includes discussion of important observations Flinders made on the effect of a ship's iron on the compass and on the marine barometer, later written up for publication by the Royal Society.

The reader looking for narrative drive will skim over the routine record of the weather and the ship-board activities in the logbooks – 'Handed the mizzen top-sail. ... Strong breezes and squally. ... Mustered the ships company and saw them clean.' Sometimes, all the excitement is in the footnotes. When the ship ran aground in the English Channel, for example, Morgan has elaborated on the bald account in the text by explaining that 'At the time Flinders was below deck in his cabin with his wife' – an inconvenient fact that had life-changing consequences for both Matthew and Ann, as the Admiralty was now alerted that she was on board and was expecting to sail with him. They moved swiftly to prevent that happening.

The richness of information provided in these volumes is immense. There is data on the weather and tides which is clearly still of use to environmental scientists. There are detailed accounts of vegetation and birdlife. There is methodological information about navigation and cartography.

And then there are descriptions of the encounters with the Aboriginal peoples – of their languages, their physical characteristics, and how both sides conducted themselves. Some meetings were 'friendly', others were hostile and aggressive. As Morgan remarks, 'Encounters between Flinders and his associates and the Aborigines were compromised by misunderstandings of gesture and language' (AC 1: 61). Flinders' policy was to maintain good relations as much as possible, as much from pragmatism as innate respect: he had to keep his crew safe and get the work of the voyage done. He regarded it as part of his duty to establish 'friendly intercourse' whenever possible, to smooth the path of future European visitors.

On Friday 22 July 1803 the daily entries finish: 'At sunset, hauled down the pendant' (AC 2: 390). The *Investigator* was condemned, and he had spent the day supervising the dispersal of its supplies and people. And that was that, though he didn't know it yet. Another ten pages or so contain correspondence relating to the arrangements to continue his work, and that of his 'scientific gentlemen'.

In this official document, Flinders occasionally allowed himself a wry or colourful turn of phrase. His well-known remarks on the pelicans of Kangaroo Island in the *Voyage* are prefigured here, with the addition of an apologetic footnote: 'I am conscious that sentimental conjectures and exclamations are very much out of their place when found in a ships logbook' (VTA I: 356). For me the most unexpected discovery is a passage of two and a half pages describing a visit to an estate in Timor in March 1803. This does not appear in any form in the *Voyage* and is decidedly personal. He writes, 'I could not prevent my ideas from dwelling upon the happiness that a man whose desires were moderate might enjoy in this delightful retreat with the beloved of his heart' (AC 2: 337). But, following this train of thought, he decides that there 'could be no collision of mind upon mind', and that without it even reading would pall. 'I energetically exclaimed No – I was not meant for this' (AC 2: 338).

The truth is that Flinders' desires were *not* moderate. His personal habits were modest and even self-denying, but his ambitions were huge. He scrupulously acknowledged the contributions of his predecessors, but he aimed to be the ultimate explorer of the Australian coast, to 'preclude the necessity of any one following after me to explore.'[9] One way of reading this publication is as the inexorable, day-by-day account of how he was prevented from fulfilling that ambition.

Kenneth Morgan. *Matthew Flinders: Maritime Explorer of Australia.* London: Bloomsbury, 2016.[10]

Kenneth Morgan writes that this book 'is a fresh appraisal of Matthew Flinders' career using for the first time the full range of documentary material available on his career' (x). Morgan, Professor of History at Brunel University in London, has recently edited Matthew Flinders' *Investigator* log books, published by the Hakluyt Society in 2015 under the title *Australia Circumnavigated*. The book under review is a biographical work drawing on this source, along with many other primary and secondary documents. As this implies, Morgan has focused his attention on Flinders as a navigator and leader of a scientific expedition rather than on his personal life. His first chapter, 'The Young Navigator', moves briskly through Flinders' family background, childhood and early education. By page 7, the 16-year-old Matthew is at sea with Captain Pasley in the *Bellerophon*.

The 13 chapters that follow recount the stages of Flinders' professional life and chart his achievements. Morgan draws on a formidable range of documents. For example, the material published in *Australia Circumnavigated*, which covers the period from 1801 to 1803 when the *Investigator* was in service under Flinders, form the basis for Chapters 5 to 10, supplemented by other primary sources: the journals of naturalist Robert Brown, gardener Peter Good and seaman Samuel Smith, correspondence to and from Flinders, Sir Joseph Banks, Governor Philip Gidley King and the 'scientific gentlemen' on the voyage, and accounts from the French officers on Baudin's expedition.

Morgan has also drawn on earlier biographies and historical works, notably Miriam Estensen's biography of Flinders from 2002 and Geoffrey Ingleton's major work on the voyage, *Matthew Flinders: Navigator and Chartmaker* (1986). Morgan's work is more in the mould of Ingleton's book than Estensen's. It is true that in the 30 years since Ingleton's book was published, more primary sources have become readily accessible and others have come to light, and Morgan has been able to include more factual details than Ingleton had available to him. However, Ingleton's work, with its extensive illustrations, maps and hydrographical detail, remains an essential reference: this new book does not supplant it. Estensen's biography is also a work of considerable scholarship, but is as concerned with Flinders the man – as a son, a brother, a husband, a friend – as with Flinders the professional navigator. Morgan often cites Estensen as a source for biographical facts.

It is hard to assess exactly where this book will find its niche in Flinders scholarship. There are no startling new revelations or interpretations. Morgan's prose is at best workmanlike and sometimes ungainly, no match for Flinders' own balanced and elegant style, so that extended summaries of what Flinders wrote in his log or his *Private Journal*, both now published and available, seem redundant. Morgan's approach is conventional and often provides little more than a summary of the primary sources. Not that he is oblivious to subtext: in an acute commentary on the correspondence between ship's surgeon Hugh Bell and Flinders during the fraught final weeks of the circumnavigation, for example, he comments that 'Bell had touched a raw nerve by criticizing Flinders' action as commander' (137), accounting for Flinders' defensive and indignant tone.

Perhaps inevitably, in subtle ways which might not be evident to a UK-based historian, this book is written from a Eurocentric perspective. Morgan uses terms such as 'native' and 'Aborigine' which would usually be avoided in current Australian scholarship. He spends only about half a page on the skirmish in which an Aboriginal man died on Morgans Island in Blue Mud Bay in January 1803, while discussing at greater length the meeting with the Malay trepangers in February, describing it as 'one of [the *Investigator*'s] most notable encounters' (128). And he ends the book by deploring as 'a sign of the times' (200) the inclusion of Bongaree, 'the main Aboriginal man on the *Investigator* expedition', in the inscription on Mark Richards' statue of Flinders unveiled at Euston

Station in 2014, instead of the scientists and the crew of the *Investigator*.

Perhaps it is 'a sign of the times' that even this slight gesture acknowledging the significance of Flinders' expedition for the Aboriginal people was made. I for one would have preferred something more substantial to recognise that Flinders' great achievement heralded irreversible changes for the people who had lived here for so long. As for Flinders' scientific colleagues, there have been publications and exhibitions on the science and art of the voyage. However, it is true that their achievements have not yet exercised the popular imagination and their acknowledgement in monuments is an idea whose time has not yet come. Morgan's account of the scientific endeavours and achievements of the *Investigator* voyage, though it is an academic book and will itself have limited reach, may pave the way for this kind of recognition.

Inspired by Flinders

Program from a 'Fridays at the Library' event held at Flinders University Library on 15 March 2002.

12 noon

A Desperate Fortune: Matthew Flinders' Australia narrated by Edward Woodward (Discovery Video).

1 pm

Readings

Life and Legend
'Matthew Flinders' by Alexander Hutchinson Barrowman (1971)
'Navigator Immortal' by William Beard (1958) – Extracts

Music

Duetto No. 6, Opus 101 - 1st movement (Presto) by Joseph Haydn (1732-1809)

'My Evening Song' - Words by Matthew Flinders, Air by Haydn (arr. G. & M. Dooley)
Matthew sent this song to Ann in a letter dated 20th November:

> *'I often retire to the little pavilion which is my study and bedroom, and with my flute in my hand and sometimes tears in my eyes I warble over the little evening song of which I sent thee a copy.'*
>
> *Why Henry didst thou leave me, thus leave me here to mourn?*
> *Ah cruel! Thou deceived'st me, I'll ne'er see thy return.*
> *Thou know'st how much I loved thee, yet could resolve to go.*
> *My grief could nothing move thee, though I was sunk in woe.*
>
> *Yet why do I thus blame thee, alas thou couldst not stay,*
> *For when stern duty calls thee, thou canst not but obey.*
> *Thy looks bespoke the anguish, the struggle in thy breast.*
> *[Though now apart we languish, together will our hearts find rest.]*[11]

Sonata No. 3 by François Devienne (1759-1803)
Devienne was a French composer and flute and bassoon virtuoso. His *Methode de flûte théoretique et pratique* first appeared in 1795, and many of his flute compositions enjoyed a great vogue for a time.

Readings

Australian Landfall

'Matthew Flinders landing on Bribie Island from the Norfolk on 16th July, 1799' by Patricia Austin (1993)

'The Missing Line' by 'T. the R.' ('Thomas the Rhymer' alias C.W.A. Hayward) (1924)

'Flinders Map' by John Blight (1975)

'The Map Maker – Kangaroo Island – South Australia' by Jeff Guess (1988)

'Colonization' by Rex Ingamells (1935) – 1st seven and last 2 stanzas.

'Mr Flinders and the Aborigines' by David P. Reiter (1994)

Music

Duo 1, Opus 8, 2nd movement (Andantino) and 3rd movement (Allegro) by Ignaz Pleyel (1757–1831)

> The enormous popularity of Pleyel's music during his lifetime is reflected in the testimony of contemporary journals and of early writers. However, he failed to fulfil the potential seen in him by Mozart and others, and in 1795 set up a successful publishing house.

Duetto No. 1, 3rd movement (Rondo) and 4th movement (Allegro Assai) by W.A. Mozart (1756–1791)

Sonata No. 2 by Georg Philip Telemann (1681–1767)

> Telemann was one of the most prolific composers that ever lived, and wrote a large amount of chamber music.

Readings

Death and Apotheosis

'The Death of Flinders, July 19, 1814' by Bernard Ingleby (1913)

'Death of Matthew Flinders, 19th July 1814' by Jeff Guess (1991)

'The Navigator's Wife after Ann Flinders (nee Chappelle) circa 1814' by Jeff Guess (2000)

'To the statue of Matthew Flinders on North Terrace' by Peter Manthorpe (1998)

Flinders in his own words:

Took up my flute and played the 1st. and 5th. Duo of Pleyels opera 9. Note, the first commences in a grand stile, and is sweetly plaintive in some parts of it.

The Andante of the 5th. is marked for minuet time, whereas the time is 2/4. Must have all Pleyel's musick when I return to England, that is set for the flute, and Mozart's, and Haydn's, and some of Hoffmeister's and Devienne's, but the whole will be too expensive, musick is so very dear in England; and indeed so is almost everything else.

...

Hope Mrs. F. will have got the better of the inflammation in her eyes; it is now fine weather in England and she will be able to ride out. Must take a house in the country when I return, and enjoy myself two or three months before I engage in any service; but, God knows, it is now three years since I heard from anybody at home; and what may have happened it is impossible to say.

...

Sat down to dinner at two o'clock. The French beans are very good in this island. Made a tolerably good dinner and drank three glasses of Madeira. Am determined to persevere in the plan of eating more of puddings and vegetables, and less meat. Find my headache better after dinner.

...

Think there must certainly be some river or large opening upon the north-west coast of Australia. Would I go out as governor of a settlement there, should it be proposed to me? I can't tell, it would depend on many circumstances. Wish to finish the examination of the whole coast of Australia before I do anything else. If there should be no great opening on the N.W. coast, it would be desirable to explore by land from the head of the great inlet on the south coast, and from Port Phillip. The asses of this island would be very useful in these excursions. Mem. To propose to Sir Joseph to touch here, when I go out again, to take in six asses, and some fruit trees; provided I can make sure of not being ill treated.

...

Hope the admiralty will not give any more passports to French ships to go out on discovery, whilst I am kept a prisoner here.

Matthew Flinders, Private Journal, 18th August 1805.

Music of the Ships - Adelaide Baroque, 22 August 2020

Program notes by Gillian Dooley

Today's program features music which may have been known to the two captains who met in what is now called Encounter Bay in South Australia, Matthew Flinders (1774–1814) and Nicolas Baudin (1754–1803). While Flinders played the flute and wrote about his musical activities and tastes, we have less evidence about Baudin's musical preferences. However, there were musicians on *Le Géographe*, including his protégé, the young artist Charles-Alexandre Lesueur, and during his eventful nautical career Baudin himself had worked for the Austrian navy as well as various French enterprises, public and private. He travelled all over the world, including to the West Indies, and the program reflects some of those influences and experiences.

W. Mozart: Quartet in D Major for Flute, violin, viola and cello K285
I. Allegro

In 1777, Mozart was commissioned by Ferdinand Dejean (1731–1797), a rich amateur he met in Mannheim, to write some quartets and concertos for the flute. Dejean had served as a surgeon for the Dutch East India Company, and after his maritime travels had retired to a life of scientific scholarship, music and continental travel. Mozart complained to his father that he couldn't stand the flute and didn't enjoy writing for the instrument, and that Dejean underpaid him, but he nevertheless produced three quartets and two concerti as a result. The D major quartet was the first, dated Christmas day 1777.

G. Paisiello: 'Nel cor più non mi sento" from La molinara
(arranged by William Gardiner for string quintet and soprano)

Giovanni Paisiello (1740–1816) was an Italian composer, well-known in his time especially for his operas. He worked in Naples and St Petersburg, where he wrote his opera *The Barber of Seville*, pre-dating Rossini's masterpiece by some decades. He was invited to Paris in 1802 by Napoleon, although he failed to please the Parisian public and returned to Naples the following year. *La molinara* (The miller-woman) was written in 1788 in Naples, and the aria 'Nel cor più non mi sento' is probably his best-known melody, with many later composers, including Beethoven, basing variations on the theme. It was originally a duet but its inclusion in anthologies such as the Schirmer *Twenty-Four Italian Songs and Arias* as a solo song has secured it a place in the standard repertoire for solo voice.

J. Haydn: Divertimento No 15 for viola, cello and Violone

1. Moderato

Joseph Haydn (1732–1809), probably the most famous composer in the 18th-century world, wrote many hundreds of chamber works as well as symphonies, concerti and operas. This divertimento is believed to be an earlier version of one of Joseph Haydn's 72 trios for baryton, viola and cello (Hob XI: 80), written for Prince Nikolaus Esterházy in the 1760s. Haydn had also written a concerto for the violone in 1763 which is now lost. The manuscript on which today's performance is based was recently discovered in a library in Vienna.

Chevalier de Saint-Georges: Andante from Overture to L'Amant anonyme for string quintet

Joseph Bologne, Chevalier de Saint-Georges (1745–1799), was born in Guadaloupe, the son of a French planter and his wife's African slave, Anne. He was educated in France and served as a colonel of the Légion St.-Georges, the first all-black regiment in Europe, during the French Revolution. Despite his many accomplishments, including fencing, he is best known today as the first known classical composer of African heritage. An early work was a set of string quartets, inspired by Haydn's quartets, said to be some of the first of the genre written in France. *L'Amant anonyme*, based on a play by Mme de Genlis, was the most successful of his half-dozen operas, but could not be performed at the Paris Opera because the singers refused to work with 'a mulatto'. It was presented in a chamber performance at the private theatre of Mme de Montesson in 1780.

J. Haydn: Sailor's Song Hob.XXVIa:31 (arranged by William Gardiner for soprano and string quintet)

Haydn's songs anticipated the tradition of Schubert and other great Lieder composers in giving the piano and voice equal importance. 'The Sailor's

Song' is an excellent example, with the accompaniment splashing and storming around a relatively straightforward melody. William Gardiner's original and witty orchestration plays beautifully with Haydn's dramatic word-painting.

This is the first of Haydn's second set of English Canzonettas, composed during his second visit to England in 1794–1795. The lyrics are sometimes attributed to Anne Hunter (1742–1821), who wrote the words to several of his better-known Canzonettas such as 'A Pastoral Song' and 'O Tuneful Voice'. They tell a simple tale of 'Britain's glory' embodied in the English seaman, who is dismayed neither by 'war nor death'.

F. Hoffmeister: Quartetto No 2 for Contrabasso, violin, viola and bass

I. Allegro moderato

Franz Anton Hoffmeister (1754–1812) was a German composer and music publisher active in Vienna, where he was friendly with both Mozart and Beethoven, and later Leipzig, where he co-founded the Bureau de Musique. This firm published the first edition of J.S. Bach's keyboard music in 1802 and was eventually taken over by C.F. Peters. He was particularly well known for his flute music – Matthew Flinders mentioned him as one of the composers whose music he was keen to buy when he returned to England – but he was a versatile musician and wrote with equal skill for the 'contrabasso', as this quartet demonstrates.

Ignaz Pleyel: Flute Quartet in D Major, B. 381 for flute, violin, viola and cello

II. Adagio

Ignaz Pleyel (1757–1831) was another composer-publisher like Hoffmeister, and another name on Flinders' sheet-music wish-list (along with Mozart, Haydn and Devienne). Pleyel was born in Austria and studied with Haydn, but moved to Strasbourg to take up a well-resourced cathedral position, with an orchestra and choir at his disposal. When the French Revolutionary government abolished music in cathedrals in 1791, he moved to London, presenting concerts in friendly rivalry with his former teacher, Haydn. Back in France during the Reign of Terror in 1793 and 1794, he managed to placate the authorities by writing compositions praising the new republic.

He set up the publisher Maison Pleyel in Paris in 1795, publishing the first complete edition of Haydn's string quartets in 1801. Later he went into piano manufacturing. He composed less in his later years, but during the last decades of the 18th century his renown was on a par with Haydn's. This Adagio is the slow movement from the first of a set of flute quartets published in Paris and London in 1789.

Matthew Flinders/J. Haydn: 'My Evening Song' (arranged by William Gardiner for Soprano and string quintet)

In November 1805, Flinders sent the melody and words of a song to his wife Ann, whom he had married in 1801 just before leaving on his voyage to Australia. At the time he was detained by the French on Mauritius. He wrote the words himself, and attributed the 'air' to Haydn. It is not certain how he came to know this tune, which is a variant on the Andante from Haydn's 'Imperial' symphony, Hob I. 53. He had little opportunity to attend symphony concerts during his life, but he often played music with the friends he had made among the French settlers on Mauritius. It seems likely that he and his friends played an arrangement of the movement – or perhaps he heard a set of variations such as that of J.B. Krumpholtz for harp and violin when visiting one of his neighbours. When he came to write the song he was evidently relying on memory, as the tune differs in several significant details. He wrote one complete verse of lyrics and three lines of a second, adding 'to be completed' at the end. The manuscript is now in the National Maritime Museum in Greenwich, along with a completion of the second verse and two more verses in Ann Flinders' handwriting.

Peter Sculthorpe: Third Sonata for strings 'Jabiru Dreaming'

I. Deciso
II. Liberamento–Estatico

Peter Sculthorpe (1929–2014) was one of the first composers to take an interest in the Indigenous music of Australia. The first movement of 'Jabiru Dreaming' (1990), Sculthorpe explains, 'contains rhythmic patterns found in the indigenous music of the Kakadu area. Some of these patterns also suggest the gait of the jabiru, a species of stork.' The second movement opens with a haunting melody on the cello, taken from the official journal of the French voyage to Terra Australis commanded by Nicolas Baudin. The scientists were instructed to take a systematic approach to collecting cultural and artistic data from Indigenous people. This resulted (inter alia) in the intercultural translation of three pieces of music from the Port Jackson area, the first pieces of Australian Aboriginal music to be committed to European notation. It is the first of these, headed 'Chant', that opens the second movement.

Epilogue:
Flinders as Romantic Hero through the Generations[1]

In the first pages of the first novel we have in English, Robinson Crusoe asks himself why we can't be satisfied with just sliding comfortably through life, why we have to go out into the world and risk ourselves, why we are driven to become 'instruments of our own destruction'. The question is as old as the novel itself, perhaps as old as storytelling: it sets storytelling in motion. (J.M Coetzee)[2]

Flinders as hero of his own life

In a letter to Ann Chappelle from Sydney on his twenty-fifth birthday in 1799 – two years before their marriage – Matthew Flinders described reading Ann Radcliffe's *Mysteries of Udolpho* and being prompted to write to his beloved with 'a heart altogether unveiled. ... but it is a strange heart, Annette. ... It is not a very insensible one, I think: but it may have acquired some degree of morbid sensibility' (PL 40). As Paul Brunton writes, Flinders 'came to manhood during the great age of sensibility' and saw himself 'as a man of feeling', although 'he understood the need for balance between the dictates of head and heart' (PL 14).

He was clearly not averse to reading novels: he claimed that he was lured to the sea by reading *Robinson Crusoe* as a child.[3] However, he did not recommend novels for his young stepsisters. Writing to his stepmother in November 1805 from his detention by the French on Mauritius, Flinders offered her some advice about the education of her teenage daughters:

> It will be well to keep them from reading novels, *Evelina, Clarissa Harlowe* and two or three others perhaps of that class excepted, at least until they

are twenty years of age. Young girls often contract such romantic notions from novel reading, that their future lives are embitted (*sic*) by not finding that perfection which for the most part is not in human nature, and is never to be expected. (PL 138)

It seems he felt in no danger from exposure to 'romantic notions' in his own case. Just three days earlier, he had written Ann a long letter full of romantic professions:

Receive, my best beloved ... my vows of constant unabated love: to love thee more than I have done, and now do, I think cannot be, thou hast the sole undivided possession of my heart. (PL 134)

Enclosed with the letter was a song he had written for her, with words addressed from a wife to her husband complaining at his desertion, but then excusing him because 'when stern duty calls thee, thou canst not but obey.'[4] This is not the only example of Flinders casting himself as the hero of his own life. A month earlier, he described in his journal 'lying under a cascade in a situation very romantic and interior' at Tamarind Falls, ruminating on 'the vicissitudes of his own life', from his childhood in the Lincolnshire fens (PJ 101).

These romantic tendencies had occasionally spilled into his official documents: when he described Pelican Lagoon on Kangaroo Island he apologised for writing what he called 'sentimental conjectures and exclamations' on the sight of baby pelicans climbing over the bones of their forbears (AC 1: 356n4); and in Timor he 'could not prevent my ideas from dwelling upon the happiness that a man whose desires were moderate might enjoy in this delightful retreat with the beloved of his heart' (AC 2: 337) – all in the Captain's log of the *Investigator* which was to be handed in to the Admiralty on his return. He was an intellectual, a scientist, a practical, hard-headed, problem-solving ship's captain. But he was also romantic to the core.

Whether this served him well or badly during his lifetime is a moot point. It is possible that his romantic image of himself as a British naval officer might have prolonged or even caused his detention on Mauritius. He later admitted that he had had 'some ambition of being the first to undertake so long a voyage in such a small vessel' when he decided to try and sail the tiny schooner *Cumberland* from Sydney to England in 1803 (VTA 2: 323). And then, a year after he landed on Mauritius seeking 'protection and assistance' and instead 'finding a prison' (PJ 14), he recounts having written a letter to Governor Decaen: 'It is likely I may be accused of wanting the spirit that I had before shewn – of an Englishman, by having suffered something for it' (PJ 55). Modern commentators are more likely to accuse him of showing too much 'spirit' – which they tend to call arrogance.

Flinders as hero of family and colleagues

After his death, Ann lived for another 38 years, mourning her 'Captain Flinders'. She wrote, in 1830, 'during the period we were permitted to live together, not a cloud cast shade over the sunshine of our affection for each other, and each day seemed but to rivet our attachment the more firmly. After such a union to seek another would be the height of folly.'[5] Although they had been married for 13 years, they were separated for nearly 10 years. For Ann the last three and a half years of his life, when they lived together in London, was, at least in retrospect, a golden age, whatever their practical difficulties and challenges had been.

In 1842 Sir John Franklin, by then the Governor of Tasmania, wrote to Ann:

> I have long been desirous of giving you the full particulars of the monument which I am about to erect on Stamford Hill above Port Lincoln to the memory of your deeply lamented husband – and my earliest friend – not that his undying fame needed such a memento for he must live in the grateful remembrance of every friend of Hydrographical Science and especially of those who navigate the shores of Australia.[6]

Franklin was Flinders' step-cousin – the nephew of his stepmother Elizabeth – and had been 'his favourite midshipman' on the *Investigator*.

Flinders himself revered Captain James Cook, and in turn he was revered by the next generation of navigators. John Lort Stokes, Captain of *HMS Beagle*, was a great admirer. On 7 July 1841 he found evidence of the *Investigator*'s visit to Sweers Island, and he wrote:

> It was thus our good fortune to find at last some traces of the Investigator's voyage, which at once invested the place with all the charms of association,

and gave it an interest in our eyes that words can ill express. All the adventures and sufferings of the intrepid Flinders vividly recurred to our memory; his discoveries on the shores of this great continent, his imprisonment on his way home, and cruel treatment by the French Governor of Mauritius, called forth renewed sympathies. I forthwith determined accordingly that the first river we discovered in the Gulf should be named the Flinders, as the tribute to his memory which it was best becoming in his humble follower to bestow, and that which would most successfully serve the purpose of recording his services on this side of the continent. Monuments may crumble, but a name endures as long as the world.[7]

The traditional owners of the country through which the Flinders River flows into the Gulf of Carpentaria, near Karumba, might find that idea unconvincing.

Miriam Estensen writes, at the end of her biography of Flinders, 'Those who wrote of him soon after his death immersed his memory in laudatory prose that was at times misleading, if the man was to be understood, and quite unnecessary.'[8] It was the custom of the time, of course, to indulge in hyperbole on such occasions. Perhaps she was thinking of the final words of the substantial obituary that appeared in the *Naval Chronicle* in late 1814:

> His private character was as admirable as his public one was exemplary: his integrity, uprightness of intention, and liberality of sentiment, were not to be surpassed; he possessed the social virtues and affections in an eminent degree, and in conversation he was particularly agreeable, from the extent of his general information, and the lively acuteness of his observations.[9]

Flinders the national legend

Flinders is now such a household name in Australia that it is difficult to imagine a time when this might not have been the case. In an attempt to gauge his celebrity over the nineteenth and twentieth centuries, I searched Trove – being careful to use all possible forms of his name, since in the nineteenth century he was usually referred to as Captain Flinders, of course.

It surprised me to find that there were only two short obituaries in

Australian newspapers, reprinted from overseas publications, in March and July 1815, both in the *Sydney Gazette and NSW Advertiser*. After a few quiet decades, his name begins to appear more frequently in the 1840s, partly because of the Franklins' proposed memorial to him in Port Lincoln, and also, no doubt, because, with the settlement of Victoria and South Australia, where he had been most active, Flinders began to be used as a geographic name.

In the twentieth century, perhaps prompted by federation and national pride, there is an explosion of interest. Beginning in the first decade of the century with 394 articles, from then until the end of the 1950s they number in the thousands. The fact that Trove has limited coverage after 1960 no doubt explains why the numbers then fall back into the hundreds for the second half of the twentieth century. The total given for the whole twentieth century is '14k' – too large a number to quantify exactly.

Ernest Scott wrote the first book-length biography of Flinders, published in 1914, the centenary of his death. Written during the early years of Federation and with the First World War looming, Scott's *Life of Captain Matthew Flinders, R.N.*, as Stuart Macintyre points out, strikes 'an unashamedly heroic tone. ... We are struck by the reverence of the author and the exuberance of his prose.' However, he also describes Scott as 'a self-conscious practitioner of the new school of scientific history' who 'insisted on going back to the original sources and testing every claim by careful assessment of the evidence.' Eschewing romance, and 'establishing the truth about Flinders, he was enhancing his status and the country's historical foundations.'[10] The fact that Scott could describe Flinders as 'an Englishman of the very best type,'[11] which is to say, a man of the very best type, and could 'celebrate Australia's good fortune to have been settled by "a race that knew how to woo her with affection and to conquer her with their science and their will"',[12] rather than one of the inferior European races, illustrates neatly the invisible blinkers that circumscribe the vision of all historical writers.

Nurungga man Professor Lester-Irabinna Rigney, in his Foreword to *Alas, for the Pelicans!: Flinders, Baudin and Beyond*, writes that 'the romantic view of colonial conquest of land and First Peoples' is quintessentially Australian, and 'derives from the legacy of colonial expeditions like those of Flinders and Baudin, and contributes to current understandings of what it means to be an Australian.'[13] These words, written in 2002, are not yet untrue. Rigney was generous enough to write that this book of essays and poems 'went beyond the politics' of the 'mischievous re-enactments' of the Flinders-Baudin encounter which saw 'facts ... passed over as the romantics gorge themselves on a feast of glorification.'[14] My own contributions to that volume were hardly iconoclastic: they were exercises in close reading arising from a fascination with the minutiae of Flinders' life as displayed in his journal, and his biography of his cat Trim, written during his post-exploration detention on Mauritius. My reckoning with Flinders' part in the imperial project and its impact on the Aboriginal peoples he encountered had to wait another fifteen years, when I co-edited *The First Wave: Exploring Early Coastal Contact History in Australia* with Danielle Clode.

Flinders in poetry

One of my contributions as an editor of *Alas, for the Pelicans!* was to curate a selection of poetry which is interleaved with the essays and allowed more or less to speak for itself. The poems ranged from the ultra-romantic to the facetious. The earliest was from 1828, by Scottish poet James Montgomery, a contemporary of Flinders. In what must have been one of the very first literary responses to Flinders writings, Montgomery takes as his cue Flinders' description of the pelicans on Kangaroo Island, spinning Flinders' 200 words of prose out into an epic religious poem of nine cantos dealing with evolution and creation, of which we extracted 80 lines or so – the section which deals most directly with the pelicans. Flinders himself does not figure in the poem, however. More than one hundred years later, South Australian poet Rex Ingamells reflected on the cost of the colonial project in 'Colonization' (1935). A long poem – covering six pages in our book – it charts the history of Adelaide from the day in late March 1802 when Matthew Flinders passed down the east coast of St Vincent's Gulf:

> *I stand upon this height that Flinders named*
> *And charted during his great voyaging. [...]*
> *For ages without name and without number,*
> *The southern hills had viewed the sail-less seas;*

> *Aeons had passed by like an easy slumber ...*
> *Seclusion wrapped the aborigines;*
> *No more ingenuous people lived than these.*[15]

Ingamells' poem explicitly counts the cost of the 'great voyaging' on 'a happy folk who loved the wind and sun, the rain / the wide-eyed stars, the bushland flowers'.[16] Romantic as this picture of pre-settlement Indigenous life is, it at least gives an alternative view, which must have seemed radical in its day, to the prevailing romanticisation of European settlement, and foreshadowed more matter-of-fact works like David Reiter's 'Mr Flinders and the Aborigines' (1994) and Patricia Austin's 'Matthew Flinders Landing on Bribie Island' (1993).

Other poems we included in the book concentrate on Flinders' personal life. Flinders' long separation from his new bride and his early and painful death inevitably inspired poetry across the generations. Jeff Guess's 1991 poem 'Death of Matthew Flinders' reflects on Flinders' own romanticism:

> *Even as an eager if a slight young man*
> *sailing out of the romance*
> *of Defoe's prose in a leaky decayed ship –*
> *he should have seen the death in that.*[17]

This is one of several poems by Guess, a well-respected poet of the present generation, in response to Flinders' life and work, which in their economy of expression are more likely to appeal to modern readers than Bernard Ingleby's 1913 version of 'The Death of Flinders' – 'Come wife, your hand! Worn little hand!' – with its dramatic ellipses and exclamatory style.

Flinders in fiction

Miles Franklin, in her inimitable style, called Flinders 'one of my pets in our early scene.'[18] In 1956, reflecting on Ernestine Hill's highly successful novel *My Love Must Wait* (1941), she wrote that Matthew Flinders was the ideal subject for Hill: 'a genius in navigation, so gallant, so young, so delayed in love, so thwarted in career, till death and honours reached him together, his story is deep in our affections.'[19] However, she privately deprecated the novel for being inaccurate and mushy.[20]

Hill's novel, because of its popularity and its broad canvas, has had a lasting effect on the image of Flinders in the broader Australian culture. Her Flinders is based on extensive archival research but she managed to elide inconvenient facts, such as that he had contracted venereal disease in Tahiti[21] – her teenage Flinders was 'shy of tar-brush charms' and 'scandalized' by suggestions that Captain Cook had had sexual relations with Tahitian women: 'such feet of clay were not for the world's appointed.'[22]

I personally find Hill's version of Flinders' life, though roughly accurate, rather overblown. A recent depiction of him is more to my taste. Catherine McKinnon's 2017 novel *Storyland* is built on an unusual pattern, unlike anything I have encountered before. It is not unprecedented to use a novel's geographical setting as the constant, while time and characters vary. McKinnon's variation on this is to nest the stories inside one another. The section titled 'Will Martin' is the base of the pyramid, which is constructed on the area around Lake Illawarra on the south coast of New South Wales.

Young Will Martin was a historical figure, one of the bit-players of history. He was George Bass's servant and accompanied Bass, with Flinders, on the Tom Thumb voyages. The reader is immediately captured by the voice of this fifteen-year-old lad from two centuries back, and then drawn further into the story by the vivid and dramatic narration and the gently acute portrayal of the two towering heroes of history who were, at this stage, young men out to prove their mettle as explorers and adventurers.

In McKinnon's version, the stereotypes are in the mind of the main character, while Hill's coquettish Frenchwomen and whining Arabs are created by the narrator, and behind the narrator, the implied author.

Conclusion

What is the harm when romanticism creeps into accounts of the lives of historical figures and they are seen in a heroic light? After all, some kind of romanticisation is perhaps inherent in all narrative, and it can even emerge from the most prosaic of record-keeping. When I was reading the new edition of Flinders' *Investigator* log, I came upon a list of items taken on board ship, including '2 horizons of quicksilver' (AC 1: 138). This excited my imagination and, although I am not prone to writing poetry myself, I suggested in a Facebook post that there was surely a poem in that. Robert Taylor rose to the challenge with a 'found poem', 'Journey to Hydrargyros', which was published in *Transnational Literature* in May 2016. This poem's genesis demonstrates the link between the urge to find an explanation and the creation of the romantic image. Taylor's poem begins

> *A shallow trough of quicksilver*
> *to form an artificial horizon, used for observing altitudes.*[23]

This string of words forms the definition of 'quicksilver horizon' on a website called 'defineitfast'. Merely taking these words and breaking them into two lines creates a poetic object, which is then reinforced with the remainder of the poem, created entirely from extracts from previously published works.

But what is lost? All narrative is, of course, a process of selection: the more one knows about a subject, the less likely one is to be impressed or charmed by a romantic description of it. Something of this is no doubt behind Miles Franklin's approach to *My Love Must Wait*: 'I have forced myself to read only a few chap[ter]s so far because it is so lush that I mistrust its scholarship and go gingerly across its flowery marshes fearing quicksands.'[24] The reviewer for the *Bulletin* noted that 'Behind all Australian fiction of this kind there seems to lie a patriotic impulse as well as an artistic.'[25] The novel's publication during the Second World War is relevant here. Eleanor Hogan notes that, although Hill 'protested that "every fact can be verified"', she 'romanticised' Flinders, 'downplaying more negative aspects of his personality and exploits.'[26] Hill defended her approach: 'if we did dramatise our country a little more for the million, it would do us much good.'[27] Like Scott's biography, published just as the First World War began, Hill's novel recruited Flinders as a national hero, someone for Australians to emulate and admire.

During times of national emergency, scrupulous accuracy and complexity are the earliest casualties. Rigney writes, 'History has no conventional climax in which the crisis is resolved.'[28] The urge to create a story from the past creates fictional closures, like 'discovery' and 'victory', but the after-effects of events persist long after the triumphant announcements are made. The consequences for the Australian

Aboriginal peoples of the European settlement, foreshadowed by the visits of explorers like Flinders and his colleagues, continue to this day in institutionalised racism and dispossession, about which there is nothing romantic.

Another loss is the quotidian nature of normal life, the ups and downs which we all experience and which can be traced in journals and letters of historic figures. Alexander Hutchison Barrowman, in his poem 'Matthew Flinders', writes that during his detention on Mauritius Flinders had 'none his sad lot to share'[29] – but we know from his journal that he had many friends and an active social life during these years. This kind of romanticism sets the famous people of the past in a kind of fantasy world rather than encouraging us to understand that they lived as we live, from day to day, with ups and downs, good days and bad days. Where is the harm in that, though? Recently at a dinner, I was speaking about Flinders' last months and describing his journal's charting of his painful fatal illness, and someone commented that I was visibly moved when talking about this. Where is the line drawn between expressing emotion in this way, and romanticising an historical person? Surely empathy with the sufferings of others is important: the danger arises when it becomes exceptionalism.

But one can't write about every person in history who has lived and died – it is just not possible. Perhaps the most damaging consequence of creating romantic heroes is the reaction it can generate. Hero status encourages iconoclasm. The more statues that are raised to the heroes of the past – the more they are held out as exceptional figures who did only exceptional, heroic deeds, the more likely they are to be attacked and their achievements denigrated. If we could see the men and women of the historic past as human beings with complex lives and contradictory impulses, who did not always act in their own best interests, let alone that of others they encountered, we would surely have a richer picture of the past and a better guide for how to proceed in the future.

Flinders' own romantic notions of the figures of the past and his urge to emulate them drove him to some extreme acts of heroism, some of which succeeded in their aims, while others failed. Would his life have been more successful in any terms – his own, or those of his admirers or his critics – without this driving force? I suspect that everyone will have their own answer to that question. His sense of heroism was, it can be seen from his personal writings, tempered by myriad other more practical considerations – financial necessity, personal loyalties, ambition, scientific curiosity. My answer is that I simply don't know – perhaps because I know too much about Flinders to think that I can ever know everything about him.

Bibliography

Archives
Flinders Papers: Letters and Documents about the Explorer Matthew Flinders (1774–1814). National Maritime Museum. Online. **[FPNMM]** flinders.rmg.co.uk/

James Fairfax Matthew Flinders Electronic Archive. State Library of New South Wales. Online. **[JFMFA]** https://collection.sl.nsw.gov.au/record/92eJV8NY

Includes (*inter alia*):
- Flinders, Matthew. Private Letters, vol. 1, 1801–1806.
- Flinders, Matthew. Private Letters, vol. 2, July 1806-Nov. 1810.
- Flinders, Matthew. Private Letters, vol. 3, 1810–1814, with letters from Ann Flinders, 1814–1821.

Flinders Collection, Special Collections, Flinders University Library.

Australian Manuscripts Collection. State Library of Victoria.

Sir John Franklin Collection, Scott Polar Research Institute, University of Cambridge.

Other Primary Sources
Banks, Joseph. *The Endeavour Journal of Sir Joseph Banks, 1768–1771*, transcribed from the manuscript held at the State Library of New South Wales. Sydney: University of Sydney Library, 1997. Web. http://setis.library.usyd.edu.au/ozlit.

Brown, Robert. *Nature's Investigator: The Diary of Robert Brown in Australia, 1801–1805* compiled by T.G. Vallance, D.T. Moore & E.W. Groves. Canberra: ABRS, 2001.

Chambers, Neil, ed. *The Letters of Sir Joseph Banks: A Selection, 1768–1820*. London: Imperial College Press, 2000.

Clarke, James Stanier. 'Biographical Memoir of Captain Matthew Flinders, RN.' *Naval Chronicle for 1814* vol. xxxii. London: Joyce Gould, 1814.

Cook, James. *The Journals of Captain James Cook on his Voyages of Discovery:*

The Voyage of the Endeavour 1768–1771 edited by J.C. Beaglehole. Cambridge: Cambridge University Press, 1955.

Cook, James and James King. *A Voyage to the Pacific Ocean ... for making Discoveries in the Northern Hemisphere ...* 2nd ed., Vol. 1. London: Nicol, 1785.

Flinders, Matthew (Snr.). *Gratefull to Providence: The Diary and Accounts of Matthew Flinders, Surgeon, Apothecary and Man-Midwife 1775–1802* edited by Martyn Beardsley and Nicholas Bennett. 2 Vols. Woodbridge: Boydell Press, 2009. **[GP]**

Flinders, Matthew. *Australia Circumnavigated: The Voyage of Matthew Flinders in HMS Investigator, 1801–1803* edited by Kenneth Morgan. 2 Vols. London: Hakluyt Society, 2016. **[AC]**

Flinders, Matthew. 'Biographical Tribute to the Memory of Trim: Isle of France, 1809.' *Overland* (Winter 1973).

Flinders, Matthew. *A Biographical Tribute to the Memory of Trim* with an introduction by Stephen Murray-Smith, Sydney: John Ferguson, 1985.

Flinders, Matthew. Narrative of expeditions along the coast of New South Wales, for the further discovery of its harbours from the year 1795 to 1799. (FLI09a) The Flinders Papers: Letters and Documents about the Explorer Matthew Flinders (1774–1814). National Maritime Museum. Online. flinders.rmg.co.uk/

Flinders, Matthew. *Matthew Flinders: Personal Letters from an Extraordinary Life* edited by Paul Brunton. Sydney: Hordern House, 2002. **[PL]**

Flinders, Matthew. *Private Journal 1803–1814* ed. Anthony J. Brown and Gillian Dooley. Adelaide: Friends of the State Library of SA, 2005. **[PJ]**

Flinders, Matthew. Narrative of expeditions along the coast of New South Wales, for the further discovery of its harbours from the year 1795 to 1799. FLI09a. *The Flinders Papers: Letters and Documents about the Explorer Matthew Flinders (1774–1814).* National Maritime Museum. Online. flinders.rmg.co.uk/

Flinders, Matthew. *A Voyage to Terra Australis.* 2 Vols. London: Nicol, 1814. **[VTA]**

Flinders, Matthew and Ann Flinders. 'My Evening Song'. Handwritten sheet music and words held in Flinders Papers, National Maritime Museum, Greenwich, UK (FLI/25).

Flinders, Matthew, Philippa Sandall and Gillian Dooley. *Trim: The Cartographer's Cat.* Oxford: Adlard Coles, 2019. **[TCC]**

McCrae, George Gordon, ed. 'Historical Sketch of Captain Matthew Flinders', *Victorian Geographical Journal* 28, 1911.

Milius, Pierre Bernard. *Pierre Bernard Milius: Last Commander of the Baudin Expedition: The Journal 1800–1804*, translated from the French and annotated by Kate Pratt; edited by Peter Hambly with an introduction by Anthony J. Brown. Canberra: NLA Publishing, 2014.

Retter, Catharine and Shirley Sinclair, eds. *Letters to Ann: The Love Story of Matthew Flinders and Ann Chappelle.* Sydney: Angus and Robertson, 2001.

Rivière, M. Serge., ed. *My Dear Friend: The Flinders-Pitot Correspondence (1806–1814) at the Carnegie Library, Mauritius*. Curepipe: Editions Le Printemps, 2003.

Stokes, John Lort. *Discoveries in Australia*. Project Gutenberg. https://www.gutenberg.org/files/12146/12146-h/12146-h.htm

Tyler, Isabella. 'Biographical Outline of Capt. & Mrs Flinders 1852.' Flinders Papers, 60/017, FLI 107, National Maritime Museum, Greenwich.

Secondary Sources

Anderson, Kay and Colin Perrin. '"The Miserablest People in the World": Race, Humanism and the Australian Aborigine.' *The Australian Journal of Anthropology* 18:1 (2007).

Baker, Sidney. *My Own Destroyer*. Sydney: Currawong, 1962.

Barber, Marcus. 'Coastal conflicts and reciprocal relations: Encounters between Yolŋgu people and commercial fishermen in Blue Mud Bay, north-east Arnhem Land.' *The Australian Journal of Anthropology* 21.3 (2010).

Barnes, Robert. *An Unlikely Leader: The Life and Times of Captain John Hunter*. Sydney: Sydney University Press, 2009.

Bastian, Josephine. *A Passion for Exploring New Countries: Matthew Flinders and George Bass*. North Melbourne: Australian Scholarly Publishing, 2016.

Bastin, Giselle et al., eds. *Journeying and Journalling: Creative and Critical Meditations on Travel Writing*. Adelaide: Wakefield Press, 2010.

Carter, Harold B. *Sir Joseph Banks (1743–1820): a guide to the biographical and bibliographical sources*. Winchester: St Paul's Bibliographies in association with the British Museum [Natural History], 1987).

Chittleborough, Anne et al., eds. *Alas, for the Pelicans! Flinders, Baudin and Beyond: Essays and Poems*. Adelaide, Wakefield Press, 2002.

Clendinnen, Inga. 'Spearing the Governor.' *Australian Historical Studies* 118 (2002).

Clode, Danielle and Carole E. Harrison. 'Precedence and Posterity: Patterns of Publishing from French Scientific Expeditions to the Pacific (1785–1840).' *Australian Journal of French Studies* 50.3 (2013).

Clode, Danielle and Gillian Dooley, eds. *The First Wave: Exploring Early Coastal Contact History in Australia*. Adelaide: Wakefield Press, 2019.

Croll, R.H. 'Matthew Flinders: Navigator and Scientist: His Services to Australia.' *Argus*, 7 November 1925, p. 10.

Dooley, Gillian. '"These Happy Effects on the Character of the British Sailor": Family Life in the Sea Songs of the Late Georgian Period.' In *Keeping Family in an Age of Long Distance Trade, Imperial Expansion, and Exile, 1550–1850* edited by Heather Dalton. Amsterdam University Press, 2020.

Douglas, Bronwen. 'Slippery Word, Ambiguous Praxis: "Race" and Late-18th-Century Voyagers in Oceania.' *The Journal of Pacific History* 41:1 (2006).

Duffy, Michael. *Man of Honour: John Macarthur – Duellist, Rebel, Founding Father*.

Sydney: Macmillan, 2003.
Estensen, Miriam. *The Life of George Bass*. Sydney: Allen & Unwin, 2005.
Estensen, Miriam. *The Life of Matthew Flinders*. Sydney: Allen & Unwin, 2002.
Fornasiero, F. Jean, John West-Sooby, and Peter Monteath. *Encountering Terra Australis: the Australian voyages of Nicolas Baudin and Matthew Flinders*. Adelaide: Wakefield Press, 2004.
Franklin, Miles. *Laughter, Not for a Cage*. Sydney: Angus and Robertson, 1956.
Franklin, Miles. *My Congenials: Miles Franklin and Friends in Letters* ed. Jill Roe, 2nd edition. Sydney: Angus and Robertson, 2010.
Gascoigne, John. *Joseph Banks and the English Enlightenment: Useful Knowledge and Polite Culture*. Cambridge, Cambridge University Press, 1994.
Gertsakis, Elizabeth. 'The Lost Letters of Ann Chappelle Flinders.' *Alas, for the Pelicans!: Flinders, Baudin and Beyond*. Adelaide: Wakefield Press, 2002.
Hill, Ernestine. *My Love Must Wait*. Sydney: Angus and Robertson, 1941.
Hogan, Eleanor. *Into the Loneliness*. Sydney: New South, 2021.
Holmes, Richard. *Age of Wonder*. New York: Pantheon Books, 2008.
Ingleton, Geoffrey C. *Matthew Flinders: Navigator and Chartmaker*. Guildford: Genesis Publications, 1986. **[MFNC]**
Joppien, Rüdiger and Neil Chambers. 'The Scholarly Library and Collections of Knowledge of Sir Joseph Banks.' In *Libraries Within the Library: The Origins of the British Library's Printed Collections* edited by Giles Mandelbrote and Barry Taylor. London: British Library, 2009.
Karntin, Jack Spear and Peter Sutton. 'Dutchmen at Cap Keerweer.' In *This is What Happened: Historical Narratives by Aborigines* edited by Luise Hercus and Peter Sutton. Canberra: Australian Institute of Aboriginal Studies, 1986.
Langham, W.H. 'Matthew Flinders: The Indefatigable.' *Register* (Adelaide: South Australia), 16 March 1925, p. 8.
Mack, James. *Matthew Flinders 1774–1814*. Melbourne: Nelson, 1966.
Morgan, Kenneth. *Matthew Flinders: Maritime Explorer of Australia*. London: Bloomsbury, 2016.
Oliver, Douglas. *Return to Tahiti: Bligh's Second Breadfruit Voyage*. Melbourne: Miegunyah Press, 1988.
Pulugurtha, Nishi, ed. *Across and Beyond*. Burdwan: Avanel Press, 2020.
'Rear Admiral Phillip Parker King', Biography. *Navy: Serving Australia with Pride*. Online. https://www.navy.gov.au/biography/rear-admiral-phillip-parker-king
Rivière, Serge M. and Kumari R. Issur, eds. *Baudin-Flinders dans l'océan Indien: Voyages, découvertes, rencontre*. Paris: L'Harmattan, 2006.
Russell, Roger W., ed. *Matthew Flinders: The Ifs of History*. Adelaide: Flinders University, 1979.
Said, Edward. *Orientalism*. London: Penguin, 1985.
Scott, Ernest. *The Life of Matthew Flinders* with Introduction by Stuart Macintyre. Sydney: Angus and Robertson, 2001.

Scott, Kim. 'Can You Anchor a Shimmering Nation State via Regional Indigenous Roots?: Kim Scott talks to Anne Brewster about *That Deadman Dance*.' *Cultural Studies Review* 18.1 (March 2012).

Shellam, Tiffany. 'Tropes of Friendship, Undercurrents of Fear: Alternative Emotions on the "Friendly Frontier".' *Westerly* 57.2 (November 2012).

Simmonds, Alecia. 'Between Sentiment and Sea: The Meaning of Friendship in the Letters of Matthew Flinders.' *The Great Circle* 38:2 (2016).

Veth, Peter, Peter Sutton and Margo Neale, eds. *Strangers on the Shore: Early Coastal Contacts in Australia*. Canberra: National Museum of Australia, 2008.

West-Sooby, John and Jean Fornasiero. 'Matthew Flinders through French Eyes: Nicolas Baudin's Lessons from Encounter Bay.' *Journal of Pacific History* 52:1 (2017).

Notes

Introduction
1. I will use the name 'Mauritius' as a general rule in this book, unless there is a particular reason to refer to the island by its French name.
2. George Gordon McCrae, 'Historical Sketch of Captain Matthew Flinders', *Victorian Geographical Journal* 28 (1911) 13.

Chapter 1 ~ Matthew Flinders: The Man behind the Map of Australia
1. Presented at the Royal Society of Victoria, 28 August 2014.
2. W.H. Langham, 'Matthew Flinders: The Indefatigable', *Register* (Adelaide: SA), 16 March 1925, 8.
3. Ernest Scott, 'Preface to Original Edition', *The Life of Matthew Flinders* xv.
4. R.H. Croll, 'Matthew Flinders: Navigator and Scientist: His Services to Australia', *Argus* 7 November 1925, 10.
5. Sidney Baker, *My Own Destroyer* 74.
6. Ingleton attributes the anonymous 'Historical Sketch of the Life of the late Captain Flinders' published in Volume 28 of the *Victorian Geographical Journal*, 1910–1911, to Samuel Flinders, and this is the basis for his statement about Samuel's opinion of Matthew.
7. James Stanier Clarke, 'Biographical Memoir of Captain Matthew Flinders, RN', *Naval Chronicle for 1814*, vol. xxxii, 178n.
8. Commodore Thomas Pasley was the commander of Flinders' first ship, later Admiral Sir Thomas Pasley (1734–1808).
9. See for example his letter to Governor King quoted in Miriam Estensen, *The Life of George Bass* 176.
10. Sir Joseph Banks, Letter to Ann Flinders, 22 May 1807, Chambers, *The Letters of Sir Joseph Banks* 281.
11. Estensen 5.
12. Ann Lisette Flinders Petrie, 'Flinders – the Family' in Russell 25.
13. James Mack, *Matthew Flinders* 239.
14. Matthew Flinders, Narrative of expeditions along the coast of New South Wales, for the further discovery of its harbours from the year 1795 to 1799. FLI09a (FPNMM).
15. T.M. Perry, 'Matthew Flinders – the Man', Russell 55.
16. Pierre Bernard Milius, 168.
17. Jean Fornasiero, John West-Sooby and Peter Monteath, *Encountering Terra Australis* 159.

18   Sidney Baker, *My Own Destroyer* 74.
19   John Franklin, Letter to Ann Flinders, 27 December 1842. (FPNMM)
20   Scott, *The Life of Matthew Flinders* 298.
21   John Franklin, Letter to Ann Flinders, 27 December 1842. (FPNMM)

Chapter 2 ~ Matthew Flinders' *Private Journal*

1   This chapter is based on two essays: 'Matthew Flinders' *Private Journal*: A Private Journey' first appeared in *Journeying and Journalling* ed. Giselle Bastin, Kate Douglas, Michele McCrea, Michael X. Savvas. Adelaide: Wakefield Press, 2010; and 'Getting to Know Matthew: A Personal Account of Editing Flinders' *Private Journal*', a paper presented (in absentia) to Encounter 2003 Conference, University of Mauritius, 20–23 October, 2003, and published in *Baudin-Flinders dans l'océan Indien: Voyages, découvertes, rencontre* (Paris: L'Harmattan, 2006).
2   Miriam Estensen, *The Life of Matthew Flinders* 477.
3   Michael Duffy, *Man of Honour: John Macarthur* 12–13.
4   Owen to Flinders, 1 August 1810. (FPNMM)
5   Owen to Flinders, 7 January 1812. (FPNMM)
6   Catherine Retter and Shirley Sinclair, *Letters to Ann* 113.
7   Stephen Milazzo, 'Flinders' Last Illness: The Final Five Months of the Journal, February to July 1814: A Medical Interpretation', PJ 511.
8   Estensen, *Matthew Flinders* 477.

Chapter 3 ~ From Timor to Mauritius: Matthew Flinders' Island Identity

1   This chapter was written for the SPACLALS conference held at the University of New England campus in Parramatta in February 2018, and was published online in *Café Dissensus* 45 (2018) and in *Across and Beyond* edited by Nishi Pulugurtha (Avanel Press, 2020).
2   Matthew Flinders, *Voyage to Terra Australis* Vol. 1, i.
3   Clarke, 'Biographical Memoir of Captain Matthew Flinders, R.N.,' *Naval Chronicle* 32 (1814): 178n.
4   Retter and Sinclair have transcribed this word as 'insulted' but a check of the manuscript at the National Maritime Museum, Greenwich confirms that Brunton's reading is correct and the word is 'insulated'. My thanks to Martin Salmon, Archivist at NMM, for checking this.
5   McCrae, 'Historical Sketch' 29–30.
6   Morgan has 'exerted' here but 'excited' seems more likely and the MS is unclear.

Chapter 4 ~ 'To perfect the discovery of that extensive country': Matthew Flinders' achievements in the exploration of Australia

1   This chapter is based on a talk given at a symposium on Flinders in Portsmouth in October 2010 commemorating the bicentenary of his arrival back in England. The text was published in 2013 on the British Naval History website which was subsequently incorporated into Global Maritime History – globalmaritimehistory.com
2   Matthew Flinders, Private Letters, vol. 3, 1810–1814, with letters from Ann Flinders, 1814–1821, 269 (JFMFA).
3   'Rear Admiral Phillip Parker King'.
4   Miriam Estensen, *The Life of Matthew Flinders* 479.

Chapter 5 ~ Matthew Flinders in South Australia, January to April 1802

1. This chapter is based on a talk given at the Proclamation Day Luncheon of the SA Pioneers' Association, 28 December 2020.
2. Matthew Flinders, letter to Ann Flinders, 31 May 1802. Flinders Papers, FLI25. (FPNMM)
3. Adelaide in South Australia regularly appears near the top of the *Economist* 'Global Liveability Index'. In 2021, Adelaide ranked third, after Auckland and Osaka.
4. The editor of *Australian Circumnavigated* (Kenneth Morgan) translates Flinders' Latin phrase as 'May their bones rest in peace, O barbarian!' I would venture: 'Let their bones rest in peace, Barbarian!'
5. Quoted in John West-Sooby & Jean Fornasiero. 'Matthew Flinders through French Eyes,' 9.

Chapter 6 ~ Matthew Flinders and the limits of empathy: first encounters with Aboriginal peoples

1. An edited version of this chapter was published in *The First Wave: Exploring Early Coastal Contact History in Australia* edited by Danielle Clode and Gillian Dooley (Adelaide: Wakefield Press, 2019).
2. Richard Holmes, *Age of Wonder* xvi.
3. Holmes xvi.
4. Matthew Flinders, Letter to Ann Chappelle, 16 March 1799. Flinders Papers, National Maritime Museum.
5. Holmes, xvi.
6. Lou Agosta, 'Empathy and Sympathy in Ethics,' *Internet Encyclopedia of Philosophy*, Online www.ieputm.edu/emp-symp/ , 30 March 2016.
7. 'The eighteenth century texts of David Hume and Adam Smith used the word "sympathy" but not "empathy", although the conceptual distinction marked by empathy was doing essential work in their writings.' (Agosta, 'Empathy').
8. Samuel Johnson, *History of Rasselas, Prince of Abyssinia*. Chapter 2.
9. Frank Kermode, *The Sense of an Ending*.
10. See Gillian Dooley, 'My Evening Song', *Alas, for the Pelicans!*
11. Flinders, *Australian Circumnavigated* Vol. 1, 356.
12. Quoted in Douglas Oliver, *Return to Tahiti* 34–5.
13. Jack Spear Karntin and Peter Sutton, 'Dutchmen at Cap Keerweer', *This is What Happened* 91.
14. James Cook, *The Journals of Captain James Cook* 399.
15. Kay Anderson and Colin Perrin, 'The Miserablest People in the World' 23.
16. Joseph Banks, *The Endeavour Journal of Sir Joseph Banks*. Emphasis mine.
17. Edward Said, *Orientalism* 7.
18. Holmes 20.
19. John Gascoigne, *Joseph Banks and the English Enlightenment* 263–4.
20. Banks.
21. Karntin and Sutton 92.
22. Matthew Flinders, 'Narrative of expeditions along the coast of New South Wales for the further discovery of its harbours from the year 1795 to 1799', 7. (FPNMM)
23. Flinders, 'Narrative' 9.
24. Flinders, 'Narrative' 13.
25. Flinders, 'Narrative' 15.
26. For more information about Bungaree, see Mark Dunn's chapter 'Exploring Connections: Bungaree and connections in the colonial Hunter Valley' in *The First Wave*.

27 Peter Sutton and Peter Veth, 'Introduction and Themes,' Veth et al. (eds), *Strangers on the Shore* 3–4.
28 Peter Sutton, 'Stories about Feeling: Dutch-Australian Contact in Cape York Peninsula, 1606–1756,' Veth et al. (eds), *Strangers on the Shore:* 43.
29 Cook 396.
30 Sutton and Veth 4.
31 Inga Clendinnen, 'Spearing the Governor,' *Australian Historical Studies* 118 (2002) 158.
32 Although many of my sources have used the alternative spelling of 'Nyungar'. I have used the spelling 'Noongar' in this paper. I am basing my choice on the official website of the South West Aboriginal Land and Sea Council http://www.noongar.org.au/
33 Len Collard and Dave Palmer, 'Looking for the residents of *Terra Australis:* the importance of Nyungar in early European coastal exploration,' in Veth et al. (eds.), *Strangers on the Shore:* 182.
34 Tiffany Shellam, 'Tropes of Friendship, Undercurrents of Fear: Alternative Emotions on the "Friendly Frontier",' *Westerly* 57.2 (November 2012) 22.
35 Kim Scott, 'Can You Anchor a Shimmering Nation State via Regional Indigenous Roots?: Kim Scott talks to Anne Brewster about *That Deadman Dance*', *Cultural Studies Review* 18.1 (March 2012) 231.
36 Sutton and Veth 2.
37 Collard and Palmer 195.
38 The identification of these people as Djalkiripuyngu, or 'footprint people', is based on the website 'Homelands and their Future: A Perspective from Bäniyala' – https://www.cdu.edu.au/northern-institute/events/homelands-and-their-future
39 Marcus Barber, 'Coastal conflicts and reciprocal relations: Encounters between Yolŋu people and commercial fishermen in Blue Mud Bay, north-east Arnhem Land', *The Australian Journal of Anthropology*, 21.3 (2010) 298–314. 298.
40 Barber 300.
41 John Whitewood, the Master's Mate, apparently recovered from his wounds: he is listed among the men discharged from the *Investigator* on 19 July 1803 in Port Jackson.
42 McCrae, 'Historical Sketch of the Life of the late Captain Flinders' 29–30.
43 I am indebted to Commander Peter Ashley, RN, for providing this information. Personal communication (email) 1 May 2016.
44 Robert Brown, *Nature's Investigator* 348, n2. Peter Good was the gardener on the *Investigator* and assisted Brown.
45 Bronwen Douglas, 'Slippery Word, Ambiguous Praxis: "Race" and Late-18th-Century Voyagers in Oceania', *The Journal of Pacific History* 41.1 (2006) 1–29.

Chapter 7 – Matthew Flinders of Donington

1 This chapter is based on talks presented to the Marion Historical Society (South Australia) in July 2020, and the Spalding Gentlemen's Society (UK) in February 2021.
2 See, for example, his letter to Elizabeth Flinders, 13 April 1806, State Library of Victoria Manuscript Collection, MS Sequence, Box 2/7.
3 Ann Flinders to Thomi Pitot, 15 December 1814. Matthew Flinders – Private Letters, vol.3, 1810–1814, with letters from Ann Flinders, 1814–1821. (JFMFA)
4 Ann Flinders to John Hursthouse, 18 March 1819. Matthew Flinders – Private Letters, vol.3, 1810–1814, with letters from Ann Flinders, 1814–1821. (JFMFA)
5 Matthew Flinders, Letter to Thomi Pitot, 22 October 1805. Matthew Flinders, Private letters, vol. 1, 1801–1806, p. 98. (JFMFA)
6 Matthew Flinders, Letter to Elizabeth Flinders, 13 April 1806. Matthew Flinders, Private letters, vol. 1, 1801–1806, p. 146. (JFMFA)

Chapter 8 ~ Ann Chappelle of Partney

1. Ernest Scott, *The Life of Matthew Flinders* 298.
2. See 'Flinders – The Family' by Ann Lisette Flinders Petrie, in *Matthew Flinders: The Ifs of History* (Adelaide: Flinders University, 1979) for details of the Chappell or Chappelle family. Some authors have given Ann's year of birth as 1772 but this seems to be an error.
3. Isabella Tyler, 'Biographical Outline of Capt. & Mrs Flinders 1852', 60/017, FLI 107 (FPNMM). Quoted in Estensen, 154.
4. Matthew Flinders, letter to Ann Flinders, 31 May 1802. (FPNMM)
5. Gill (35–40) uses the Flinders marriage as an example of the importance of letters in maintaining intimate and familial relations at a distance.
6. Retter and Sinclair, 41.
7. Flinders, 'Handwritten Sheet Music and Words'. (FPNMM)
8. Matthew Flinders, letter to Ann Flinders, 5 January 1807. Matthew Flinders: Private Letters Vol.2 July 1806-Nov. 1810, p. 41. (JFMFA)
9. For a discussion of these songs, see my chapter '"These Happy Effects on the Character of the British Sailor": Family Life in the Sea Songs of the Late Georgian Period' in *Keeping Family in an Age of Long Distance Trade, Imperial Expansion, and Exile, 1550–1850* edited by Heather Dalton (Amsterdam University Press, 2020). The section of this chapter on the Flinders song is extracted from this chapter, p. 246–247.
10. This correspondence remains in a private collection but is discussed and quoted in Elizabeth Gertsakis, 'The Lost Letters of Ann Chappelle Flinders', in *Alas, for the Pelicans!* (Adelaide: Wakefield Press, 2002).
11. Ann Flinders, letter to George Pearson, 20 August 1830, quoted in Gertsakis, 106.
12. Tyler, quoted in Estensen, 157.
13. Matthew Flinders Letter book. (JFMFA)
14. Isabella Tyler to Matthew Flinders, 10 July 1810, FL/I01. (FPNMM)
15. Anne Flinders, quoted in Scott, *The Life of Matthew Flinders* 286.
16. Ann Flinders to Thomi Pitot, 7 December 1814. Matthew Flinders – Private Letters, vol.3, 1810–1814, with letters from Ann Flinders, 1814–1821. (JFMFA)
17. Ann Lisette Flinders Petrie, 'Flinders – the Family', in *Matthew Flinders: the Ifs of History* (Adelaide: Flinders University, 1979) 23.

Chapter 9 ~ Matthew Flinders and his Friends

1. 'Biographical Memoir of Captain Matthew Flinders, RN', *Naval Chronicle for 1814* vol. xxxii (London: Joyce Gould 1814) note, p. 178.
2. Scott, *The Life of Matthew Flinders* 298.
3. Alecia Simmons, 'Between Sentiment and Sea: The Meaning of Friendship in the Letters of Matthew Flinders', *The Great Circle* 38:2 (2016) 38.
4. Matthew Flinders, Letter to Thomas Franklin, 6 July 1806. Matthew Flinders, Private letters, vol. 1, 1801–1806, p. 163. (JFMFA)
5. This section is based on a talk given to the Sir Joseph Banks Society, Lincoln, UK, in October 2016.
6. Trailblazers Exhibition: Joseph Banks. Australian Museum. Online. https://australian.museum/about/history/exhibitions/trailblazers/joseph-banks/
7. Australian National Herbarium. Sir Joseph Banks (1743–1820). Online. https://www.anbg.gov.au/biography/banks-joseph.html
8. Kenneth Morgan, Matthew Flinders: Maritime Explorer of Australia (London: Bloomsbury, 2016) 13.
9. Morgan, Matthew Flinders 49.

10   Morgan, Matthew Flinders 54.
11   Flinders, Letter to Banks, 24 January 1801, Brunton 58.
12   Banks letter to Ann Flinders, 22 May 1807. *The Letters of Sir Joseph Banks: A Selection 1768–1829* edited by Neil Chambers (London: Imperial College Press, 2000) 281.
13   See Chapter 14, 'The Library at Soho Square', for a detailed discussion of Flinders' research for his *Voyage*.
14   Banks letter to John Barrow, 24 October 1810. Letters 297.
15   This section is based on my review of A Passion for Exploring New Countries: Matthew Flinders and George Bass by Josephine Bastian. Historical Records of Australian Science, 28:2 (2017) 196–196.
16   Bastian xi.
17   Bastian 51.
18   Bastian 51.
19   Bastian 153.
20   Bastian 51.
21   William Kent to Matthew Flinders, 17 September 1811, FL/I01. (FPNMM)
22   Matthew Flinders to Charles Desbassayns, 10 October 1807. Matthew Flinders: Private Letters Vol.2, July 1806-Nov. 1810. (JFMFA)
23   Matthew Flinders, Letter to Louise / Labauve d'Arifat, April 1813. Matthew Flinders – Private Letters, vol.3, 1810–1814, with letters from Ann Flinders, 1814–1821. S1/57, p. 227. (JFMFA)
24   Matthew Flinders to 'the captain or commander of any of His Majestys ships', 23 July 1806. Matthew Flinders: Private Letters Vol.2 July 1806-Nov. 1810. S1/56, p. 3. (JFMFA)
25   Matthew Flinders to Thomi Pitot, 4 September 1807, in *My Dear Friend: The Flinders-Pitot Correspondence (1806–1814) at the Carnegie Library, Mauritius* edited by Marc Serge Rivière (Curepipe: Editions Le Printemps, 2003), 18.
26   Ann Flinders to Thomi Pitot, 7 December 1814. Matthew Flinders – Private Letters, vol.3, 1810–1814, with letters from Ann Flinders, 1814–1821. S1/57, p. 283–284. (JFMFA)
27   This section is extracted from a short essay on the friendship between Flinders and Owen written at the request of Jane Merrill, the author of a forthcoming book on the Owen family of Campobello Island, Canada.
28   W.F. Owen to Matthew Flinders, 1 August 1810. (FPNMM)
29   W.F. Owen to Matthew Flinders, 10 September 1810. (FPNMM)
30   W.F. Owen to Matthew Flinders, 7 January 1812. (FPNMM)
31   Matthew Flinders to W.F. Owen, 22 February 1813. Matthew Flinders – Private Letters, vol.3, 1810–1814, with letters from Ann Flinders, 1814–1821. S1/57, p. 216–217. (JFMFA)
32   Ann Flinders to W.F. Owen, 29 July 1814. Matthew Flinders – Private Letters, vol.3, 1810–1814, with letters from Ann Flinders, 1814–1821. S1/57, p. 268. (JFMFA)

Chapter 10 ~ 'The sporting, affectionate, and useful companion of my voyages': Matthew Flinders and Trim

1   This chapter is partly drawn from my 2002 essay 'The Uses of Adversity' in *Alas, for the Pelicans!*, and the essay 'Matthew Flinders: Trim's Shipmate and Bedfellow' in *Trim: The Cartographer's Cat* (2019).
2   Samuel Richardson, letter to Miss Mulso, quoted in Miriam Allott (ed.), *Novelists on the Novel* (London: Routledge and Kegan Paul, 1959) 41.
3   George Eliot, quoted in Andrzej Gasiorek, *Post-War British Fiction: Realism and After* (1995) 10.

4 Stephen Murray-Smith, 'Introduction', *A Biographical Tribute to the Memory of Trim* by Matthew Flinders (Sydney: John Ferguson; Halstead Press, 1985) 5.
5 Perry, 3.
6 Jane Austen to Francis Austen, 25 September 1813, no. 90 of *Jane Austen's Letters*, ed. Deirdre Le Faye, 3rd ed. (Oxford: Oxford University Press, 1995) 229.
7 Perry, 2.
8 Quoted in Philippa Sandall, *Seafurrers: the ships' cats who lapped and mapped the world* (South Melbourne: Affirm Press, 2018) 14.
9 Bongaree (Bungaree, c.1775–1830) was the first Aboriginal to circumnavigate mainland Australia as far as we know. He was possibly more familiar with Australia's coastline than anyone else at the time, since he had taken part in more voyages of exploration than anyone else. He dipped his exploration toe in the water with Henry Waterhouse in the *Reliance* on a round trip to Norfolk Island in 1798. Then he sailed with Flinders in the *Norfolk* in 1799 to examine the northern parts of the coast of New South Wales, and in the *Investigator* "to explore the whole of the coasts" of New Holland (1802–03); with James Grant in the *Lady Nelson* to Port Macquarie (1804); and with Phillip Parker King in the *Mermaid* to survey Northwest Cape and Arnhem Land (1817). [Note from *Trim: the cartographer's cat*]
10 A "kid" is a small wooden tub for grog or rations.
11 George Gordon McCrae, 'Historical Sketch of Captain Matthew Flinders', *Victorian Geographical Journal* 28, 1911, p. 13.
12 Matthew Flinders Memorial Statue website
http://www.flindersmemorial.org/the-matthew-flinders-memorial-statue/
13 Murray-Smith, Introduction, 5.

Chapter 11 - Matthew Flinders, life-writer
1 This chapter is based on an online lecture given at Flinders University in May 2020.
2 This section is extracted from 'The Uses of Adversity: Matthew Flinders' Mauritius Writings' in *Alas, for the Pelicans!*.
3 Joan Didion, 'On Keeping a Notebook', *Slouching Towards Bethlehem* (New York: Farrar Strauss Giroux, 2008) 132–133.
4 Didion, 133.
5 See Chapter 13 for a discussion of the melody.
6 Flinders, 'Handwritten Sheet Music and Words'. (FPNMM)
7 Gillian Dooley, 'My Evening Song', *Alas, for the Pelicans!* 124.
8 In a letter of January 1807, Matthew wrote, 'thank thee, my love, for the verses thou hast sent me.' It is possible this was response to his song lyric.

Chapter 12 - Books in Matthew Flinders' life
1 Published in *Journal of Australian Studies*. Vol 90, 2007, 43–48.
2 'Biographical Memoir of Captain Matthew Flinders, R. N.' *Naval Chronicle* 32 (1814). This could be an intertextual reference to *Robinson Crusoe*, who on the first page of his account writes that his 'Inclination' for going to sea' was 'against the Will, nay the Commands of my Father, and against all the Entreaties and Perswasions of my Mother and other Friends.'
3 Matthew Flinders to Hydrographer, *Naval Chronicle*, 5 July 1814. Brunton 239.

Chapter 13 - Music in Matthew Flinders' Life
1 The article on which this chapter is based was first published in *The Britannia Naval Research Association 'The Journal'* 5:1 (2011) 9–13, and reprinted in The Friends of the State Library of SA journal *Bibliofile*, 13:2 (2012) 32–38.

2   National Maritime Museum, *Research guide M7: Music and the sea: Sources of information in the National Maritime Museum*. Online. Accessed 27 December 2010. <http://www.nmm.ac.uk/researchers/library/research-guides/general-maritime/research-guide-m7-music-and-the-sea-sources-of-information-in-the-national-maritime-museum>
3   Don Michael Randel, *The Harvard Dictionary of Music* (Cambridge, Mass: Harvard University Press, 2003) 320.
4   Quoted in Adam Carse, *Musical Wind Instruments* (New York: Da Capo Press, 1965) 87.
5   Robert Barnes, *An Unlikely Leader* 27.
6   Mike Parker, 'Tidings of my harp,' *Jane Austen's Regency World* (44: Mar/Apr 2010) 35.
7   Flinders, 'Handwritten Sheet Music and Words'. (FPNMM)
8   Ann Flinders to Thomi Pitot, 15 December 1814. Matthew Flinders – Private Letters, vol. 3, 1810–1814, with letters from Ann Flinders, 1814–1821, S1/57. (JFMFA)

Chapter 14 ~ The Library at Soho Square: Matthew Flinders, Sir Joseph Banks and the Publication of *A Voyage to Terra Australis* (1814)

1   First published in *Script & Print: Bulletin of the Bibliographical Society of Australia and New Zealand*, 41:3 (2017) 169–186.
2   Geoffrey Ingleton gives a full financial account of the publication of Flinders' *Voyage* in *MFNC* 421–3. A search of Abebooks.com in January 2018 shows two sets of all three volumes, including the large format atlas, are on the market for $135,000 & $87,500. The higher price is explained by an inscription in Flinders' handwriting in Volume 1 reading 'From the author', making it extremely rare if not unique. Sets of the two text volumes without the atlas sell for between $5,000 and $10,000. (Values in Australian dollars.)
3   Danielle Clode and Carol E. Harrison, 'Precedence and Posterity' 364–365.
4   Sir Joseph Banks, Letter to William Marsden 28 October 1810, quoted in Kenneth Morgan, *Matthew Flinders* 184.
5   Rüdiger Joppien and Neil Chambers, 'The Scholarly Library and Collections of Knowledge of Sir Joseph Banks', *Libraries Within the Library* 243.
6   Morgan, *Matthew Flinders* 185.
7   A list of the books Flinders consulted when writing his *Voyage* is given in an appendix to this chapter. Where possible, information about his source for each book is also provided.
8   James Cook and James King, *A Voyage to the Pacific Ocean* Vol. 1, i.
9   Cook and King, *Voyage*, iv.
10 Cook and King, *Voyage*, v.
11 Joppien and Chambers, *The Scholarly Library* 231.
12 Joppien and Chambers, *The Scholarly Library* 238.
13 Harold B. Carter, *Sir Joseph Banks* 226.
14 Edwin Rose, Personal Communication (Email), 19 September 2017.
15 Carter, *Joseph Banks*, 225.
16 Joppien and Chambers provide several examples of other such acknowledgements (234).
17 Matthew Flinders, Letter to Captain Farquarson Stuart, 11 September 1813. MS 13020, Australian Manuscripts Collection, State Library of Victoria.
18 John Franklin to Robert Brown, 9 June 1815, MS 248/296/5, Sir John Franklin Collection, Scott Polar Research Institute, University of Cambridge. Quoted in Morgan, *Matthew Flinders*, 195.
19 Franklin, 195.

20 Ann Flinders, Letter to G. Nicol, 22 September 1815. Matthew Flinders–Private Letters, vol. 3, 1810–1814, with letters from Ann Flinders, 1814–1821, S1/57. (JFMFA)
21 Morgan, *Matthew Flinders* 194.
22 George Nicol, Letter to Ann Flinders, 6 September 1815. (FPNMM)
23 Morgan, *Matthew Flinders* 49.
24 L. A. Gilbert, 'Sir Joseph Banks', *ADB Online* (http://adb.anu.edu.au/biography/banks-sir-joseph-1737).

Occasional pieces

1 Miriam Estensen, *The Life of Matthew Flinders* 5.
2 Matthew Flinders, Narrative of expeditions along the coast of New South Wales, for the further discovery of its harbours from the year 1795 to 1799, FLI/09a (FPNMM).
3 Jean Fornasiero, John West-Sooby and Peter Monteath, *Encountering Terra Australis* 159.
4 Published in *Australian Book Review*, No. 245, October 2002, p. 22–23.
5 Published in *Australian Book Review* no. 277 December-January 2005–2006, p. 48.
6 Published in *Australian Book Review* 310 (April 2009), p. 50.
7 Published in the *Adelaide Review* 22 September 2006, p. 16.
8 Published in *Journal of the Historical Society of SA*, 2016.
9 Brunton 69.
10 Published in *Australian Historical Studies*, 48:1 (2017), 122–124.
11 Last line of lyrics added by Gillian Dooley for this arrangement.

Epilogue

1 This paper was written for the conference of the Romantic Studies Association of Australasia, 'Romantic Generations', held at La Trobe University in December 2021.
2 J.M. Coetzee and Arabella Kurtz, *The Good Story* (London: Harvill Secker, 2015) 190–191.
3 James Stanier Clarke, 'Biographical Memoir of Captain Matthew Flinders', *Naval Chronicle* 32 (1814) 178.
4 Quoted in Gillian Dooley, 'My Evening Song', *Alas, for the Pelicans!* 124.
5 Ann Flinders, Letter to George Pearson, 20 August 1830, quoted in Elizabeth Gertsakis, 'The Lost Letters of Ann Chappelle Flinders' in *Alas, for the Pelicans!* 106.
6 John Franklin, Letter to Ann Flinders, 27 December 1842. (FPNMM)
7 John Lort Stokes, *Discoveries in Australia*.
8 Estensen, *The Life of Matthew Flinders* 480.
9 Clarke 191.
10 Stuart Macintyre, 'Introduction', *The Life of Matthew Flinders* by Ernest Scott with an introduction by Professor Stuart Macintyre, x-xi.
11 Scott, *The Life of Matthew Flinders*, xvii.
12 Macintyre, x.
13 Lester-Irabinna Rigney, Foreword, *Alas, for the Pelicans!* xiv.
14 Rigney, Foreword, xiii.
15 Rex Ingamells, 'Colonization', *Alas, for the Pelicans!* 186.
16 Rex Ingamells, 'Colonization' 191.
17 Jeff Guess, 'Death of Matthew Flinders', *Alas, for the Pelicans!* 126.
18 Miles Franklin, Letter to the Grattan family, 10 February 1942, in *My Congenials* 450.
19 Miles Franklin, *Laughter, Not for a Cage* 212.

20 Carole Ferrier (ed.) *As Good as a Yarn with You: Letters between Miles Franklin, Katherine Susannah Pritchard, Jean Devanny, Marjorie Barnard, Flora Eldershaw and Eleanor Dark* (Cambridge: Cambridge university Press, 1995) 137, 271.
21 See Morgan, *Matthew Flinders* 9.
22 Ernestine Hill, *My Love Must Wait* 67.
23 Robert Taylor, 'Journey to Hydrargyros', *Transnational Literature* 8.2 (May 2016). Online. https://dspace.flinders.edu.au/xmlui/bitstream/handle/2328/36074/Journey_to_Hydrargyros.pdf?sequence=1&isAllowed=y
24 Miles Franklin, Letter to the Grattan family, 450.
25 Quoted in Eleanor Hogan, *Into the Loneliness* 184.
26 Hogan, 184.
27 Quoted in Hogan, 185.
28 Rigney, xiv.
29 Alexander Hutchison Barrowman, 'Matthew Flinders', in *Alas, for the Pelicans!* 95.

Index

A

Aboriginal Australians, 4, 5, 20, 47, 68, 74–93, 209, 211, 214, 226, 227, 229–230
Aboriginal languages, 209
Aboriginal music, 219–220
Adelaide Baroque, 216–220
Adelaide, South Australia, 71, 226
Admiralty, 2, 13, 16, 21, 40, 57, 58, 62, 110, 120–123, 139, 159, 172–175, 181, 186, 189, 209, 215, 222
Aken, John, 38, 60, 88, 90, 166
Alas! For the Pelicans: Flinders, Baudin and Beyond, 225
Albany, Western Australia, 83
Arrowsmith, Aaron, 184, 185, 190, 191
Ashley, Peter
   Indomitable Captain Matthew Flinders, The, 206–207
astronomy, 64, 102, 148, 175
Austen, Jane, 75, 110, 137
Austin, Patricia, 214, 227
Australia Circumnavigated. See logbook on *Investigator*
Australian flora, 66, 197
Austrian navy, 216
autobiography, 147

B

Baker, Sidney
   My Own Destroyer, 10
Bampton, William, 190
Banks Strait, Tasmania, 118
Banks, Joseph, Sir, 5, 11, 12–13, 15, 16, 34, 40–41, 57, 58, 64, 77–79, 82, 93, 107, 110, 117–123, 125, 149, 160, 164–165, 173–191, 196, 210
Banksia, 118–119
Banksia Park, South Australia, 119
Barngarla people, 70
Barrow, John, 122, 175, 178
Barrowman, Alexander Hutchinson, 213, 230
Bass Strait, 72
Bass, Elizabeth, *see* Waterhouse, Elizabeth
Bass, George, 13, 15, 18, 46, 62, 66, 79, 86, 117, 123–125, 196, 202–206, 228
Bastian, Josephine
   Passion for Exploring New Countries, A, 123–125
Baudin, Charles, 29, 30, 128
Baudin, Nicolas, 2, 16, 29, 42, 60, 72, 128, 198, 199, 201–202, 210, 216, 220
Bauer, Ferdinand, 66, 112, 197
Beagle (ship), 223
Beard, William, 213
Bell, Hugh, 62, 91, 211
Bellerophon (ship), 207, 210
billiards, 28, 166
biographies, 201

Bishop, Charles, 124
Bligh, William, 14, 18, 76, 77, 91, 119, 178, 179, 196, 199
 Voyage to the South Sea, 188
Blight, John, 214
Blue Mud Bay, Northern Territory, 47, 87–92, 211
Marion Body
 Fever of Discovery, The, 206–207
Bolger, Etienne, 22, 23
Bologne, Joseph, Chevalier de Saint-Georges, 217
Bolton, Mary Ann, 104
books, 3, 14, 18, 24, 28, 29, 48, 50, 52, 74, 98, 122, 124, 128, 151, 160–165, 174, 176–182, 186, 188–191, 196, 199, 212
Boston Island, South Australia, 70
Bounty (ship), 179, 189
breadfruit, 76, 119
British Library, 180
British Museum, 164, 180, 181
British Navy, 13, 14, 17, 23, 24, 29, 43, 105, 110, 124, 125, 134, 152, 153, 160, 202, 203, 204, 206, 207, 222
Brosses, Charles de, 177
 Terra Australis cognita, 190
Brown, Anthony J., 2
 Ill-Starred Captains, 201
Brown, Robert, 41, 65–66, 91, 122, 164, 168, 180, 181, 184–185, 197, 210
Buffalo (ship), 110, 126
Bungaree, 80–81, 138, 211
Burney, Charles, 168
Burney, Frances
 Evelina, 104, 221
Burney, James, 165, 177, 181, 190
 Chronological History of the Discoveries in the South Seas, 190

C

Café Marengo, 27, 43, 166
Cape Catastrophe, South Australia, 70
Cape Donington, South Australia, 70
Cape Leeuwin, Western Australia, 83, 89
Cape of Good Hope, 24, 50, 121, 130, 132
cascades, 37, 44, 151–152, 222
Chambers, James, 105
Chappelle, Ann, 1, 16, 20, 21, 26, 36–37, 40, 42, 44, 46, 47, 49, 52, 57–58, 76, 101–105, 108- 115, 117, 120, 124, 125, 126, 142, 156–159, 163–165, 171–172, 186, 200–201, 204, 208–209, 213–214, 219, 221–223
 correspondence, 14, 33, 36–37, 39, 50, 52, 64, 70, 74, 90, 101–105, 121, 127, 131, 133, 139–140, 156, 161, 185, 200–201, 221
charts, 2, 24, 27–28, 33, 45, 58, 61–65, 72, 147–150, 162, 174–176, 182–185, 196–197, 205, 208
Chazal family, 30, 42, 172
Chazal, Anne, 30, 128, 136, 170
Chazal, Toussaint Antoine de, 29, 30, 64, 128, 135–136, 170
chess, 30, 42, 128, 163
China, 49, 63, 205
circumnavigation of New Holland 1801–1803, 12–13, 45, 49, 60, 68, 79, 82, 98, 156, 166, 199, 202, 211
circumnavigation of Tasmania, 45–46
climate, 34, 149
Coffin Bay, South Australia, 68
Columbus, Christopher, 150
Cook, James, 10, 13, 14, 23, 59, 64, 77, 79, 81, 118, 149, 150, 174, 177, 179, 188, 189, 196, 223, 228
Coupang, Timor, 48
Couve family, 170
cross-cultural encounters, 76–93
Crozet, Julien Marie.
 Nouveau voyage a la mer du Sud, 191
Cumberland (ship), 14, 16, 17, 19, 23, 44, 49–50, 63, 90, 125, 139, 140, 160, 223

Index

D

d'Arifat family, 18–19, 30–36, 64, 125–128, 153, 169, 170
d'Arifat, Aristide, 34
d'Arifat, Delphine, 18, 33–36, 127, 164, 200
d'Arifat, Labauve, 29, 38, 127–128
d'Arifat, Lise, 29, 39, 127, 171
d'Arifat, Louise (Mme), 18, 29, 31, 32, 40, 51, 114, 115, 127–128, 138
d'Arifat, Marc, 34
d'Arifat, Sophie, 34, 36, 112
Dalrymple, Alexander, 189, 205
Dampier, William, 179
  Voyage to New Holland, A, 188
dancing, 39, 81, 86, 167
Decaen, Charles Mathieu Isadore, 3, 16–17, 19, 20, 22–30, 33, 34, 38, 63, 121, 135, 154, 156, 162, 201, 207, 223
Defoe, Daniel
  Robinson Crusoe, 11, 14, 45, 53, 74, 98, 105, 165, 195, 221
deforestation, 34, 50
Dejean, Ferdinand, 216
Dell, Joseph, 11
depression, 31–33, 51, 121, 151, 162
Desbassayns, Charles, 29, 36, 39, 127, 128, 130, 172, 179, 184
Desbassayns, Lise (Mme). *See* d'Arifat, Lise
Desperate Fortune, A, 213
Devienne, François, 169, 213, 215
Dharawal people, 80
Dodd, Joseph, 105
dogs, 20, 38, 68, 154
Donington, Lincolnshire, 11, 70, 97, 105, 109, 140, 167
Dryander, Jonas, 180, 184
dysentery, 47, 151

E

Elder, John, 20, 31, 38, 43, 154

Encounter Bay, South Australia, 2, 60, 72, 216
Encounter celebrations, South Australia, 2
Encyclopaedia Britannica, 156, 160–162
Endeavour (ship), 78, 179, 188, 189
English prisoners on Mauritius, 28, 162, 166
Enlightenment, 13, 74–79, 124, 202
escape plans, 26, 31, 52
Estensen, Miriam,
  Letters of George & Elizabeth Bass, 204–206
  Life of George Bass, The, 202–204
  Life of Matthew Flinders, The, 42–43, 199–201, 207, 211, 224
Euclid, 14
Euston Station, London, 6, 9, 106, 141, 211
Eyre Peninsula, South Australia, 69

F

firearms, 80, 81, 85, 86, 87
fires, 68, 89
First Wave, The: Exploring Early Coastal Contact History in Australia, 226
Flinders Bar, 34, 65
Flinders family, 26, 106, 199
Flinders Island, Bass Strait, 60, 62, 104, 119, 202
Flinders Island, South Australia, 104, 119
Flinders Park, South Australia, 118
Flinders Petrie, Lisette, 116
Flinders Ranges, South Australia, 119
Flinders River, Queensland, 224
Flinders Street, Adelaide, 119
Flinders Street, Melbourne, 119
Flinders University, 2, 112, 118, 119, 195–198, 213
Flinders, Ann, (wife). *See* Chappelle, Ann
Flinders, Anne (daughter), 40, 114, 115, 116, 131, 133, 172, 200
Flinders, Betsey (sister), 99, 101

Flinders, Elizabeth (née Weeks)
(stepmother), 12, 100, 101, 104, 105, 106, 109, 115, 221, 223
Flinders, Hannah (step-sister), 97, 104–105
Flinders, Henrietta (cousin), 11, 105, 152
Flinders, Henrietta (step-sister), 104–105
Flinders, John (brother), 100, 102
Flinders, John (cousin), 14, 105, 152
Flinders, Matthew
  Final illness and death, 41, 184–185
  Works
    Biographical Tribute to the Memory of Trim, 19–20, 33, 43, 136–143, 147
    My Evening Song, 36, 111–112, 156–158, 171, 213, 219, 222
    Observations on the Coasts of Van Diemen's Land, 161
    Private Journal, 22–43, *passim*
    Voyage to Terra Australis, A, 105, 173–191, *passim*
    Atlas, 183
Flinders, Matthew (Senior), 11–12, 14, 74, 97–100, 102, 106, 109, 117, 152, 167
Flinders, Samuel, 10, 17, 65, 90, 98, 100, 102–104, 105, 114, 119, 122, 133
Flinders, Susanna (née Ward) (mother), 97, 98–100, 102
Flinders, Susanna (sister), 99, 101, 112
Flindersia, 119
flute, 28, 36, 50, 64, 157, 166–170, 213–214
Forrest, Thomas
  Voyage to New Guinea, 190
  Voyage to Terra Australis, to New Guinea and the Moluccas, 177
Fowler, Robert, 63, 68
Fowler's Bay, South Australia, 68
Franklin family, 105
Franklin, Betsey, 105
Franklin, Hannah, 100, 105
Franklin, James, 105
Franklin, John, 18, 21, 100, 102, 105–106, 185, 223

Franklin, Mary, 105, 109
Franklin, Miles, 1, 227, 229
Franklin, Willingham (Junior), 105, 174
Franklin, Willingham (Senior), 105
French language, 18, 50, 155, 163, 196
French prisoners in England, 18, 197
French Revolution, 163, 217, 218

G

Galinyala, 70
Garden Prison. *See* Maison Despaux
Géographe (ship), 16, 72, 191, 216
geographic names, 225, 226
geology, 64, 164, 197, 203
geophysics, 37, 51, 64, 152, 197
George III of England, 42, 59, 86
Good, Peter, 91, 210
Grant, Charles, Vicomte de Vaux.
  History of Mauritius or the Isle of France, 19, 135
Greek, 167
Guess, Jeff, 214, 227
Gulf of Carpentaria, 59–60, 69, 70, 140, 184, 224
Gulf St Vincent, South Australia, 70, 226
Guringai people, 80

H

harp, 170–171, 219
harpsichord, 30, 170, 172
Harris, John,
  Navigantium atque itinerantium bibliotheca, 177, 191
Harvey, James (brother-in-law), 101
Harvey, James (nephew), 101
Harvey, Susan (niece), 101
Hawkesworth, John, 177, 179
  Account of the Voyages ..., 188
Haydn, Franz Joseph, 111–112, 157, 169, 171, 213, 215, 217–219
Hayward. C.W.A., 214

Hill, Ernestine, 1, 228
  My Love Must Wait, 227–229
Hoffmeister, Franz Anton, 169, 215, 218
Hope, Hugh, 133
Hull, 109
Hunter, John, 15, 16, 62, 168, 186, 204
  Historical journal of the transactions at Port Jackson, An, 191
hurricanes, 50
Hursthouse, John, 103

I
Inconstant (ship), 133
indigo, 34, 64, 197
Ingamells, Rex, 214, 226
Ingleby, Bernard, 214, 227
inland sea, 69
Investigator (ship), 9, 14, 60–62, 68–69, 80, 87, 89, 93, 150, 160–161, 167–168, 188–189, 223–224
islands, 44–53

J
Jamaica, 76
Johnson, Samuel, 75

K
Kangaroo Island, South Australia, 71, 76, 209, 214, 222, 226
kangaroos, 71
Karta, 71
Karumba, Queensland, 224
Kaurna people, 71
Kent, Eliza, 110, 125–126
Kent, William, 110, 125–126
Kermode, Frank, 75
King George Sound, 83, 86
King, Anna Josepha, 110–111
King, James, 177
King, Philip Gidley, 14, 19, 49, 62–63, 128, 140, 210
King, Phillip Parker, 66, 104, 119, 138
Kooranup, 86

L
La Billardière, Jacques-Julien Houtou de
  Voyage in search of La Pérouse, 189
La Chaise, Mr, 29
La Pérouse, Jean-François de Galaup, Comte de, 179
Lacretelle, Jean Charles D. de, 163
Langham, W.H., 1, 9
languages, 4, 80, 116, 169, 176, 203
Latin, 28, 39, 46, 71, 74, 166, 167
Le Refuge, Plaines Wilhems, Mauritius 31, 51
Lesueur, Charles-Alexandre, 216
libraries, 98, 124, 160, 164, 165, 173–191
Lincolnshire, 15, 27, 97, 105, 109, 112, 152, 204
logbook on *Investigator*, 2, 4, 28, 44–40, 68, 70–72, 76, 82–88, 90, 92, 148, 151, 159, 162, 166, 207–210, 222, 228
Louis XV, 163

M
Macarthur, Elizabeth, 111
Macarthur, John, 25
Mack, James, 15
Macquarie, Lachlan, 123
Madagascar, 178
magnetism, 34, 65, 161
Maison Despaux, 28, 31, 128, 139, 153–156, 162, 166, 168–169
maize, 34, 64, 197
Major, Mrs, 175
Malay traders, 211
Manthorpe, Peter, 214
marine barometer, 34, 64, 161, 208
marines, 85, 86
marriage, 21, 40, 58, 108–114, 158, 201
Marsden, William, 174
Martin, Will, 228
mathematics, 18, 64, 74, 167
McCrae, George Gordon, 6, 141

McKinnon, Catherine
   Storyland, 228
Memory Cove, South Australia, 69, 70
Meteorology, 156, 160
Milius, Pierre Bernard, 16
Milton, John
   Paradise Lost, 47, 74, 161
Mineng people, 84, 85
Mirning people, 68
money, 98, 106
Monistrol, Louis Augustin, 24
monkeys, 38, 78
Montesquieu, 78
Montgomery, James, 226
Moore, John Hamilton
   New Practical Navigator, The, 14, 195
morality, 12, 35, 39–40, 75–76, 163
Morgan Island, Northern Territory, 47, 83, 87–92
Morgan, Kenneth (ed.)
   Australia Circumnavigated, 207–210
Mortimer, George
   Observations &c made during a voyage in the brig Mercury, 191
Mount Brown, South Australia, 70
Mount Lofty, South Australia, 71
Mozart, Wolfgang Amadeus, 169, 214–218
music, 28–29, 64, 128, 156–157, 166–172, 197, 213–219

N
Napoleon, 173, 216
natural history, 65, 112, 119, 181, 183, 197, 203
Naturaliste (ship), 72, 191
Nautical Almanac, 175
Naval Academy, Portsmouth, 118
Naval Chronicle, The, 161, 165, 224
Nawu people, 68
Nepean Bay, Kangaroo Island, SA, 46
Netherlands, The, 182
New Guinea, 182

Ngarrindjeri people, 2, 72
Nicol, George, 185–186
Noongar people, 83–87, 117
Nore, UK, 120
Norfolk (ship), 57, 62, 66, 80, 138, 202, 214
novels, 1, 34, 86, 104, 221–222, 227–229
Nukunu people, 70
Nuyts Land, 68

O
obituaries, 224
Odiham, Hampshire, 18
Owen, Edward, 133
Owen, William Fitzwilliam, 39, 131–134
Pailleux, Mr, 36
painting, 112, 116, 135, 172
Paisiello, Giovanni, 216
parenthood, 114–115
parole, 26, 31
Partney, Lincolnshire, 108–109
Pasley, Thomas, 11, 14, 105, 152
passport, 3, 16, 22–23, 63, 64, 72
Paterson, Elizabeth, 110
Paterson, William, 110
Peace of Amiens, 50
Pearson, George, 101, 112–113
Pelican Lagoon, Kangaroo Island, SA, 71, 222
pelicans, 46, 71, 76, 222, 226
Péron, François, 72
   Voyage de découvertes aux terres australes, 191
Petrie, Ann Flinders, 207
Petrie, Lisette Flinders, 14
Petrie, William, 116
Petrie, William Matthew Flinders, 116
philosophy, 34, 37, 48, 134, 163
Pitot, Edouard, 28, 128, 168
Pitot, Thomi, 28–31, 103, 106, 115, 128–131, 163, 164, 168–169, 172
Plaines Wilhems, Mauritius, 31, 37, 64

Pleyel, Ignace, 28, 166, 169, 214–215, 218–219
poetry, 1, 74, 163, 213, 226–229
politics, 30, 37, 51, 111–112, 152, 226
Porpoise (ship), 14, 23, 49, 62, 63, 138, 196
Port Jackson, New South Wales, 23–24, 60–63, 66, 80, 110, 124, 203, 220
Port Lincoln, South Australia, 20–21, 68, 70, 82, 119, 223, 225
Port Louis, Mauritius, 18, 20, 23, 125, 128, 131, 132, 153, 163, 198
Port North-West. *See* Port Louis, Mauritius
portrait, 64, 135–136, 170
Portsmouth, UK, 113, 120
Prévost, Abbé
Histoire general des voyages, 177, 189
Princess Royal Harbour, Western Australia, 83
promotion, 26, 122, 155, 173
Providence (ship), 14, 18, 91, 102, 119, 178, 196
Purchas, Samuel
Purchas his pilgrimage, 189
Radcliffe, Ann
Mysteries of Udolpho, The, 221

R

reading, 36, 44–46, 48, 50, 74. 160–165
Reiter, David P., 214, 227
Reliance (ship), 15, 70, 76, 102, 109, 124, 138, 168, 196, 204
religion, 39–40, 48, 99, 112, 126, 134, 200–201, 226
Richards, Mark (scupltor), 6, 141, 211
Richardson, Samuel
Clarissa, 104, 221
Rigney, Lester-Irabinna, 225, 229
rivers, 69
Robertson, John
Elements of Navigation, The, 14, 195
Robertson, Walter, 29, 37

Rollo (ship), 49
Romanticism, 13, 42–43, 74–75, 158–159, 221–231
Rossel, E.P.E.
Voyage de Dentrecasteaux, 191
Rousseau, Jean-Jacques
Emile, 163
Royal Observatory, 175
Royal Society, 15, 34, 64, 122, 161, 181, 197, 208

S

Salem, United States, 38
Sandall, Philippa
Seafurrers, 137
Savanne, Mauritius, 22
scientists, 83, 174, 181, 201, 209, 212, 220
Scipio (ship), 11, 98
Scott, Ernest,
Life of Captain Matthew Flinders, 225
Scott, Kim
That Deadman Dance, 86
Sculthorpe, Peter, 219
Seaflower (ship), 131
sharks, 69
ships' cats, 137
shipwreck, 14, 23, 28, 33, 45, 49, 142
singing, 81, 170
Sir Joseph Banks Islands, South Australia, 118–119
slave trade, 131
slaves and slavery, 20, 37–38, 48–49, 76, 13–131, 217
Smith, Christopher, 117
Smith, Samuel, 210
Smith, William, 154
Soho Square, London, 121–122, 173, 179–181, 186, 188–191
South Australia, 2, 9, 20, 68–73, 82, 118–119, 123, 141, 199, 216, 225–226
South Hummocks, South Australia, 70
Spalding, Lincolnshire, 11

spears, 68, 80–81
Spencer Gulf, South Australia, 69–70
Spilsby, Lincolnshire, 109
Spithead, UK, 70, 110, 114
St James's Churchyard, London, 114
St Paul (island), 45
St Thomas's Church, Charlton, 113
Stamford Hill, South Australia, 21, 223
statues, 6, 9, 10, 136, 140–141, 211–212, 214, 230
Steibelt, Daniel, 170, 172
Sterne, Laurence
    Tristram *Shandy*, 136
Stokes, John Lort, 223–224
Struyck, Nicolaas, 190
Stuart, Farquarson, 41, 183
Sweers Island, 223
sword, 17, 113

T
Tahiti, 76–78, 206, 228
Tamarin Falls, Mauritius, 37
Tasman, Abel Jansz, 181–182
Tasmania, 15, 21, 45, 46, 66, 72, 118, 123, 161, 196, 202
Taylor, Robert
    'Journey to Hydrargyros', 229
Taylor, William, 69
Telemann, Georg Philip, 214
Tenerife, 109
Thévenot, Jean de
    Relations de divers voyages curieux, 189
Thistle Island, South Australia, 70
Thistle, John, 69–70
Tiarks L., 182
Tidd, Lincolnshire, 109
Timor, 3, 44, 46–50, 59, 121, 151–152, 159, 209, 222
Tom Thumb (boat), 15, 79, 123, 196, 202, 228
Torres Strait, 60, 63, 178, 190
translation, 36, 136, 164, 182, 190

Trim (cat), 1, 5, 19–20, 33, 43, 117, 135–143, 147, 148, 159, 196, 207, 226
turtles, 79
Tyler, Anne, 111, 113
Tyler, Isabella, 41, 109, 113–114, 140

V
Vacouas, Mauritius, 30
Valentijn, François
    Oud en Nieuw Oost-Indien, 182, 190
Van Diemens Land. *See* Tasmania
Van Este, Mrs, 47–49
Vancouver, George, 83
    Voyage of Discovery to the North Pacific Ocean, 179, 188
venereal disease, 41, 199, 206, 228
Venus (ship), 203, 205
Victoria, Australia, 1, 3, 73, 225
Vlaming, Willem De, 182
Voltaire, 40, 78, 163
voyage publications, 173, 177

W
war with France, 16, 119, 158, 173
Waterhouse, Elizabeth, 124–125, 203–204
Waterhouse, Henry, 15, 138
West Indies, 105, 189, 216
Westall, William, 66, 197
Whitewood, John, 87, 89
Wiles, James, 52, 117–119, 174
Woide, C.G., 182
Woolwich, UK, 113
Wreck Reef, 33, 49
York Lunatic Asylum, 102
Yorke, Charles Philip, 58, 122

Wakefield Press is an independent publishing and
distribution company based in Adelaide, South Australia.
We love good stories and publish beautiful books.
To see our full range of books, please visit our website at
www.wakefieldpress.com.au
where all titles are available for purchase.
To keep up with our latest releases, news and events,
subscribe to our monthly newsletter.

Find us!

Facebook: www.facebook.com/wakefield.press
Twitter: www.twitter.com/wakefieldpress
Instagram: www.instagram.com/wakefieldpress